Interpreting a Classic

The Joan Palevsky Imprint in Classical Literature

In honor of beloved Virgil—

"O degli altri poeti onore e lume . . ."

—Dante, *Inferno*

Interpreting a Classic

Demosthenes and His
Ancient Commentators

Craig A. Gibson

UNIVERSITY OF CALIFORNIA PRESS
Berkeley · Los Angeles · London

The publisher gratefully acknowledges the generous
contribution to this book provided by Joan Palevsky.

University of California Press
Berkeley and Los Angeles, California
University of California Press, Ltd.
London, England
© 2002 by
The Regents of the University of California

Library of Congress Cataloging-in-Publication Data

Gibson, Craig A., 1968–.
    Interpreting a classic : Demosthenes and his ancient
commentators / Craig A. Gibson.
        p.   cm.
    Includes bibliographical references (p.) and indexes.
    ISBN 0-520-22956-8 (alk. paper)
        1. Demosthenes—Criticism and interpretation—
History.   2. Speeches, addresses, etc., Greek—History
and criticism—Theory, etc.   3. Oratory, Ancient.
I. Title.
PA3952.G53   2002
885'.01—dc21   2001048055

Printed in the United States of America
10   09   08   07   06   05   04   03   02   01
10   9   8   7   6   5   4   3   2   1
The paper used in this publication meets the minimum
requirements of ANSI/NISO Z39.48–1992 (R 1997)
(*Permanence of Paper*). ♾

For William T. Jolly
Teacher, mentor, friend

Contents

Preface

This is a book about ancient writers and readers who shared an interest in the orations of the Athenian statesman Demosthenes. There has been no full modern discussion of the nature of this branch of the ancient reception of Demosthenes; it is a story that has been told only in part and with various aims. In addition, the texts themselves have never been assembled in one place, translated into a modern language, and provided with explanatory notes. This book is intended to address these gaps in the scholarship.

Part I consists of three chapters. Chapter 1 describes the physical form of the commentaries and discusses their transmission. A diachronic history of their transmission would have been preferable, but the fragmentary nature of our evidence and the lack of securely known names, dates, and cultural contexts for the commentators make that a difficult if not impossible project. Therefore, the chapter is largely descriptive, relying on a series of illustrative snapshots from a rich history of ancient responses to Demosthenes. Chapter 2 considers the role of Didymus and the sources, agenda, and readership of the commentaries. Chapter 3 argues that Didymus's *On Demosthenes* (P.Berol.inv. 9780) may be a series of excerpts from a lost original commentary, made by someone with interests primarily in classical Athenian history.

Part II presents the ancient philological and historical commentaries on Demosthenes, together with their Greek texts (except that of the lengthy P.Berol.inv. 9780) and detailed notes. The translations are in-

tended to convey the content and method of the commentators, wherever possible, but like all translations, they are acts of interpretation and
are therefore necessarily argumentative.

This book is the product of many years of interest in the ancient philological and historical commentaries on Demosthenes. I wish to thank
John F. Oates of Duke University for introducing me to Didymus's commentaries on Demosthenes, which I first examined in my 1995 dissertation; portions of that study have been revised and incorporated in the
present work. I am grateful also to Peter Burian, Diskin Clay, Francis
Newton, and especially Kent Rigsby for their advice in the early stages
of the project. A postdoctoral fellowship in the Western Traditions Program at the University of Nevada, Reno, provided the time and insti-
tutional support needed to write the first draft of the book. I wish to
thank Phil Boardman, Gaye McCollum-Nickles, and Bernie Schopen of
UNR for their collegiality and interest in the project; the program's man-
agement assistant, Susan Kempley, for running interference while I re-
searched and wrote; and the Interlibrary Loan service for so quickly
locating and delivering needed materials. I wish also to thank my colleagues in the Department of Classics at the University of Iowa, particularly Helena Dettmer and Mary Depew, for their advice and support
as I completed revisions. I am very grateful to Kate Toll of the Press for
her initial enthusiasm, continual encouragement, and invaluable assistance, and to Dore Brown and Cindy Fulton for overseeing the final stages
of production. To M. R. Dilts and the two anonymous readers for the
Press I offer my sincere gratitude for their helpful suggestions and corrections. Christopher Blackwell, Peter Burian, Diskin Clay, Francis Newton, Andrea Purvis, Rebekah Smith, and Joshua D. Sosin read portions
of the manuscript at various stages and helped improve it in a number of
ways, and Kent Rigsby graciously served as a final reader of the whole.
Mark Thorne assisted with indexing. Any errors or infelicities that remain are my own. Above all, I wish to thank my wife Kristal for her love
and understanding; I could not have accomplished this without her.

Abbreviations

Berol. 5008   P.Berol.inv. 5008. Edited by F. Blass, "Lexikon zu Demosthenes' Aristokratea," in "Neue Papyrusfragmente im Ägyptischen Museum zu Berlin," *Hermes* 17 (1882) 148–63.

Berol. 9780   P.Berol.inv. 9780. Edited by L. Pearson and S. Stephens, *Didymi in Demosthenem Commenta* (Stuttgart, 1983).

Berol. 21188   P.Berol.inv. 21188. Edited by H. Maehler, "Der Streit um den Schatten des Esels," in *Proceedings of the XIXth International Congress of Papyrology,* vol. 1, ed. A. H. S. El-Mosalamy (Cairo, 1992) 625–33.

Didymus fragments   See text 2 in part II.

D-S¹   H. Diels and W. Schubart, eds. *Didymos Kommentar zu Demosthenes.* Berliner Klassikertexte 1. Berlin, 1904.

D-S²   H. Diels and W. Schubart, eds. *Volumina Aegyptiaca Ordinis IV, Grammaticorum Pars I, Didymi de Demosthene Commenta cum Anonymi in Aristocratem Lexico.* Leipzig, 1904.

FGrH	F. Jacoby. *Die Fragmente der griechischen Historiker.* Berlin, 1923–58.
Harpocration	See text 2 in part II.
Pack²	R. A. Pack. *The Greek and Latin Literary Texts from Greco-Roman Egypt.* 2d ed. Ann Arbor, 1965.
P.Lond.Lit. 179	Edited by F. G. Kenyon, *Aristotle: On the Constitution of Athens,* 3d ed. (Oxford, 1892) 215–19.
P-S	L. Pearson and S. Stephens, eds. *Didymi in Demosthenem Commenta.* Stuttgart, 1983.
Rain. 7	P.Rain.inv. 7. Edited by C. Wessely, "Fragmente eines alphabetischen Lexikons zu Demosthenes Midiana," *Studien zur Palaeographie und Papyruskunde* 4 (1905) 111–13.
RE	A. F. von Pauly, G. Wissowa, et al., eds. *Real-Encyclopädie der klassischen Altertumswissenschaft.* Stuttgart, 1894–.
Stras. 84	P.Stras.inv. 84. Edited by H. T. Wade-Gery and B. D. Meritt, "Athenian Resources in 449 and 431 B.C.," *Hesperia* 26 (1957) 163–97.

Introduction

The Athenian statesman and orator Demosthenes (384–322 B.C.) was one of the most influential authors of Greek and Roman antiquity. The writings passed down under his name in the manuscript tradition include sixteen speeches delivered before the Athenian Assembly, nine others from important public trials, thirty-three from private law cases, six letters, a funeral oration, an essay on love, and a large collection of generalized introductions *(prooemia)*.[1] Of these writings, the speeches delivered in the Assembly and in public trials were generally considered to be his best. Demosthenes was also one of the orators included in the canon of ten Attic orators, a list of recommended authors that probably reached its final form in the second century C.E.[2]

Demosthenes was read more than any other ancient orator; only his Roman admirer Cicero offered any real competition. For hundreds of years he was studied by schoolboys eager to embark upon careers as pub-

1. The genuineness of some of these is doubtful; see Sealey, *Demosthenes,* 222–40. On the authenticity of the letters, see Goldstein. For ancient papyri containing texts of Demosthenes, see most recently Clarysse. See Drerup on the manuscript tradition. Modern editions of Demosthenes are based on four main manuscripts: the tenth-century Marcianus 416 (called F), the tenth- or eleventh-century Monacensis 485 (A), the tenth- or eleventh-century Parisinus 2935 (Y), and the ninth- or tenth-century Parisinus 2934 (S).

2. On the canon of the ten Attic orators, see Douglas, "Canon of Ten Attic Orators"; Smith. The other nine were Lysias, Isaeus, Hyperides, Isocrates, Dinarchus, Aeschines, Antiphon, Lycurgus, and Andocides.

lic speakers, politicians, and patriarchs. Writers of all periods studied and imitated Demosthenes' style. Literary critics tried to describe the effects of his style on the reader or listener, and to explain how such effects were achieved. Biographers supplied their hungry reading publics with extensive discussions of Demosthenes' political career, his speeches, and even his personal quirks and sense of humor. Commentaries and dictionaries provided generations of readers with valuable discussions of the finer points of classical Athenian history and definitions of unusual or archaic words. Just as Homer was "the poet" of Greek and Roman antiquity, Demosthenes was "the orator."

Postclassical readers of Demosthenes faced a number of challenges, not the least of which was their distance from the world of classical Athens. In his speeches Demosthenes addresses the Athenians of his own day in terms calculated to advise, inform, and move them. There was no particular reason for him to assume that his published speeches would still be read hundreds of years later. There was no way to predict that a proper name or other word in those speeches would be unfamiliar to a reader six hundred years in the future, and no real reason to concern himself with that fact. Likewise there was no reason to provide footnotes to current events and well-known episodes from Athenian history. When Demosthenes refers in his tenth oration to the Persian king's previous restoration of the city's affairs (10.34), his original audience presumably knew what that meant. They did not need to be told that he was referring, as one ancient scholar argues, to a Persian-sponsored Athenian defeat of the Spartans in a naval battle at Cnidus in the 390s B.C.[3]

Even if Demosthenes wanted to give his audience such details, it is also possible that he *could* not. As J. Ober has argued, for political reasons an ancient orator had to "avoid taking on the appearance of a well-educated man giving lessons in culture to the ignorant masses."[4] Demosthenes had to portray himself as knowledgeable (and therefore trustworthy), but at the same time he had to avoid giving the impression that he believed that he was better than anyone in his audience (and therefore untrustworthy). For these reasons Demosthenes' speeches did not and perhaps could not provide the philological and historical explanations that later readers might need. Nevertheless, Demosthenes was a "classic"

3. See Didymus's comments in Berol. 9780, cols. 7.7–8.2.
4. Ober, 178–79. On the Attic orators' use of history, see also Pearson, "Historical Allusions; S. Perlman, "Historical Example"; Nouhaud.

author on a recommended reading list, and if such an author was to have relevance for each new generation of readers, these readers needed help.

The scholars who provided this help had no special title in antiquity. Given their interests and agenda, we may call them the philological and historical commentators.[5] Unlike many ancient readers, these philological and historical commentators were not interested in mining Demosthenes' speeches for rhetorical gems or biographical data. Rather, they devoted themselves to reacquiring the factual knowledge that Demosthenes had apparently taken for granted in his original audience. Through their efforts Demosthenes could function in their own times and places as a historical eyewitness to a period universally recognized by subsequent generations as the greatest in Greek military, political, and cultural achievement.

Some of the tools and techniques of our commentators had already been applied in Hellenistic Alexandria to other authors, such as Homer and the dramatic poets.[6] In addition to the traditional questions of grammar, word choice, and etymology, the commentators on Demosthenes also discussed the dates and authenticity of the orations, identified the historical persons mentioned in them, and explained references to unfamiliar facets of life in classical Athens. Our commentators were most interested in discussing philological and historical questions evoked directly by the literal details of the text. There was no discussion of rhetorical theory or its practical application, no moralizing, no discussion of Demosthenes the man, and no use of allegory. Cases of insurance fraud did not invite philosophical speculation on the immortality of the soul, and Philip of Macedon was never likened to the primordial chaos.

That the commentators devoted themselves to factually oriented topics has had a curious effect on modern scholars. Over the past century and a half, classicists have tended to approach such fragmentary and

5. This title is intended to reflect the content and agenda of the commentaries, which include analyses of individual words and discussions of historical topics such as key names, dates, and events. Other possible names for them are less satisfactory. The term "grammatical" is sometimes used to describe them, in reference to the interests of the ancient *grammatici.* But this term could mislead a modern audience, as it implies an interest in morphology and syntax that is not well represented in the commentaries. Furthermore, the ancient *grammatici* rarely take up detailed historical investigations of the type seen in some of our texts. The term "antiquarian" is also unsuitable, as antiquarian authors tend to arrange their material topically and do not usually provide point-by-point explications of texts. On ancient antiquarianism, see Momigliano, "Ancient History"; Rawson, *Intellectual Life,* 233–49.

6. For a good overview of this subject, see Pfeiffer, *Classical Scholarship.*

practical texts in a fragmentary and practical manner, efficiently reducing the whole to the sum of its parts. Correct etymologies are transported into our modern etymological dictionaries. Incorrect ones are dismissed in footnotes. Primary historical sources quoted in the commentaries are lifted out of their ancient context, reassembled elsewhere, used to reconstruct the writings of the Atthidographers, lifted again for historical essays, marshalled in columns, evaluated, accepted, dismissed. Ancient claims for authenticity are believed and noted in prefaces, or disbelieved and reduced to brackets. Identifications of persons, places, and things are whisked away to our dictionaries and encyclopedias as derivative *comparanda* for things we supposedly know much better from Cornelius Nepos or Plutarch or the scholia to Apollonius of Rhodes. Tidy, efficient, and utterly scientific, the modern scholarship on these sorts of texts unfortunately tells us little about the target authors, and even less about their commentators.

A modern philologist or historian, however, may hold that the fragmentary and practical nature of such writings fairly well justifies our rating them by degree of accuracy. Considerable sympathy with this view is understandable. Facts are important. The truth of history, though it is increasingly unfashionable and perhaps naïve to say so aloud, is important. And the hard questions with which the modern reader of ancient oratory must always come to terms are important: Is this speaker telling the truth? Does he really expect his audience to know the historical details that he seems to assume of them, or is he trying to capitalize on their ignorance, patriotism, or fear? Can this speech provide an accurate understanding of the historical persons, places, and events mentioned in it?[7] This modern quest for the truth about the past sends us to the ancient commentators, whom we tend to hold to modern standards of accuracy regarding this particular historical detail, the use or faithful transmission of that source, or the true meaning of this or that word or phrase.

This approach has proved valuable in a number of areas. If it were not for careful modern studies of the ancient commentaries on Demosthenes, we would know less about a great many topics: the chronology of Philip's campaigns, the fate of the philosopher-king and tyrant Hermias of Atarneus, the authenticity of some of Demosthenes' speeches (which directly affects our understanding of Greek history), and the contents

7. On which see Pearson, "Historical Allusions"; Todd.

of some lost comedies, to name a few examples. But this piecemeal approach has also left two groups largely to the side: the educated scholars through whose diligence the text of Demosthenes was supplied with commentaries and lexica, and the other ancient readers who eagerly sought out not only Demosthenes' writings but also these secondary companion-pieces. In other words, modern scholarship has already as thoroughly as possible answered the question, what can these commentators tell us about Demosthenes and the fourth century? However, the question that has never been asked of these texts as a group, and which is to be examined in detail here, is, what can these commentators tell us about commentators, about commentaries, and about the ancient readers who consulted them?

Approached in this way, the ancient commentaries on Demosthenes have a fascinating new story to tell. This book attempts to give a detailed and generous portrait of a scholarly industry that touched generations of ancient readers from the first century B.C. to the fifth century C.E. and beyond. The story of the ancient philological and historical commentaries on Demosthenes begins with the first-century commentaries of the Alexandrian scholar Didymus Chalcenterus. These commentaries, as we shall see, were soon dismembered into special lexica to individual speeches and also into other commentaries. Some of these new scholarly works were read and adapted in the second century C.E. by Harpocration in his *Lexeis of the Ten Orators,* as well as by even later lexicographers and commentators. Down to the end of antiquity, lexica and commentaries were involved in a kind of scholarly symbiosis, alternately feeding and being fed by one another. Some words and ideas from the ancient philological and historical commentaries even found their way —largely via excerpts from popular reference sources—into the Byzantine scholia to Demosthenes.[8] Written and revised in some cases hundreds of years after the latest of the ancient writings surveyed in this book, these comments in the margins of mediaeval manuscripts of Demosthenes show that it was almost exclusively his rhetoric that interested scholars after the end of the ancient world.

Long study of the ancient philological and historical commentaries on Demosthenes has led me to formulate three working hypotheses that

8. I use the word "scholia" to denote comments written in the margins of manuscripts, and "commentaries" to denote texts written separately from the text of the target author, but modern scholars are not always uniform in this practice.

inform much of this book. It will be useful to state them here at the out-
set rather than frequently repeating them throughout:

I. "FRAGMENTS" OF ANCIENT SCHOLARSHIP
CANNOT BE TAKEN AT FACE VALUE.

Quotations from otherwise lost works (called "fragments") have been
stripped from their original contexts and redeployed in new, foreign contexts. This impedes our ability to assess their original significance accurately, for several reasons. First, a "fragment" is not necessarily an accurate representation of a scholar's idea, much less the specific language
with which it was conveyed. There were no generally accepted scholarly
principles in antiquity that dictated how one should represent the ideas
of another scholar, and no regularly observed conventions of denoting
when an excerpted passage was an exact quotation, a quotation with el-
lipses, a quotation containing some paraphrase, a paraphrase, or a summary. Second, commentators in the ancient world rarely preserve the
evidence and arguments used by previous scholars. They may, for example, report that an earlier scholar believed that a certain speech was
never delivered, but they do not usually state on what evidence their
source based this conclusion, if in fact that evidence was even provided
in the original source. Third, and most important, "fragments" of ancient scholarship are often situated in a polemical context and thus tend
not to represent the excerpted author at his best. We shall see this clearly
illustrated in Harpocration's responses to Didymus, as well as in Didymus's responses to earlier, anonymous views.

Modern practitioners of source criticism *(Quellenforschung)* have not
always paid adequate attention to the rhetorical strategies of ancient
scholars, whose purpose is seldom simply to record accurately and completely the views of earlier scholars in an objective, value-free medium.[9]

---

9. Similarly, Whittaker, 65 n. 4, points out that Plutarch, the prolific biographer and
literary critic of the second century C.E., did not intend "to preserve for posterity the fragments of texts which he quoted, but only to exploit them according to current literary con-
vention." M. L. West, 18, notes that scribes "may deliberately adapt the [grammatical]
construction or some other aspect of the quotation to suit [their] own purposes." Montanari has written recently on the need for a more sensible approach to the fragments of Hellenistic scholarship. See also Daintree on misapplications of *Quellenforschung* in modern
treatments of late-ancient and mediaeval commentaries on Vergil. For a discussion of the
problems and possibilities associated with fragments of historians, see Brunt, "Historical
Fragments." A good recent discussion of these issues as they pertain to the study of ancient
history is found in Potter, 59–66, 70–78, 90–95.

Throughout this study, therefore, I have endeavored to consider the original context of fragments, the alterations to which they may have been subjected, and the rhetorical aims of the scholars providing them.

2. ANCIENT COMMENTATORS WERE WRITING FOR ANCIENT AUDIENCES.

Ancient commentators purposefully used excerption and paraphrase to emphasize one particular point at the expense of all the other points that could have been emphasized. Their choices are often not the ones that modern scholars—in our eagerness to use the commentaries for quite different purposes—would like them to have made. Any sense of disappointment that we may feel, however, may simply be a reflection of an unexamined assumption that the purpose of such texts is to provide us with "parallels" and other "information." Take, for example, this selection from the lexicographer Harpocration, in which he relates Didymus's interpretation of the Greek verb *dekateuein*, "to pay a tithe":

> To pay a tithe: . . . When Demosthenes says as follows about a certain young woman in *Against Medon*, namely that "she has neither paid her tithe nor celebrated the mysteries," Didymus the scholar in his book on the subject/speech says that Lysias, in *Concerning the Daughter of Phrynichus*, said that "to pay a tithe" means "to act the she-bear." . . .[10]

In this lexical entry, Harpocration reports that Didymus had adduced a parallel from the orator Lysias in order to explain a certain passage in Demosthenes. In both of the orations cited, "paying a tithe" is said to be a euphemism for taking part in a ritual dance in honor of Artemis, in which young girls dressed as bears. So far Didymus. But some of the questions that modern researchers might bring to this passage are left unanswered. There is no summary of either of the orations cited; this is regrettable, because neither survived antiquity. There is no full list or discussion of the civic duties of young Athenian girls to complement or contradict what is known from elsewhere. There is no perceptive analysis of the role of the goddess Artemis in Greek life. The list of what the passage does *not* provide for a modern scholar could easily be extended. But Harpocration and Didymus were not writing for a modern audience. Harpocration's purpose was to provide his readers in the second century C.E. with material that he deemed useful for understanding the vocabu-

---

10. See fragment 9 from Harpocration (text 2), below.

lary of the Attic orators: some alternative meanings of a Greek verb for "to pay a tithe," a demonstration of how the word is used in classical Greek oratory, and a brief reference to relevant secondary source material. And that is all. It is important to keep in mind that ancient scholars, like other ancient authors, were writing for audiences with educational backgrounds, expectations, and needs that were often quite different from our own. They could not anticipate our interests, and so should not be faulted excessively for failing to cater to them.

3. DATE AND PLACE OF COMPOSITION DO NOT NECESSARILY DETERMINE A COMMENTARY'S ACCURACY.

A well-stocked library at one's fingertips and an Alexandrian pedigree do not necessarily result in a brilliant commentary based on the earliest and (hence) most infallible source materials;[11] likewise, a late-ancient date alone does not necessarily result in a work consisting of mindlessly cut-and-pasted, diluted, misunderstood mishmash.[12] To assume otherwise would be, at worst, demonstrably incorrect; at best, counterproductive and misleading. I do not raise this point out of a misguided desire to mount a defense of, lavish undeserved praise upon, or boost the self-esteem of those ancient scholars who, by any reasonable standard, should properly remain at the bottom of the class. I raise it in order to suggest that the burden of proof *should* be (but usually is not) on anyone who would assume that there is a necessary cause-and-effect relationship between an ancient commentary's brilliance, accuracy, or usefulness —or substitute any other word denoting its value to modern scholars— and its date, place, or social circumstances of composition. The scholars of late antiquity, it should go without saying, did not suffer from a mental disability caused by their spatial or temporal distance from Hellenistic Alexandria. To accept this sort of view requires implicit commitment to an overall "decline" model of intellectual life in late antiquity that seems more often to have been assumed for historiographical convenience than rigorously demonstrated. Therefore, I have resisted the

---

11. Douglas, review, 191, argues that one must actively avoid falling into the trap of assuming "that the Alexandrians did all the work and did it perfectly, and that the records in our papyri and scholiasts, whatever their date, are but fragmentary, abbreviated and often garbled remains of a comprehensive Alexandrian achievement, that in short, nobody did any original research after c. 150 B.C. and nobody ever got anything wrong before that date."

12. Daintree discusses similar problematic assumptions in modern treatments of medieval Latin scholarship.

temptation to construct a rise-and-fall narrative of the ancient philological and historical scholarship on Demosthenes, which might place
the Alexandrian Didymus and Berol. 9780 at its apex and hold up later
commentaries and lexica as examples of the supposedly sad state into
which the supposedly unoriginal, rehashed scholarship of late antiquity
had devolved.

As has long been recognized, commentaries in general are a most useful
source for the intellectual historian. Even though they survive only in a
fragmentary state, the ancient philological and historical commentaries
on Demosthenes allow us to pose questions about the intellectual world
of antiquity that his texts alone—stripped of the ancient scholarly apparatus that was meant to accompany them—cannot even begin to answer. Commentaries serve as records of the interactions between reader
and target author, between reader and scholarly apparatus, and between
reader and scholar. They allow us to catch a glimpse of ancient readers
at work and, if only for a moment, to see Demosthenes through their
eyes. They reveal that different ancient readers of Demosthenes—other
commentators, students and teachers, historians, and others—had different needs and interests. The commentaries show us how ancient scholars locate topics of interest (either in the text of Demosthenes or in another scholarly aid), cast them as worthwhile questions or problems, and
then explain them for varied purposes and audiences. In addition, these
texts reveal the interaction of generations of scholars both with the
text of Demosthenes and with the received views of other scholars. They
show, for example, how the Alexandrian scholar Didymus evaluates and
dismisses the allegedly unfounded views of his ill-informed predecessors.
They also show, a century or so later, how the lexicographer Harpocration criticizes Didymus for his allegedly illogical, improbable, and ridiculous assertions. The ancient philological and historical commentaries
on Demosthenes thus serve as a record of fierce intellectual battles fought
in the schoolrooms, libraries, and published writings of Greek and Roman antiquity. At stake was nothing less than the correct interpretation
of a classic.

PART ONE

The Ancient Commentaries on Demosthenes

CHAPTER I

Form and Transmission

The ancient commentaries on Demosthenes were particularly volatile and subject to various sorts of excerpting and reorganization. This resulted in the creation of different reference works for different purposes and audiences. None of these works represented any sort of advance over the others, and with the exception of the much later marginal scholia, one might have expected to find any of them in circulation at any given time. This phenomenon is, of course, not unique to the ancient scholarship on Demosthenes. J. E. G. Zetzel characterizes the transmission of late-ancient scholarship in Latin as "a continuous flow . . . into and out of variorum commentaries, margins, glossaries, and the like. At various times different sources might meet by chance, as in the Bembine Terence, or be recompiled intentionally, as in our Donatus." [1]

This chapter examines the several commentaries that survive, and those that have been excerpted for use as entries in general or special lexica. We shall also consider the relationship between our commentaries and the Byzantine scholia to Demosthenes, comments written in the margins of mediaeval manuscripts which mainly reflect their authors' interest in rhetoric.

---

1. Zetzel, "Latin Scholia," 354; see Zuntz, 76–79, on the transmission of ancient scholarship on Aristophanes.

COMMENTARIES

Let us begin with the commentaries on Demosthenes, commonly referred to as *hypomnemata,* that are preserved in ancient papyri. These commentaries consist of a series of remarks on individual passages from an oration, arranged in the order in which a reader of Demosthenes would normally encounter them. Three of these are currently known: Berol. 9780, a commentary on twenty passages from orations 9–11 and 13;[2] Stras. 84, a commentary that discusses eight passages from oration 22; and Berol. 21188, a fragment of a commentary on oration 5 that preserves a discussion of only one passage.

The usual practice in ancient commentaries was to introduce each comment or group of comments with a brief lemma (quotation) from the target author, in this case Demosthenes. The lemma was just long enough to help the reader locate the passage in question; it was not necessarily intended to provide a complete thought or sentence.[3] In Berol. 9780, col. 11.14–26, for example, the lemma "that we must neither fear his power nor oppose him in a base manner" is given in order to draw attention to the word "fear" (ὀρρωδεῖν), whose etymology is then discussed at length. By contrast, the longer lemma from Dem. 10.1 in col. 1.26–29 is not specifically discussed at all but is used simply to indicate the beginning of the commentary on oration 10: "Athenian gentlemen, since I consider the things that you are debating as very important and necessary for the city, I shall try to say some things on the subject that I consider useful." In the absence of a standardized system of reference by edition-and-page or oration-and-section numbers (e.g., Dem. 21.4), reference to specific passages through the use of lemmata was the only available method that was likely to make sense to readers,[4] provided their text of the author did not differ substantially from the one used by the commentator.[5]

---

2. Many have doubted that Berol. 9780 is a commentary. For detailed consideration of this question, see chapter 3.

3. By contrast, the Byzantine scholia to classical authors sometimes include lemmata, sometimes not. It was less important to include a lemma when the comment could be placed in the margin near the target word or phrase.

4. However, Slater, "Interpreting Scholia," 58, states that "[b]y Roman times a commentary could be tied by line numbering to an edition," adducing Asconius's commentary on Cicero as the best example of this.

5. The commentator's text, for example, could have been one that contained misspellings, duplications, omissions, or transpositions of words or phrases. On the causes of such

Even though our commentators presumably have a text of Demosthenes in front of them, they still sometimes choose to paraphrase or otherwise adapt lemmata and source material rather than to quote it. Stras. 84, for instance, contains heavily paraphrased lemmata. One lemma reads, "That they helped the Euboeans in three days" (ὅτι τρισὶν ἡμέραις ἐβοήθησαν [Εὐβοεῦσιν]), instead of the more precise "Just recently you helped the Euboeans within three days" (πρώην Εὐβοεῦσιν ἡμερῶν τριῶν ἐβοηθήσατε). The lemma from Dem. 5.25 in Berol. 21188 —"Therefore silly . . . to fight against everyone about the shadow at Delphi"—may, if the editor's restorations are correct, omit as many as fourteen words,[6] providing the reader with only the beginning and end of the passage to be discussed. Similarly, the huge quotation of the *Athenian Constitution* in Rain. 7 is interrrupted in the middle with the words "and after a few words" ([καὶ με]τ᾽ ὀλίγα), indicating that the commentator has omitted a passage deemed irrelevant to his purpose. The adaptation of lemmata, in any case, is not a sign of laziness or sloppy scholarly standards. It simply shows that lemmata in commentaries were never intended to replace an actual text of the author: their sole purpose was to help readers locate the passages in question.

After providing an appropriate lemma, ancient commentators on classical authors proceed to interpret the passage in question.[7] The most common target for their attention is an obscure word or proper name that their contemporary readers were unlikely to understand. There is considerable variety in the angles taken by the commentators in this regard. For example, Didymus assembles an impressive array of evidence from oratory and comedy in order to identify Aristomedes, a buffoon who is singled out of the audience for abuse in Dem. 10.70 (Berol. 9780, cols. 9.52–10.10). Stras. 84 contains a basic identification of the "treasurer" (ταμίας) of Dem. 22.17: "This man was the treasurer of the money for the trireme builders that was voted on by the Council toward the yearly expenses." But the commentator goes on to add a historical footnote to the effect that "the old *colacretae*" used to fulfill the same function. This additional information on Athenian constitutional history

---

discrepancies in the texts of ancient authors, see M. L. West, 15–29. See D-S¹, xliii–li, for speculations on the nature of the Demosthenes text used by Didymus in Berol. 9780.

6. καὶ κομιδῇ σχέτλιον πρὸς ἑκάστους καθ᾽ ἕν᾽ οὕτω προσενηνεγμένους περὶ τῶν οἰκείων καὶ ἀναγκαιοτάτων.

7. The sources and agenda of the commentators on Demosthenes are discussed more fully in chapter 2.

does little to illuminate Dem. 22.17, but it may have been interesting for its own sake to ancient students of history.

Didymus's commentary on the unusual word meaning "mixture of dregs of wine" (ἑωλοκρασία), which is preserved as fragment 3 in Harpocration, defines the word ἑωλοκρασία by paraphrasing the passage in which it occurs. In oration 18.50 Demosthenes says, "But that man is to blame, as he has splashed on me the ἑωλοκρασία of his own wickedness." The commentator recasts this sentence as "This man pours on me today the things that he mixed up (ἐκέρασε) yesterday and the day before (ἐχθὲς καὶ πρώην) and says that I did them." Not only does the paraphrase clarify the sense of the word ἑωλοκρασία by replacing it with presumably more familiar words, but it also cleverly reveals that the word is derived from ἕωλος (yesterday's) and κρασία (mixture).

Besides individual words, phrases, and proper names, the ancient commentators on Demosthenes also discussed more complex issues such as the dates of events that are alluded to in the speeches, the dates of the speeches themselves, questions of authenticity, and long-standing interpretative problems. Many of these discussions were prompted by disagreements in the secondary literature or in other existing interpretations. For example, the commentator in Berol. 21188 states that "Demosthenes did not use the expression ('about the shadow of an ass') because of the decree made by the Amphictyons"—note the implied disagreement with an alternate view—"but because of Philip, on account of his behavior with regard to Delphi and the Phocian affairs." In Berol. 9780, Didymus notes his disagreement with quite a few previous scholars: those who say that the "previous restoration" mentioned in Dem. 10.34 refers to the failed Peace of Antalcidas (col. 7.11–62); those who believe that Dem. 13 should be included among the *Philippics* (col. 13.16–25); and those who depict the tyrant Hermias of Atarneus as a completely good or a completely bad man (cols. 4.48–5.63), to name a few examples. The practice of openly disagreeing with predecessors, anonymous or otherwise, is of course a general characteristic of ancient scholarship.

If ancient commentators do not find any of the existing interpretations adequate, they often advance and defend new interpretations of their own. After giving two explanations from Didymus on the phrase "the law below," a commentator represented in Berol. 5008 appends a third interpretation: "But it is also possible that 'from below' is said because Ephialtes moved the *axones* and the *cyrbeis* from the Acropolis down to the Bouleuterion and the Agora, as Anaximenes says in the (n)th book of the *Philippica*."[8] Didymus's remarks at the beginning of his commentary on Dem. 13 are also instructive here:

> And some include this speech (Dem. 13) with the *Philippics,* which seems to me to be incorrect. For there is no mention of Philip in it at all, nor of the Macedonians, nor of the cities that he took in violation of the treaties and oaths—Perinthus, Olynthus, Potidaea—rather, the speech is about the freedom of the Rhodians and Mytilenaeans, neither of which cities has anything to do with Macedonia. (Berol. 9780, col. 13.16–25)

According to Didymus, it makes no sense to label oration 13 as a *Philippic,* and so an alternate schematization of the speeches that did so must be flawed.

Commentators in antiquity had various reasons for accepting one interpretation over another. One such reason was the claim of plausibility or reasonableness. Upon rejecting the view that the "previous restoration" of Dem. 10.34 is a reference to a failed Peace of Antalcidas in 392/1, Didymus comments that, under the circumstances, "Demosthenes probably was not reminding (the Athenians) of this peace, but of some other benefaction" (Berol. 9780, col. 7.28–31). According to Didymus, the failed peace agreement did not suit the background implied by the passage in Demosthenes. The availability of conflicting primary or secondary evidence could provide additional grounds to accept one interpretation over another. Didymus argues that oration 10 was delivered in 340/39, because Demosthenes "never would have said these things, if the Athenians had already actually broken the peace agreement" (Berol. 9780, col. 1.66–67). He then supports this contention with a quotation from Philochorus to demonstrate that the peace was still in effect in 340/39.

TRANSMISSION OF COMMENTARIES THROUGH EXCERPTION

As with most ancient commentaries and scholia, each isolated section of the commentaries on Demosthenes ends without a formal conclusion or transition to the next section. Punctuation and the introduction of a new lemma signal the beginning of the next independent section of the commentary. This distinctiveness of the different sections of the commentary had interesting consequences for the history of ancient scholarship.

---

8. Text from Blass, "Lexikon." See notes ad loc.

Ancient scholars often culled and copied out isolated, self-contained sections—that is, the comments that are intended to accompany the lemmata, and sometimes the lemmata themselves—from longer original commentaries. The material thus excerpted often fell into particular patterns: for example, etymologies, definitions of words from tragedy, or historical investigations. I use the term "excerption" to distinguish this almost surgical practice of copying out and redeploying distinct sections of a commentary from more holistic reductions of the length and scope of a work through overall paraphrase or summary, like Photius's *Bibliotheca,* the *periochae* of Livy, or Heraclides' epitome of the Aristotelian *Athenian Constitution.* Other terms, such as "condense," "epitomize," and "abridge," are simply too vague and do not accurately describe either the process or the results. Excerption could be followed up by reduction within the excerpted passages (through further cuts or paraphrase), but the section-by-section targeting of particular passages preceded any subsequent editorial changes.[9] The section-by-section organization of ancient commentaries in general, and those on Demosthenes in particular, made it easy for scholars to extract sections with a particular agenda to use in new scholarly works of their own.

SPECIAL AND GENERAL LEXICA

Excerption was routinely used in the imperial age to produce individual entries for special and general lexica to Demosthenes.[10] The special lexicon is a lexicon devoted to one particular oration, while the general lexicon is devoted to a larger collection of orations (such as the *Philippics*) or even the collected writings of the ten canonical Attic orators. Special lexica are represented by Rain. 7 (a lexicon to Dem. 21 dating to the fourth or fifth century C.E.) and Berol. 5008 (a lexicon to Dem. 23 also dating to the fourth or fifth century C.E.). General lexica are represented in this tradition only by Harpocration's *Lexeis of the Ten Orators* (second century C.E.).

In ancient lexica, individual entries were usually arranged either al-

9. As is clear from the differences between the discussion of "the law below" in P.Berol.inv. 5008 and in a corresponding entry in Harpocration; see Gibson, "P.Berol.inv. 5008"; and notes on text 3.

10. On ancient lexica in the papyri, see the excellent overview of Naoumides, "Greek Lexicography."

phabetically or in the order in which readers would normally encounter them in the text. Other methods of organizing lexica were possible, however. The entries in Rain. 7 were ordered by the initial sounds of the words, rather than strictly by their spellings. Pollux, a lexicographer of the second century C.E., organized his vast glossary-lexicon thematically. He used such themes as festivals (ἑορταί, book 1), types of dances (εἴδη ὀρχήσεως, book 3), words associated with philosophy (τὰ ἐπιστήμη συνημμένα ὀνόματα, book 4), diseases of dogs (περὶ νοσημάτων κυνῶν, book 5), and things at the baths (περὶ τῶν ἐν τῷ βαλανείῳ, book 10). This sort of organization would have made the lexicon difficult to consult for help in understanding the occurrence of a particular word in context, but this was apparently not the purpose of the book, as Pollux seems to have expected his addressee to read it from cover to cover.

Alphabetical order in antiquity rarely meant "absolute" alphabetical order in the modern sense—that is, extending to the final letter of each word in question.[11] It meant only that words beginning with the same letter were grouped together, with irregular attention paid to letters beyond the first letter. So long as the prospective reader could locate the word or phrase in question, there was little obsession with carrying out alphabetization to its logical conclusion. In general, as M. Naoumides has suggested, the larger the dictionary, the stricter its alphabetization.[12]

In the ancient scholarship on Demosthenes, the special lexicon did not give way to the general lexicon, nor did the general lexicon give way to the special lexicon. Both forms are found early, and both are found late. There was no "evolution" from the special lexicon to the commentary, or from the commentary to the special lexicon. The extant commentaries often focus on the etymology and usage of particular words, material that may well have been drawn from lexica. There are also some individual lexical entries that explicitly state that a particular bit of information on a word was found in a commentary *(hypomnema).*[13] Long entries in lexica (such as those in Berol. 5008) were almost certainly drawn from commentaries.[14] These different reference works were constantly in flux, as one might well expect with any reference works that were frequently consulted by successive generations of readers. No doubt there

11. On alphabetization in antiquity, see Daly.
12. Naoumides, "Greek Lexicography," 187–89.
13. See fragments 5 and 20 from Harpocration (text 2), below.
14. Naoumides, "Greek Lexicography," 195.

were times when one would find a commentary on Dem. 10 more useful than either an alphabetical special lexicon to the speech or a general
lexicon to the Attic orators. Each type of reference work answered a particular readerly need.

Individual entries in lexica resemble those of commentaries.[15] *Paragraphoi,* reverse indentation, and enlargement of the first letter of the
lemma were sometimes used to separate individual entries. The simplest
lexical entries supply a "gloss" of the word or phrase in question, replacing an unfamiliar word with a familiar synonym. In fragment 21 in Harpocration, Didymus glosses the phrase "they openly sell something in
the Agora" (ἐν τῇ ἀγορᾷ πωλῶσί τι ἀποπεφασμένως) with the less ambiguous "they publicly prostitute themselves" (πορνεύωσι φανερῶς). In
fragment 19, Didymus glosses the word ἐξένιζε (literally, "he foreignized") with the phrase "he spoke foreign-ly rather than Attic-ly" (οὐκ
Ἀττικῶς διελέγετο, ἀλλὰ ξενικῶς). Harpocration rejects Didymus's interpretation in favor of the meaning "he was a foreigner" (ξένος ἦν).

In addition to glosses, ancient lexicographers sometimes add references to the name of a work in which the word occurs and a brief lemma
containing the word. All the Harpocration entries surveyed in this book,
for example, open with the name of the Demosthenic oration in which
the word is found, while only about a third supplement that with an additional lemma.[16] This absence of lemmata should come as little sur-
prise, however, given that the reader of a lexical entry presumably comes
to that particular entry only after encountering the unknown word in
context.

Like commentaries, ancient lexica also sometimes quote from primary
and secondary source materials, or at least mention where corroborating sources can be found. The author of the comment on "Miltocythes"
in Berol. 5008 had consulted the historians Philochorus, Theopompus,
and Anaximenes. Rain. 7's discussion of the Athenian officials called *di-
aetetae* includes a large quotation from the Aristotelian *Athenian Constitution.* Didymus, as Harpocration informs us, had discussed the word
οἰκίσκος with references to parallels from the comic poets Aristophanes
and Metagenes (fragment 4 in Harpocration).

15. For information on surviving ancient lexica other than the ones examined in this
book, I refer the reader to Naoumides' excellent and insightful study, "The Fragments of
Greek Lexicography in the Papyri."
16. See fragments 3, 9, 13, 18, 19, and 21.

THE BYZANTINE SCHOLIA TO DEMOSTHENES

In late antiquity and in some cases possibly as late as the ninth century,[17] freestanding ancient commentaries on many classical authors were transferred to the wide margins of vellum manuscripts, where the material in them was continually supplemented, reduced, and reorganized down through the Byzantine period.[18] These marginal commentaries are commonly referred to as "scholia." The scholia to Demosthenes,[19] some of which may have originated in rhetorical commentaries written by Zosimus of Ascalon around 500 C.E.,[20] are today found in mediaeval manuscripts ranging in date from the ninth through the fifteenth century.[21] Nothing can better demonstrate the continuing popularity and relevance of Demosthenes in the Byzantine period than the existence of these copious notes written in the margins of his texts.

The scholia to an individual oration of Demosthenes typically open with a prologue that summarizes the contents of the oration, discusses its authenticity and date, and describes its organization using the traditional but flexible vocabulary of ancient and Byzantine rhetorical criticism. The scholia then proceed point by point to analyze Demosthenes' use of particular rhetorical figures and clarify terse or ambiguous expressions. Philological interests are represented in the form of basic etymologies and brief glosses. Discussions of historical figures and events are kept to a minimum and are accomplished in as few words as possible.

One would like to think that a great many mediaeval readers—or at

---

17. Wilson, "History of Scholia," discusses the evidence for dating the original composition of marginal scholia.

18. On this process, see Wilson, "History of Scholia," esp. 255–56. The history of most scholia is difficult to determine. According to Herington, 38, the Medicean scholia to Aeschylus's *Prometheus Bound*, for example, may "represent the remains of a large commentary pieced together (in the late Roman period?) from a number of *hypomnemata*, somewhat as the far better preserved Homer scholia are definitely known to have been assembled."

19. See the introductions to Dilts, vols. 1–2, for overview and bibliography on this subject.

20. Wilson, "History of Scholia," 254–55; G. Kennedy, *Greek Rhetoric*, 88, 170.

21. Marginal scholia are found in only two ancient texts of Demosthenes. There are two single-word "glosses" on Dem. 25.63–67 (actually only repetitions of words found in the accompanying text) in *P.Flor.* VIII.39 (Pack² 325), a text on vellum dating to the fifth century C.E. Scholia also appear between the two columns of a text of Dem. 23.103–4 dating to the third century C.E.; for the text, see Schwendner, text 7. Some of these scholia correctly explain Demosthenes' reference to τοὺς μὲν ἀσθενεῖς as τοὺς ἑτέρους βασιλ(έας), and identify the referent of τὸν δ' ἕνα ὄντα ἰσχυρόν as Cersobleptes; the others are illegible.

least their teachers—were able to read Demosthenes with such notes in the margin to assist them. When they did so, they would have found that the scholiasts consistently recommended to them a particular interpretative agenda, a particular way of reading Demosthenes. To the Byzantine scholiasts, reading Demosthenes mainly meant reading the public speeches[22]—his famous rhetorical masterpieces—and interpreting them primarily from a rhetorical perspective.

In an early and influential article on Berol. 9780, F. Leo assumed that Didymus's lost commentaries on Demosthenes—he did not mean the ones represented by fragments in Harpocration[23]—were rhetorical in nature and were the main source for the Byzantine scholiasts. A. Gudeman followed Leo's suggestion in an entry on scholia in a standard classics encyclopedia, asserting with great conviction that Didymus was definitely the ultimate source of the Demosthenic scholia.[24] No doubt this assumption was encouraged by the appearance of Didymus's name in the scholia to other classical authors. Some years later, R. Pfeiffer—the author of the most frequently read and consulted book on ancient scholarship of the last generation—not only adopted Leo's idea but essentially made it the key to understanding the genres of ancient scholarship.[25] Despite authoritative assurances to the contrary, however, it is unlikely that Didymus ever wrote extensive rhetorical commentaries on Demosthenes, or that these supposed commentaries were used by the Byzantine scholiasts.

To begin with, there are only two comments attributed to Didymus by name in the Demosthenic scholia, and neither demonstrates an interest in rhetoric. In fact, both are selections already known from the ancient philological and historical tradition. Didymus fragment 7 (from Harpocration) has been picked up by the B scholia to Dem. 21.17, and Didymus fragment 11 (from Harpocration) has been picked up by the B scholia to Dem. 24.105.[26] The tenth-century encyclopedia called the *Suda*,[27]

---

22. They preferred the public over the private speeches. There are over ten times as many scholia to oration 19, for example, as there are to all the private speeches combined. Among the private speeches, there are no scholia to orations 28, 31, 36, 41–45, 47–53, and 56. The ninth-century scholar and patriarch Photius says that, in his day, the public orations were generally considered better specimens of composition (*Bibliotheca* 490b–491a; ed. Henry).

23. Leo, "Didymos," 260.

24. Gudeman, "Scholien," 699.

25. Pfeiffer, *Classical Scholarship*, 278 (see also 29, 213, 218).

26. The B scholia are edited by Baiter and Sauppe; on which see Dilts, xvii.

27. For an overview of this work, see Adler.

which adapted both these entries from Harpocration or an intermediary, is probably the source for the scholiasts' comments here.

Furthermore, Didymus's surviving writings on Demosthenes show little if any interest in rhetoric. In Berol. 9780, Didymus analyzes a complicated sentence from Dem. 10.34 to show how its "hyperbatic phrasing" (ὑπερβάτωι τῆι φράσει) should be "reconstrued" (καταστατέον) (cols. 6.66–7.7). Perhaps this represents an interest in rhetoric; it is far from certain, though. The limited technical vocabulary used in the passage does not correspond to other ancient discussions of Demosthenes' rhetoric or to discussions in the Byzantine scholia. In addition, Didymus never says precisely what the term "hyperbatic phrasing" means or why it might be important to the aspiring orator, as we might well expect a rhetorical commentator to do.

A certain Ammonius appears to cite a collection of "rhetorical commentaries" by Didymus: "Didymus in Book 11 of the *Rhetorica Hypomnemata* says the following: that ships are different from boats. For boats are rounded, while ships have oars and carry troops."[28] The name or description of the work from which this information comes (ῥητορικὰ ὑπομνήματα) could be translated as *Rhetorical Commentaries*. And certainly, it is conceivable that rhetorical commentaries might contain this sort of information. However, given that this single fragment so closely resembles what we find in Didymus's surviving philological and historical commentaries—especially fragment 8 (from Harpocration)—the correct sense of the title or description is more likely to be *Commentaries on the Orators* (like ὑπομνήματα εἰς τοὺς ῥήτορας), a multivolume collection of exactly the sort of commentaries studied in this book.

In summary, Didymus—like most intellectuals in the ancient world —may well have been conversant with the prominent rhetorical theories of his day, but there is little evidence that this affected how he approached the task of commenting on Demosthenes. On the evidence currently available, there is no reason to accept Leo's supposition that Didymus wrote rhetorical commentaries on Demosthenes or that these commentaries served as the main source for the Byzantine scholia. We shall reserve discussion of how this apparently mistaken assumption affected Leo's reading of Berol. 9780 for chapter 3.

Rather than seeking evidence for the influence of texts that may never

---

28. Δίδυμος ἐν ἑνδεκάτῳ ῥητορικῶν ὑπομνημάτων φησὶν οὕτως· ὅτι διαφέρουσιν αἱ νῆες τῶν πλοίων. τὰ μὲν γάρ ἐστι στρογγύλα, αἱ δὲ κωπήρεις καὶ στρατιώτιδες (no. 334, ed. Nickau). Fragment also given in Schmidt, 321.

have existed, it is more relevant to our purposes to consider two other questions: Was the content of the Demosthenic scholia influenced by the ancient philological and historical commentaries on Demosthenes? And can the scholia provide us with further independent evidence by which to reconstruct those commentaries? The answer seems to be a qualified "no" in both cases.

In comparing the ancient commentaries and lexica with the Byzantine scholia that discuss the same passages, one finds only a few correspondences. The scholiasts did not use any material from the texts in Rain. 7, Berol. 5008, Berol. 21188, or Stras. 84. Two selections from Didymus that appear in the scholia and are attributed to Didymus by name have already been mentioned. There are also two other scholia that draw on Didymus but do not attribute the remarks to him. Didymus fragment 3 (from Harpocration) is picked up by the scholia to Dem. 18.50 (Dilts 102a), and Didymus fragment 8 (from Harpocration) appears in the scholia to Dem. 21.133 (Dilts 471b), both with only slight alterations. In the case of the scholia to Dem. 21.133, the scholiast's use of the words εἶδος ἐκπώματος shows that he is reading Harpocration's report of Didymus's view, not reading Didymus in the original. Although the words εἶδος ἐκπώματος are found in Harpocration's entry for *cymbion,* they come from a part of the entry that is not attributed to Didymus and so presumably are Harpocration's own contribution.

A third example provides no verbal similarities but may nevertheless reveal Didymus's influence. In an overview of Dem. 10, the scholia briefly gloss the "former restoration" of Dem. 10.34 as "Conon's sea-battle" (τὴν διὰ Κόνωνος ναυμαχίαν).[29] This identification cannot be made from reading Demosthenes alone; it must have come from a secondary source. In Berol. 9780, Didymus argues at length for this identification and against others (col. 7.7–62). If the scholiasts got this idea from Didymus, someone in the course of its transmission has stripped a very detailed and amply illustrated argument down to a four-word punch line.

With the exception of this curious final example, it seems that the Demosthenic scholiasts knew only those parts of the ancient philological and historical commentaries that made their way into large, general lexica like Harpocration's *Lexeis of the Ten Orators* and the *Suda.* Whether the scholiasts were also able to draw directly or indirectly on philologi-

---

29. Dilts, vol. 1, p. 153, lines 8–9 (Dilts 9).

cal and historical commentaries that are lost to us—and thus are largely beyond our ability to detect—is unknown.

Throughout this chapter we have presupposed generations of scholars who brought to the task of commenting their different needs and interests, their different assumptions about their audiences, and their own unique ways of posing and answering questions about the text of Demosthenes. With this account of the form and transmission of the commentaries constantly in mind, we shall turn now to consider the sources, critical agenda, and readership of these largely unknown ancient scholars.

CHAPTER 2

Sources, Agenda, and Readership

Information, ideas, and arguments about Demosthenes' orations were passed among various sorts of commentaries and lexica from at least the first century B.C. down to the end of antiquity and beyond, as we have seen in the previous chapter. But to characterize this exchange and transfer as the mechanics of transmission, and to stop at that, is to privilege the process over the purpose, the raw data of exchange over the commentators who developed and shaped it and the audiences for whom they did so. The intent of the present chapter, therefore, is to use the surviving texts to illuminate the sources, methods, and agenda of the commentators and—to the extent that it is possible—to reconstruct their intended audiences.

SECONDARY SOURCES: DIDYMUS AND HIS PREDECESSORS

Any discussion of the sources used by the commentators should begin with Didymus. Little is known about Didymus's life. He was born and raised in Alexandria, and he lived and worked in the second half of the first century B.C.[1] He was part of the last generation of Alexandrian scholars before Rome became the new center of Greek learning.[2] He

---

1. On his life and dates, see Cohn; Pfeiffer, *Classical Scholarship*, 274–79; Fraser, 1: 471–74.
2. Fraser, 1: 467–75; see Pöhlmann, 1: 61–68, on the first Greek philologists at Rome.

wrote commentaries on the full range of classical Greek authors. He also compiled lexica of rare and obscure words from tragedy, comedy, and the Hippocratic corpus.[3] None of these writings survives except in quotations preserved in later authors ("fragments"). Also lost, except in fragments, are Didymus's commentaries on the Attic orators Demosthenes (except Berol. 9780), Aeschines, Hyperides, Isaeus, and possibly Isocrates, Dinarchus, and Antiphon.[4] More fragments of Didymus's commentaries on Demosthenes survive than of his commentaries on all the other orators combined. These fragments show that Didymus commented on the orations we know as numbers 4–5, 9–11, 13, 18–19, 21–25, 30, 43, 46, 49, 53, 57, and 59. Based on the apparently random distribution of these fragments from speeches throughout the Demosthenic corpus, we may conclude that Didymus produced commentaries on the whole of the corpus as it was known to him.[5]

By all accounts Didymus is the key figure in the ancient philological and historical tradition of commentaries on Demosthenes. But how important was Didymus, actually? We shall begin by noting two undisputed facts: Didymus is the only philological and historical commentator on Demosthenes whose name we know, and his dates are earlier than the dates of the earliest surviving texts from the tradition. These two facts could be due merely to the chance survival of evidence from a period in which survival was the exception rather than the rule. Nevertheless, they have helped to elevate Didymus to the rank of most important commentator in nearly every existing account of this tradition.[6] Regardless of how important he actually is (a question to which we shall return momentarily), it is worth considering in some detail the other factors that have contributed to Didymus's prominence in the story. Some of this discussion should also be applicable to the study of ancient scholarship in general.

First and foremost, histories of ancient scholarship have traditionally been oriented toward the names of prominent individuals. Since Didymus's name is the only one known in the philological and historical tradition of commentaries on Demosthenes, the modern author of a nar-

---

3. On which see Wilamowitz, *Einleitung,* 158–66; Fraser, 1: 473. For the fragments of Didymus's lexica, see Schmidt, 15–111.

4. Discussion in Cohn, 458–60; for the fragments, see Schmidt, 310–20.

5. There is no evidence that he knew or commented on the letters, the *Essay on Love,* the *Funeral Oration,* or the *prooemia.*

6. Lossau's *Untersuchungen zur antiken Demosthenesexegese,* Palingenesia 2 (Bad Homburg, 1964) is the one exception.

rative history is compelled to assign him a key role in the story. From there it is only a short but slippery step to the unprovable assumption that Didymus is the filter through which any pre-Didymean scholarship on Demosthenes passed, and the source from which all post-Didymean commentary on Demosthenes emanated. Such a tidy account is unlikely to be correct.

A second and closely related factor contributing to the historiographical prominence of Didymus is the desire of philologists to attribute all that is unattributed.[7] While the impetus to connect unknown works with known authors and thereby produce a semblance of order is understandable, this practice has produced a number of unconfirmed "sightings" of Didymus throughout the unattributed ancient responses to Demosthenes. Such attributions seem to have the effect of discouraging further comment on the texts, as though attribution to a known author has already essentially "explained" them. But it is important to remember that no other names have been passed down to us. Had we but one more name of a philological and historical commentator who is said to have written on Demosthenes, modern scholars might have been a bit more reluctant to credit Didymus with authorship of the unattributed lexical entries in Rain. 7,[8] the unattributed commentary in Stras. 84,[9] and the lexical entries in Harpocration that "seem Didymean."[10] It is certainly not impossible that some anonymous fragments of Didymus survive in these texts, but even if they do, each of them is still the result of some other scholar's work of selection, organization, and perhaps revision. There is still work to be done, then, after texts and their presumed authors have been reunited.

A third reason for Didymus's prominence in histories of ancient scholarship is the periodization of ancient intellectual history in accordance with models from political history. The usual periodization results in the portrayal of Didymus as a third-shift custodian to Hellenistic scholarship, who swept up around the worktables of his more illustrious predecessors and guarded their collective achievement through mindless copying and compilation. The best known of such portrayals is that of

---

7. Daintree notes the common desire in modern discussions of late-ancient and medieval commentaries "to provide valuable anonymous scholia with a respectable paternity, certainly with a late antique pedigree if a classical one cannot be managed" (69).

8. Wessely in *Archiv*.

9. Laqueur, 220.

10. D-S[1], xvii.

J. E. Sandys in *A History of Classical Scholarship*. Didymus, according to Sandys,

> deserves our gratitude for gathering together the results of earlier work in criticism and exegesis, and transmitting these results to posterity. The age of creative and original scholars was past, and the best service that remained to be rendered was the careful preservation of the varied stores of ancient learning; and this service was faithfully and industriously rendered by Didymus.[11]

Despite its attractions and widespread acceptance, this portrayal of Didymus is not primarily based on the evidence provided by surviving ancient texts. Rather, it seems mainly to be a reflection of the storyteller's need for periodization and closure. Diachronic narratives of the history of Greek scholarship tend to break off with the end of the period known to us (but not to antiquity) as the Hellenistic Age. This break provides the historian a convenient opportunity to backtrack and narrate the story of Roman scholarship from its beginnings. The story of Greek learning is then typically resumed, after a break of a century or so, with the colorful personalities of the Second Sophistic.

Were intellectual histories not so constrained by the equally problematic periodizations of political history, Didymus might find a more congenial home—and one with as much or more textual evidence to recommend it—in a chapter on commentaries and lexica to classical Greek authors. The recurrence of his name in a wide variety of sources certainly leads one to suspect that no matter what classical Greek author an imperial-age scholar was researching, the published opinions of Didymus simply could not be ignored. Didymus's influence alone—as measured by the frequency with which later sources mention him, whether favorably or unfavorably—recommends against portraying him as a suffering servant longing nostalgically for the heyday of Alexandrian scholarship. Rather, insofar as he collects, studies, reports, modifies, and rejects the findings of his predecessors, Didymus differs little from the vast majority of scholars who have ever lived.

It has sometimes been assumed, mainly owing to the absence of earlier Hellenistic evidence to the contrary, that Didymus's commentaries on Demosthenes are based on fewer secondary sources than are his commentaries on other authors.[12] Nevertheless, there is evidence in Didy-

---

11. Sandys, *Classical Scholarship*, 1: 143.
12. Cohn, 458.

mus's surviving commentaries to show that even in this area he is working within an established field of scholarly inquiry. Before we turn to consider how Didymus uses ideas that he encounters in his predecessors' commentaries, we should examine how Didymus uses the potential optative in his commentaries, and whether this can provide any additional evidence for understanding the relationship between Didymus and his sources.

Didymus frequently uses the potential optative in Berol. 9780.[13] In several passages a "someone" is included as the agent of the action:

> Someone might perhaps perceive (τάχ' ἄν τ[ις σ]υν[ίδοι]) the date of the speech from what Philochorus says, putting it under the archonship of Nicomachus. (col. 1.29–30)

> And someone might be able to point out (ἄν κ(αὶ) . . . τις ἔχοι παρα-[δ]ε[ι]κνύναι) many other benefactions of the king to the city, such as the peace proposed before the Assembly by Callias, son of Hipponicus, and the monetary contributions—both individual and public—to the city, of which Demosthenes might perhaps be reminding them here, as in a summary (τάχ' ἄν . . . ὡς ἐν κεφαλαίωι τὰ νῦν ὑπομιμνήσκοι). (cols. 7.71–8.2)

> And someone might conjecture (στοιχάσαιτο δ' ἄν τις) that the king's magnanimity toward the Athenian people arose from his suspicion against the Macedonian, against whom he intended to bring war, because he had heard from Hermias of Atarneus that war was being prepared against him. (col. 8.26–32)

> But someone might suspect (ὑποτοπήσειε δ' ἄν τις)—not far from the mark—that a derivative little speech has been assembled, compiled from certain orations of Demosthenes. (col. 11.7–10)

> Someone might perceive (συν[ί]δοι τις ἄν) the date of the speech as being the archonship of Callimachus, the one after Apollodorus. (col. 13.40–42)

On other occasions Didymus omits the "someone" from the formulation, but the potentiality of the situation still remains:

---

13. A brief explanation of this construction may be helpful for the Greekless reader. The verb in the English language has three moods: the indicative, which is used to state facts and ask questions; the imperative, which is used to issue commands; and the subjunctive, which is used mainly in certain conditional sentences. To these three moods Greek adds a fourth, the optative. The optative mood is used in a number of ways in Greek. Most relevant to our purposes, it can be used in the future less vivid (or "should-would") conditional sentence; for example: "If it *should* rain tomorrow, the turtle *would* get wet." If the "if" clause (the protasis) is dropped from such a sentence, the result in Greek is a construction called the potential optative. Now the turtle would get wet, could get wet, may get wet, or might get wet: English provides several ways of expressing the "potential" for its getting wet. To extend this example more generally, one may say that the potential optative is used in Greek to describe situations that may or may not happen ("The turtle could/may/would get wet").

And his connection by marriage with Aristotle and the paean written for him might seem (δόξε[ιεν ἄν]) to bear witness to his *arete,* and it might not be a bad idea (κοὺκ ἄν [ἔ]χ[ο]ι φαύλως) to give this text, because it is not easily accessible for most people. (col. 6.18–22)

And Anaximenes in book 6 of his histories *On Philip*—of which I omit any quotation, for it is not useful—might seem (δόξ[ειε] δ' ἄν) to have set forth the stories about him, as it were, deficiently. (col. 6.59–62)

But in the present passage Demosthenes might possibly be recalling (δύναιτο δ' ἄν . . . μνημονεύειν) another peace proposal from the king, one which the Athenians gladly accepted. (col. 7.62–65)

But it might be (ε[ἴ]η δ' ἄν) better to note briefly the words of Philochorus. (col. 8.15–16)

This date might be (εἴη ἄν) when they were beaten and humbled at Aegospotami and when, for a short time, the people were curtailed, since the foreign revenues were cut off. (col. 8.49–53)

This might be (τοῦτ' ἄν εἴη) the date of the deliberative speech and the end of the *Philippics.* (col. 11.5–7)

Alexander might seem (δόξειε δ' ἄν) to have enjoyed a better fortune than his father with regard to wounds and blows. (col. 13.7–10)

When we have examined this passage, (we can see that) the speech—which contains a recommendation for things needed for war, in preparation for the event that there should actually be a war—might have been composed (εἴη ἄν . . . συντεταγμ(έν)ος) after this archonship. (col. 13.58–62)

M. J. Lossau has argued that the potential optative in such passages indicates Didymus's close dependence on anonymous authorities.[14] In other words, Lossau might expand the phrase "Someone might think" with the parenthetical "and indeed an anonymous authority *does* think so." This view does not seem to be well founded. In each of the above examples, the optative mood is used to describe something that is merely "potential": something that may or may not happen. The potential optative cannot be made to bear more than this semantic load. Against Lossau's view, K. T. Osborne has argued that these same passages are precisely the ones in which we can see Didymus venturing, albeit cautiously, to advance new theories of his own.[15] Osborne thus might expand the phrase "Someone might think" with a parenthetical "and indeed I, Didymus, do, though perhaps only tentatively." Osborne's view seems more likely to be correct. We shall proceed under the assumption that the po-

14. Lossau, 93–95.
15. Osborne, 31–33, 43–44.

tential optative cannot tell us anything about the pre-Didymean history of Demosthenic criticism.

More concrete evidence for the relationship between Didymus and his predecessors is found in Didymus's references to "some," anonymous authorities who had expressed various views on Demosthenes:

> Some (ἔνιοι) say that the speech (Dem. 10) was composed in the archonship of Sosigenes. (col. 2.2–3)

> Some say that by the 'previous restoration' he (Demosthenes) means the Peace that came down in the time of Antalcidas the Spartan. (col. 7.11–14)

> There are those who ((εἰσὶν) οἵ) say that this deliberative speech is by Anaximenes of Lampsacus, because of the fact that it has been inserted in Book 7 of his *Philippica* with almost these very words. (col. 11.10–14)

> Some interpreted his words as being rather 'vulgar,' since ὀρρωδεῖν, and whatever words there are like it, are hardly Demosthenic. (col. 11.14–17)

> Some include this speech with the *Philippics*. (col. 13.16–18)

In each case, "some" are most likely the authors of other commentaries on Demosthenes that Didymus has consulted. It is also worth mentioning the possibility—though it is one supported by no surviving physical evidence—that Didymus possessed annotated texts of Demosthenes containing brief introductory notes about dates of delivery and authenticity, and perhaps marginal glosses that briefly identified and dated historical allusions or commented on word choice.[16] In this scenario, Didymus's commentaries might consist in part of responses to anonymous notations in a text of Demosthenes.

Didymus's references to "some" have sometimes been discussed as though Didymus were a modern scholar who has failed to give proper credit to his sources. But Didymus's habits in this regard conform to those of most ancient authors.[17] In contrast with the practices of modern scholars, most ancient authors in general make little explicit reference to their use of source material, and ancient scholars are no excep-

---

16. There would not have been much room for such comments in most ancient texts (Zuntz, 74–75). On the use of annotated texts as source material, see Sealey, *Demosthenes*, 227, for a suggestion about the sources used by Dionysius of Halicarnassus in his *First Letter to Ammaeus*.

17. For example, in his study of the P scholia to Aeschylus's *Prometheus Bound*, Herington says that "what [the scribe of P] did was no different from what any serious student would have done at his time and in his circumstances, or indeed from what any serious student does now, with one important exception: we usually add our source references" (22).

tion.[18] When Didymus refers to his source material, he does so for the same reasons that most educated scholars in antiquity do. When he agrees with his predecessors or at least can find no fault with their views, he simply says, "Some say X," and leaves it at that without further comment. This is standard practice in ancient scholarship. When Didymus disagrees with them, he says something like "Some say X, but they are wrong," and follows this statement with a discussion of the evidence that leads him to disagree with them. Again, this is standard practice. And when Didymus simply wants to show that other views exist—views that he has no particular desire to discuss in detail—he tacks them on to the end of the discussion, after he has shown that other views are wrong and his view is right. Take, for example, Didymus's closing comments on the meaning of the "previous restoration" mentioned in Dem. 10.34:

> But in the present passage Demosthenes might possibly be recalling another peace proposal from the king, one that the Athenians gladly accepted. . . . And someone might be able to point out many other benefactions of the king to the city, such as the peace proposed before the Assembly by Callias, son of Hipponicus, and the monetary contributions—both individual and public—to the city, of which Demosthenes might perhaps be reminding them here, as in a summary. (Berol. 9780, cols. 7.62–8.2)

Didymus had opened this discussion by arguing that a predecessor's view —namely that the "previous restoration" was a failed Peace of Antalcidas in 392/1—was incorrect. He went on to argue that the "previous restoration" was actually an allusion to Conon's Persian-sponsored defeat of the Spartans at Cnidus in 394 (but described by Philochorus under the year 397/6). He now closes the discussion by appending the above list of theories, which might also conceivably explain the "previous restoration." These views are offered without elaboration, without confirmation or rejection. They simply exist. And although Didymus apparently does not find them worth his full attention, he may have felt a responsibility at least to note their existence.[19]

One thing is clear: Didymus is actively engaged in evaluating what previous scholars had contributed to the interpretation of Demosthenes. His purpose is not simply to rehash the available bibliography on the subject at hand. Such is H. Yunis's characterization of Didymus, whom

---

18. In general on ancient historians' attitudes toward their sources, see Veyne, 5–15.

19. It seems unlikely that Didymus treated these scholars anonymously simply because he felt their ideas were of poor quality, as Sealey, *Demosthenes*, 228, suggests; he is here following D-S[1], xliii.

he sees simply as a tour guide through a survey of "what had by his day become standard discussions of classical literature."[20] To the contrary: to the extent that "standard discussions" of Demosthenes existed in Didymus's day, it was largely Didymus's goal to subvert them.[21] In particular, Didymus's purpose in quoting views with which he disagrees is to provide himself with convenient positions against which to argue and then to advance his own theories. His identification of the "previous restoration" in cols. 7.7–8.2, discussed above, is a good example of this. The beginning of his discussion of Dem. 13 is also relevant: "And some include this speech with the *Philippics,* which seems to me to be incorrect" (col. 13.16–18). After stating that it is incorrect to include Dem. 13 among the group of speeches called the *Philippics,* Didymus goes on to demonstrate why the label "*Philippic*" does not accurately describe it: "For there is no mention of Philip in it at all, nor of the Macedonians, nor of the cities that he took in violation of the treaties and oaths. . . . Rather, the speech is about the freedom of the Rhodians and Mytilenaeans, neither of which cities has anything to do with Macedonia" (col. 13.18–25). As with much of ancient scholarship, Didymus sometimes mentions the views of his predecessors for the express purpose of correcting them.

Ancient philological and historical scholarship on Demosthenes apparently regarded Didymus as a "must consult" source. Harpocration and the authors of the lexica in Berol. 21188 and Berol. 5008 cite Didymus (and only Didymus) by name, and other surviving texts may also betray his influence. Perhaps Didymus's name was the only one that later generations remembered. In any case, Didymus's references to "some" in Berol. 9780 show conclusively that he was not the first to conduct philological and historical investigations into Demosthenes' orations, and the other surviving texts and literary fragments show that he was far from the last to do so. As Didymus did with his predecessors' views, so also his anonymous successors sometimes report his theories without further discussion (Berol. 21188, Berol. 5008, Harpocration) and sometimes use his theories as occasions against which to define their own views (Harpocration). In short, Didymus was at least as important as—and perhaps a great deal more important than—the other unnamed scholars

---

20. Yunis, 1055; see also 1049–50.
21. Similarly, Osborne, 7–9 and passim; also Sealey, *Demosthenes,* 228: "Even before the time of Didymos the speeches of Demosthenes had been studied and expounded, but the work of exposition had not been done well."

who were working to correct the views of their predecessors and to make Demosthenes accessible to readers in their own times and places.

PRIMARY SOURCES

Ancient scholars who wrote on Demosthenes from a philological and historical perspective drew on their broad acquaintance with Greek poetry and criticism thereon, fourth- and third-century historians, and other assorted literary sources in order to illuminate Demosthenes' orations for their contemporary audiences.

Alexandrian scholarship on epic, tragedy, and comedy provides the Demosthenic commentators with parallels for curious expressions in Demosthenes, etymological discussions, and other kinds of information. Didymus quotes the *Odyssey* in order to prove that a peculiar word for "to fear" in Demosthenes (ὀρρωδεῖν) derives etymologically from the fact that fearful people have sweaty rear ends (Berol. 9780, col. 11.22–23). Homer's *Iliad* is cited in Berol. 5008 to prove that "on the road" (ἐν ὁδῷ) was an ancient Greek euphemism for "in ambush." A line from the *Iliad* is also quoted in Didymus's discussion of the etymology of "Orgas" (col. 14.18–20), along with relevant lines from the tragedians Aeschylus and Sophocles.

Parallels from the comic poets Aristophanes and Metagenes, according to Harpocration (fragment 4), misled Didymus into thinking that Demosthenes was talking about a "bird coop" in *On the Crown,* when he was actually only talking about a "small house." Aristophanes also provides Didymus with parallels for two etymological discussions in Berol. 9780. One is the aforementioned discussion of "to fear" (ὀρρωδεῖν) (col. 11.23–26). The other demonstrates that the verb "to abuse" (σκορακίζειν) derives from the proverbial expression "to the crows" (ἐς κόρακας) (cols. 11.52–12.33). Longer passages from the fourth-century comic poets Philemon and Timocles help Didymus fill out his identification of the famous Athenian thief named Aristomedes "the Brazen" (cols. 9.62–10.11). The "comic poets" may also have been invoked as a group at the end of Stras. 84.

The commentators also consulted later classical and Hellenistic poetry. Aristotle's hymn and epigram in honor of the tyrant Hermias (Berol. 9780, col. 6.22–43) is answered by the vicious reply of Theocritus of Chios to the effect that Aristotle despised Platonic philosophy in preference to Macedonian patronage and sex with a barbarian

(col. 6.43–49). The Hellenistic poets Euphorion and Callimachus figure in Didymus's etymological discussions of "Orgas" in Berol. 9780
(cols. 14.17–18 and 31–35), and Euphorion's lost epyllion called *Apollodorus* is somehow relevant to Didymus's contention that particular
kinds of ancient legal texts were written in the style called "boustrophedon," each successive line running left-to-right and then right-to-left
(fragment 10 in Harpocration).

The most prominent sources in the ancient commentaries on Demosthenes, however, are fourth- and third-century historians who wrote on
Athens, Macedonia, and the world. There is only one citation of Ephorus's universal history (Berol. 5008), and only one of Xenophon's *Hellenica* (fragment 1 in Harpocration). The rest of the commentators'
citations of historians come from fourth- and third-century historians
of Athens and Macedonia. According to Harpocration, when Didymus
cites the Atthidographer Phanodemus for the fact "that a wedding feast
was given at weddings to one's fellow clansmen," he is mistaken; this information, he says, cannot be found anywhere in Phanodemus (fragment 20 in Harpocration). The historians of Macedonia, Marsyas and
Duris, give conflicting accounts of how Philip lost his eye (Berol. 9780,
col. 12.43–55). The historian Callisthenes provides a favorable account
of the life and times of Hermias, which balances the unfavorable one by
Theopompus (Berol. 9780, cols. 5.64–6.18).

The Atthidographer Anaximenes does not fare well at the hands of
the commentators on Demosthenes. His account of Hermias is dismissed
as useless (Berol. 9780, col. 6.59–62); he is tacked on as a corroborating footnote to the preferred accounts of Philochorus and Theopompus
(Berol. 5008); and he is explicitly rejected at one point in favor of Philochorus (Berol. 9780, col. 8.14–16). Yet Anaximenes was read. Didymus names his *On Alexander* as a source for the "wrong" Aristomedes of Berol. 9780, col. 9.43–52; he also briefly mentions the theory
that Anaximenes may have been the author of Dem. 11 (Berol. 9780,
col. 11.10–14). Anaximenes' *Philippica* also provides another commentator with information about Ephialtes' legal reforms (fragment 10
in Harpocration).

Along with Anaximenes, the Atthidographer Androtion is apparently
rejected in favor of Philochorus in Berol. 9780, col. 8.14–16. However,
he is later quoted in full in a second account of Athenian-Megarian dealings at the "no-man's-land" called Orgas (Berol. 9780, col. 14.35–49).
The historian Theopompus gives an unfavorable account of Hermias
(Berol. 9780, cols. 4.66–5.64), is said to have narrated the arrest and

death of Miltocythes (Berol. 5008), and is mentioned as providing corroborating evidence in the discussion of the Spartan *morae* (Berol. 5008).
Theopompus's *On Philip* provides Didymus with historical information about fourth-century Athenian revenues (Berol. 9780, cols. 8.58–
9.9), the "wrong" Aristomedes (col. 9.43–52), Philip's theft of the
boats at Hieron (col. 10.39–50), and Athenian troubles with Megara
(cols. 14.52–15.10).

Though the Atthidographer Philochorus is cited for details about Miltocythes and the procedure of ostracism in Berol. 5008, it is Didymus
who makes the most use of him. Philochorus is Didymus's main source
for chronological arguments in Berol. 9780. He helps Didymus date
the Athenian aid to Eretria and Oreus (col. 1.1–25), the tenth oration
(col. 1.29–30), the breakdown of the peace with Philip (cols. 1.53–
2.2), the Athenian rejection of the Peace of Antalcidas (col. 7.14–
28), the Persian king's failed embassy to Athens (col. 8.17–23), Philip's
theft of the ships at Hieron (cols. 10.50–11.5), and the affair at Orgas
(col. 13.40–58).

The ancient commentators also draw quite a bit of their information
from various other literary sources. The Peripatetic Hermippus's biography of Aristotle is used in Didymus's discussion of Hermias (Berol. 9780,
col. 6.51–53), and the aforementioned quotation of Theocritus of Chios
was obtained at second hand from a work of Bryon called *On Theocritus* (col. 6.43–49). Timosthenes' geographical work *On Harbors* helps
Didymus identify the city of Nicaea (Berol. 9780, col. 11.28–37), while
Aristotle's *Customs of the Barbarians* provides him with certain information about Scythian customs (Berol. 9780, col. 4.14–15). Theophrastus's *Laws* furnishes Harpocration with information about the Attic theatre, directly contradicting a view expressed by Didymus (fragment 7 in
Harpocration). The author of the commentary in Stras. 84 apparently
had access to a collection of fifth-century Athenian inscriptions.[22]

An accomplished and important figure in paroemiography (the collection and study of proverbial expressions),[23] Didymus uses proverb
collections to explain certain colloquial expressions in Demosthenes. In
Berol. 9780, cols. 11.62–12.33, Didymus explains the verb σκορακίζειν
by quoting at great length from the paroemiographer Demon's aetiology
of the expression "to the crows" (ἐς κόρακας). In the quoted selection,
Demon relates how certain young men who went into voluntary exile

22. On the use of inscriptions by ancient Greek authors, see most recently Higbie.
23. For a history of the genre, see Rupprecht, "Paroimiographoi," esp. 1747–68.

because of a prank involving crows were consequently themselves called
Crows; ever since that day, says Demon, anyone who is exiled is told to
go "to the Crows." This is a good example of how Didymus's research
on other subjects may have helped shape his agenda in writing commentaries on Demosthenes. Didymus is also cited in Harpocration and
in Berol. 21188 for his intepretation of the phrase "about the shadow of
an ass," an ancient proverbial expression referring to useless quarreling
over inconsequential matters. In the context of Dem. 5.25, Didymus had
taken the Demosthenic "about the shadow at Delphi" to be an adaptation of this proverb referring to Philip's "behavior with regard to Delphi
and the Phocian affairs" (Berol. 21188).

Among the most useful of these other literary sources were the constitutional histories of Greek city-states. Spartan constitutions by Xenophon and Aristotle are used by one commentator to clarify the relationship between the military contingents called *morae* and the other
divisions of the Spartan army (Berol. 5008). The fifth-century tyrant Critias's *Spartan Constitution* provides Harpocration and Athenaeus with
a reference to a "Milesian-made bed" (κλίνη Μιλησιουργής), which
helps them argue that Didymus's interpretation of the word Λυκιουργεῖς
in Dem. 49 is morphologically impossible (fragment 17 in Harpocration). A large section of the Aristotelian *Athenian Constitution* is quoted
by another commentator in order to define the duties of a particular
Athenian political office (Rain. 7), and an unknown constitutional history seems to be the source behind several discussions in Stras. 84.

AGENDA

The philological and historical commentators on Demosthenes are characterized by their interest in identifying historical allusions, assigning
dates to speeches and events, and using their knowledge of life in ancient
Athens to illuminate Demosthenes.[24] They quote from fourth- and third-
century historians mainly to support proposed dates, but also to help
identify historical individuals, to support their interpretations of obscure
references in Demosthenes, and to corroborate Demosthenes' facts. This
range of discussions, supported by extensive use of quotations, suggests
that the commentators and lexicographers who worked on Demosthenes

---

24. Bühler provides an excellent overview of the interests and methods of ancient
Greek scholars.

had a genuine interest in some of the key players and events of fourth-century Greek history, an interest in history for history's sake.

Careful identification of allusions to historical people and events is a marked feature of Didymus's commentary on Demosthenes in Berol. 9780. An offhand reference to the arrest of an informer in Dem. 10.34 motivates Didymus not only to identify him as the tyrant Hermias of Atarneus, but also to evaluate and try to find a balance among the heavily slanted contemporary accounts of Hermias (cols. 4.48–6.62). Similarly, in writing on Dem. 10.70, Didymus points out that the Aristomedes named there is not the one from Pherae who fought against Philip and Alexander, but rather is the silly figure known from elsewhere in oratory and comedy (cols. 9.38–10.10). Demosthenes' reference to the Persian king's previous and recent restorations of Athens motivates Didymus to discuss the value of competing theories that tried to explain these allusions (cols. 7.7–8.32). While some had identified Demosthenes' phrase "fighting about the shadow at Delphi" as a reference to a decree made by the Amphictyonic Council, Didymus rejected this view and instead explained it as a reference to Philip's behavior toward Delphi and Phocis (Berol. 21188). Likewise, the allusion to Themistocles' expulsion from the city in Dem. 23.205 is explained as ostracism, and the commentator then quotes Philochorus to show how ostracisms were carried out (Berol. 5008).

Upon identifying an allusion to a historical event, the commentators often proceed to date that event.[25] The eponymous archon is used in the usual fashion to specify the year. The reference in Dem. 21.161 to "a second call for donations after this" is identified as having taken place "in the archonship of Callimachus" (349/8) (Rain. 7), but any source for the date has been lost in lacuna. In Stras. 84, the commentator somehow relates the financing and construction schedule of the Propylaea and Parthenon (Dem. 22.13) to a decree of Pericles dated to either 450/49 or 431/0. In his commentary on Dem. 9–11 and 13 (Berol. 9780), Didymus also frequently discusses the dates of events mentioned or alluded to in the speeches: Athenian aid to Oreus and Eretria (col. 1.1–25), the deaths of Philistides of Oreus and Clitarchus of Eretria (col. 1.46–49), the end of a peace agreement (cols. 1.53–2.2), the failed Peace of Antalcidas (col. 7.11–28), Conon's defeat of the Spartans (cols. 7.28–62), the Persian king's offer to Athens (col. 8.2–32), Philip's theft of the merchants'

25. On methods of dating in ancient scholarship, see Bühler, 46–49.

boats at Hieron (cols. 10.50–11.5), and the Athenian-Megarian affair at Orgas (col. 13.25–62). As noted above, Philochorus is Didymus's main source for these chronological discussions.

The dates of Demosthenes' speeches are also discussed in commentaries. In Berol. 9780, Didymus opens his commentary on orations 10, 11, and 13 with discussions of their dates. In dating Dem. 10 to 341/0, he combines internal evidence from the speech with four references to Philochorus in order to reject alternate dates and situate Dem. 10 in its historical context (cols. 1.1–2.3 ff.). He dates Dem. 11 to the year 340/39 on the basis of references in a letter of Philip (not our Dem. 12) and a sketch of the historical background obtained from Philochorus (cols. 10.13–11.5). After first rejecting a post-346 date for Dem. 13, Didymus then uses internal evidence from the speech and a dated quotation from Philochorus to support a date of 349/8 (col. 13.25–62).

Athens figures prominently in the ancient commentaries on Demosthenes, from the workings of its ancient constitution to the mysterious details of life in the past.[26] The commentators and lexicographers discuss a tremendous range of topics. Berol. 5008 discusses the location and format of ancient Athenian legal texts, the procedure for ostracism, and the Eleusinian Mysteries.[27] Rain. 7 shows an interest in public arbitration, loans, taxation, and religious officials and their activities. In Stras. 84 the commentator discusses the chairmanship of governmental committees, the Periclean building program, fifth-century Athenian finance, treasury officials, the jurisdiction of the *thesmothetae,* and the names and duties of archons and other officials. Finally, the fragments of Didymus in Harpocration reveal Didymus's interests in the layout of the theatre, the shapes of classical-era drinking cups, tithing, imprisonment, architectural elements, the requirement for advance deposits in court cases, guardianship and attainment of the majority, the arrangement of olive trees in groves, and clan-sponsored wedding feasts.

Discussions of authenticity are preserved only in Didymus's commentary in Berol. 9780, where he calls into question the authenticity of oration 11 (col. 11.5–26).[28] In this discussion, Didymus reports three observations that relate to the authenticity of the speech. First, he says that

---

26. On "Sacherklärung" in ancient Greek scholarship, see Bühler, 57–58.

27. It also discusses the composition of and terminology associated with the Spartan military.

28. On ancient Greek discussions of authenticity, including style and word use, see Bühler, 49–53.

in Dem. 11 "someone might suspect—not far from the mark—that a derivative little speech has been assembled, compiled from certain orations of Demosthenes." But he does not note which parallel passages from other speeches might give rise to such a suspicion, and he does not draw from this any explicit conclusions about the speech's authenticity. He also mentions the theory that the historian Anaximenes wrote it, noting that something similar to Dem. 11 appears in book 7 of Anaximenes' *Philippica*. Next, he reports the opinion that an unusual word meaning "to fear" appears in the speech, but that this word and other "vulgar" words like it are "hardly Demosthenic." A full discussion of the word's etymology follows. However, even after reporting these three observations, Didymus never commits himself to any particular view on the speech's authenticity. Since he does in fact go on to comment on the speech, one might assume that he does not find in these three observations sufficient grounds for declaring the speech spurious. But it is even more likely that Didymus and the other commentators simply dealt with the Demosthenic corpus as it was passed down to them. In their eyes, a fourth-century text falsely attributed to Demosthenes was still a fourth-century text worthy of study and commentary.

In addition to their interests in history and authenticity, what we might call philological interests are also heavily reflected in these commentaries and lexica. Philology and history of course are not mutually exclusive categories, as interest in a word or proper name might easily lead the commentators to discuss a date or sketch out a historical background suggested by that word or phrase. In addition to the examples already mentioned above, the author of Stras. 84 discusses the terms used to designate periods within the Peloponnesian War. The meanings of certain proverbial expressions are investigated in Berol. 21188, Berol. 9780, and the Didymus fragments in Harpocration. The papyrus lexica to Dem. 21 and 23 mention alternate ways to say "putting on arms" and "ambushing" (Rain. 7, Berol. 5008). Commentators also identify minor historical figures such as Miltocythes (Berol. 5008), Aristomedes (Berol. 9780), and Polystratus (Didymus fragment 1 in Harpocration), and they discuss the meanings and etymologies of words such as "to fear," "to abuse," and "Orgas" (Berol. 9780), as well as "mixture-of-dregs-of-wine," *oikiskos* (little house), "crumb cakes," "it was bladed," "he foreignized," and "they sell" (Didymus fragments in Harpocration). The commentators' discussions of the meanings and etymologies of words range from simple and very matter-of-fact glosses to much more elaborate discussions such as the treatment of "Orgas" in Berol. 9780, col. 14.2–35.[29]

The ancient commentators are familiar with existing opinions about interpretative problems in Demosthenes' orations, and they draw freely on Homer, the dramatists, other poets, historians, and various other literary sources to interpret them. Their aims are threefold: to explain allusions and expound upon explicit references to the events, people, places, and facets of classical Athenian culture that figured in Demosthenes' speeches; to offer glosses and etymologies of difficult or unusual words and expressions; and (perhaps to a lesser extent) to use this and other information to decide which speeches were actually written by Demosthenes.

READERSHIP

We have discussed the physical form and layout of the commentaries and lexica, and we have seen the predominantly historical and philological questions and concerns that are reflected in them. Our next goal is to try to use these texts to help identify their ancient readership. As with many such ancient texts, our commentaries do not have addressees and do not explicitly describe the intended reader.[30] Yet an examination of their contents in the light of ancient research, teaching, and writing practices does yield certain suggestive possibilities.

We have seen that commentators and lexicographers who studied Demosthenes also consulted each other's research. These scholars read earlier commentaries and lexica when they excerpted them to produce new works of scholarship. Their frequent references to the opinions of other scholars are also a reminder that they were reading other commentaries and lexica. One might think here of Didymus's references to anonymous predecessors, as well as later scholars' references to Didymus. Parallel discussions in different commentaries and lexica suggest the sense of shared agenda and purpose that the commentators must have felt as they

---

29. Our commentators gloss unfamiliar words with familiar ones in order to explain them, but there were also other reasons for giving glosses. For example, in the long series of glosses and synonyms in the A scholia to Aeschylus's *Prometheus Bound,* according to Herington, "elucidation may be only a secondary purpose. The main aim of the commentator, in this matter, may well be pedagogic, to exercise and widen the student's Greek vocabulary" (29). For a discussion of scholarly and literary treatments of etymology up to the late first century, see O'Hara, 1–56.

30. One exception to this general statement is discussed below.

read and responded to each other's works.[31] And all the intense effort directed at solving historical and philological problems allowed and perhaps even encouraged the ancient commentators on Demosthenes, like most ancient scholars, to engage in overt polemic against their supposedly less intelligent predecessors.

An excellent case in point is Harpocration's use of Didymus's commentaries on Demosthenes. In the twenty-one entries of Harpocration's lexicon where he explicitly notes that he is drawing on Didymus for information about Demosthenes, Harpocration often cites Didymus for information that he does not question (fragments 2–3, 8–12, 14–16, 18, 21). He twice pits Didymus's opinion against that of other scholars while he himself remains outside of the debate: Didymus and Theophrastus weigh in on the meaning of the theatre's *parascenia* in fragment 7, and Didymus is pitted against an anonymous authority on the derivation of the word *podokakke* in fragment 11. In both situations, Harpocration offers his readers two competing explanations, commits to neither, and thus forces readers to choose for themselves.

There are also several instances in which Harpocration cites Didymus's opinion and then modifies or rejects it. In the entry on Polystratus (fragment 1), Didymus is said to have claimed that he could not find a reference anywhere to a Polystratus who was in charge of a mercenary force at Corinth; this motivated Harpocration to suggest (incorrectly) that the text should be altered to read "Polytropus." Harpocration also criticizes Didymus's use of parallels from comedy in fragment 4: "From these examples, Didymus seems to have offered a misleading interpretation of the Demosthenic usage of this word." Similarly, in fragment 5, Didymus's suggestion that the word " 'crumb cakes' has a meaning that is clear and recognizable from the sound itself" is regarded by Harpocration as "overwrought" (περιεργότερον) and "without a parallel" (ἀμάρτυρον). Likewise, he says that Didymus's nontraditional accentuation of the word for "scapegoat" does not occur elsewhere, to his knowledge (fragment 13). He thinks that Didymus has misunderstood the age range denoted by the term *hebe* (fragment 16). On the word "Lycianmade," which Didymus interprets as meaning "made by a man named Lycius," Harpocration accuses him of apparently not knowing "that one would not find such a form made from individuals' names, but rather

31. See Harpocration fragment 10 (text 2) and Berol. 5008 (text 3) on "the law below"; and see Harpocration fragment 2 (text 2) and Berol. 21188 (text 4) on "about the shadow of an ass."

from the names of cities or peoples" (fragment 17). The verb form mean-ing "he foreignized" (ἐξένιζε), Harpocration also tells us, refers to the man's actually being a foreigner and not, as Didymus would have it, to his speaking with a foreign accent (fragment 19). Harpocration even ac-cuses Didymus of providing faulty bibliographical references: Didymus, as Harpocration reports, "says that a wedding feast was given at wed-dings to one's fellow clansmen, adducing an expression of Phanodemus, in which no such thing is written. In the *Commentaries on Demosthe-nes,* the same author again says that a wedding feast is the introduction of wives to the clansmen, but he gives no evidence for this interpreta-tion" (fragment 20). Harpocration does not know what a wedding feast is. He knows only that Didymus got it wrong.

While we might well regard some of this polemic as unproductive, particularly where a scholar curses the darkness but refuses to light a candle, this exchange of ideas across the generations also helps us to en-vision a real and vibrant scholarly community that took as its agenda the explication of Demosthenes in his historical, linguistic, and cultural context.

Not much is known about the direct availability of commentaries and lexica to students in the ancient world. Much of what they learned from such texts must have been transmitted only indirectly through their teachers' lectures and distillations of published research. Regardless of whether students had direct or only indirect access to our commentar-ies, however, we may still get some sense of their potential usefulness to students at different levels by examining their contents. A beginning student, someone who is encountering Demosthenes for the first time under the instruction of a teacher, would easily be able to use the brief glosses like those found in the lexicon in Rain. 7 to aid in reading and getting a basic understanding of a text. The discussion of hyperbaton in Berol. 9780 (cols. 6.66–7.7) might be accessible to a beginning reader who had learned about hyperbaton in school from the *grammaticus.* Didymus shows the reader in this passage how to get at the core mean-ing of Dem. 10.34 without becoming distracted by Demosthenes' use of hyperbaton.

With but few exceptions, however, our commentaries in general do not seem to provide the basic grammatical and background information one might expect to be provided to a first-time reader. They certainly do not reflect the teaching concerns of a work like Servius's commentary on the *Aeneid* (fourth century C.E.), whose purpose was to teach young students how the classical author Vergil uses the Latin language, and to show them how they themselves might learn something useful from Vergil for their own development as speakers and writers.[32] But a more advanced student or a teacher who is already familiar with the basics of reading Demosthenes' speeches might want to use our commentaries to learn more about the historical people and events alluded to in Demosthenes. Our commentaries, then, might have served a function similar to Asconius's commentaries on Cicero (first century C.E.), whose purpose, as B. A. Marshall argues, was to supplement a young man's rhetorical education by discussing important historical exempla used in oratory.[33] An advanced student or teacher might also be interested in learning more about classical Athenian history and culture through studying Greek oratory. Lucian and Plutarch (both second century C.E.) and the hypothetical excerptor of Berol. 9780 (to be discussed in chapter 3) come to mind as this sort of reader. Such readers might want to have a historical situation, a name, a date, or a peculiar expression clarified for them; they might be interested in reading an overview of what various scholars (e.g., the "some" of Berol. 9780) say about a given problem in the text; or they might be mining the commentaries and lexica for some other project of their own. A good example of this last is Athenaeus (second century C.E.), whose monumental *Deipnosophistae* includes Didymus's discussion of "Lycian-made" cups (11.486C–D), a discussion that is also preserved in Harpocration (fragment 17).

Were these mostly imperial-era texts consulted at all by Latin-speaking Roman readers? Cicero's fondness for the writings of Demosthenes, in addition to his own popularity, encouraged Caecilius, Quintilian, and Plutarch to compose comparisons of the two authors. Education in the Greek classics and the popularity of Cicero might have done something for the popularity of Demosthenes among other Roman readers as well. Generally speaking, Roman scholars and other readers from the late Republic onward are known to have enjoyed reading about Greek history, and there was much interest in Greek intellectual and cultural traditions.[34] But in our commentaries and lexica to Demosthenes, there are no references to historical Romans, Roman authors, or Roman institutions. There is no specific tip of the hat to a Roman audience or

---

32. Kaster, 169–97.
33. B. A. Marshall, 37; Asconius is edited by Squires.
34. See, for example, Rawson, *Intellectual Life,* esp. 61–65. See Wardman, 85–101, on Roman attitudes to classical Athens and Macedonia. In general on Roman attitudes toward the Greeks and Greek culture, see Rawson, "Romans"; Balsdon, 30–58; Petrochilos.

to devotees of Latin literature. Perhaps this is not too surprising.[35] But it takes only one text to remind us of what we may be missing: In the fourth century C.E., the rhetorician Libanius addressed a set of overviews (*hypotheseis*) of the speeches of Demosthenes to a Roman proconsul who apparently had expressed some fondness for the orator. These overviews draw on Dionysius of Halicarnassus, rhetorical and stylistic analyses of the speeches, biographies of Demosthenes, and historians, all conveniently distilled by an expert for a busy but intellectually curious Roman official who was already an accomplished student of Latin literature.[36]

Although the authors of biographies of Demosthenes seem not to have imported much content from our commentators (and vice versa), biographers do use some of the same primary sources that our commentators use, and they readily draw on other scholarly traditions to help their readers understand the life and writings of Demosthenes. One biography of Demosthenes (Ps.-Plutarch *Moralia* 844a-848d) includes dates for the delivery of some of the speeches, as our commentators often do, and cites the comic poet Timocles and the historian Philochorus, as does Didymus in his commentary on Demosthenes' *Philippics* (Berol. 9780). Similarly, Plutarch's biography of Demosthenes cites the biographer Hermippus and the historians Theopompus, Marsyas, and Duris, all of whom again appear in Didymus. The Byzantine scholar Photius (ninth century) applies stylistic criteria from ancient rhetorical scholarship to the question whether Demosthenes was really the author of the speech *On Halonnesus* (Dem. 7).[37]

Teachers of rhetoric, declaimers, and authors of rhetorical commentaries and handbooks could perhaps have found some use for our commentaries.[38] Like Libanius, Greek rhetoricians in general probably drew on a number of different kinds of scholarly aids to support their teaching, though we see little solid evidence in their published writings of any contact with materials like ours. The only definite correspondence that

---

35. Rawson, *Intellectual Life*, 64–65, calls attention to the difficulty of detecting when a Greek author is writing for a Roman audience.

36. Ed. Foerster, 8: 575–681; the dedicatory preface is on p. 600. See Gibson, "Libanius' Hypotheses."

37. Photius *Bibliotheca* 491a. On the *Bibliotheca*, see Wilson, *Scholars*, 93–111; Treadgold, 16–36. McComb, 86–113, argues for Photian authorship of the literary criticism in the *Bibliotheca*.

38. The recent Dilts and Kennedy translation of two imperial-age treatises on Greek rhetoric provides an excellent introduction to the methods and concerns of this type of reader. The scholiasts to Demosthenes show little evidence of familiarity with our commentaries; see pp. 21–25.

I have located is a mutual interest in the loss of Philip's eye.[39] In ancient Greek and Roman education, students typically studied the texts of the historians and orators after advancing beyond elementary studies with a grammarian *(grammaticus)* and going on to study with a rhetorician.[40] In the course of explaining the texts of the poets and other authors, grammarians gave explanations of the *historiae* appearing therein.[41] This practice is in keeping with the prescriptive overview of the grammarian Dionysius Thrax, who says that the third of the six parts of grammar is "a ready response to unfamiliar words and to *historiae*" (γλωσσῶν τε καὶ ἱστοριῶν πρόχειρος ἀπόδοσις).[42] In this context, the very flexible Greek and Latin term *historiae* probably refers to what we call "allusions" or "references," but *historia* is also a term used in the ancient world to denote any details about people or events that are commonly accepted as historical fact, or are so well known that they are included in the realm of "history," despite the fact that they may never have occurred. Under such a broad conception, the *historia* of the assassination of Abraham Lincoln, for example, would be on an equal footing with the *historia* of George Washington and the cherry tree.[43]

According to Quintilian, the analysis of *historiae* in a text—stories, references, allusions, or historical or quasi-historical details—"should be done very carefully, but not overdone to the point of superfluous effort: for it is sufficient to lay out the versions received or recounted in very famous authors" (1.8.18).[44] Quintilian's purpose is, granted, the education of the prospective orator. Still, it is worth noting that this recommendation to keep the analysis of *historiae* within reasonable limits is quite different from the regular practice of our commentators on De-

39. Kohl, no. 203; compare Berol. 9780, cols.12.37–13.12. On ancient discussions of Philip's eye wound, see Riginos, 106–14.

40. Marrou, 164; see Quintilian 2.5.1. On the *grammaticus* and the *rhetor* in Hellenistic Greek and Roman education, see Marrou, 142–205, 265–91; Rawson, *Intellectual Life,* 66–79. The boundaries of their teaching responsibilities were apparently not very firm. The orator and teacher Quintilian (first century C.E.) laments a recent trend whereby the grammarians were beginning to cover topics more properly taught by the rhetoricians (2.1.1–6). On Quintilian's life and writings, see G. Kennedy, *Quintilian,* 11–38. On the relationship between educational theory and practice in antiquity, see, most recently, Morgan, 190–239.

41. Quintilian 1.8.18; Cicero *De Oratore* 1.187.

42. *Ars grammatica* 1 (ed. Uhlig).

43. See notes on *P.Lond.Lit.* 179, lines 37–39. For a discussion of *historia* and related terms, see Potter, 9–19.

44. His accedet enarratio historiarum, diligens quidem illa, non tamen usque ad supervacuum laborem occupata: nam receptas aut certe claris auctoribus memoratas exposuisse satis est.

mosthenes, who revel in analyzing complex problems and contradictory source materials. From reading the most popular versions of particular *historiae,* Quintilian suggests, the aspiring speaker can expect to gain a "recognition of things and exempla with which [he] ought to be especially familiar" (10.1.34).[45] According to Quintilian, *historiae*—which seem here to mean popular accounts of historical people and events— serve primarily as a source of illustrative anecdotes, not unlike poems or stories that you might hear on the street (12.4.1).

Whether Quintilian is specifically interested here in what we would call "historical" details is not absolutely clear. Nevertheless, some ancient writers thought that Greek rhetoricians, at least, were prone to mishandle history. In his *Professor of Rhetoric,* the satirist Lucian portrays a fictitious professor as recommending that prospective orators throw in gratuitous references to classical Greek history whenever possible, whether relevant or not. "If you're speaking at Athens in a case of assault or adultery," the caricatured professor is made to say,

> be sure to talk about events in India and Ecbatana. In every case you should mention Marathon and Cynegirus, the sine qua non's of history. And always mention sailing through Athos and marching across the Hellespont and the sun being blocked out by Persian arrows, and talk about Xerxes fleeing and Leonidas being admired and the inscription of Othryades being read, and make many frequent references to Salamis and Artemisium and Plataea. (18)

As this passage humorously suggests, a basic familiarity with classical Greek history was regarded as being helpful to the prospective speaker. Among Greek declaimers, Demosthenes' life and writings were very popular subjects.[46] The rhetorician Himerius (fourth century C.E.) composed a declamation, or fictional speech, in the character of the orator Hyperides on behalf of Demosthenes (*Or.* 1), and one in the character of Demosthenes on behalf of Aeschines (*Or.* 2). Here is an author who obviously acquired some of his knowledge of the history of the fourth century B.C. from reading the orators. In addition to his introductions to the speeches of Demosthenes, Libanius (also fourth century C.E.)

45. . . . ex cognitione rerum exemplorumque, quibus in primis instructus esse debet orator.
46. Kohl has collected and discussed 350 rhetorical themes adapted from Greek history, 125 of which deal with the period of Demosthenes; see 56–60 (on Philip) and 66–82 (on Aeschines and Demosthenes). On the use of history in Greek rhetorical exercises, see Russell, *Greek Declamation,* 106–28, esp. 118–20.

wrote fifteen declamations on topics from Greek history (9–23). Seven of these concerned relations between Athens and Macedon (17–23); the background reading that he did in preparing to write his hypotheses to Demosthenes' speeches must have helped. A certain familiarity with classical Greek history was also required for writing a kind of declamation that the Romans called *suasoriae*, short fictional pieces in which one attempts, hypothetically, to convince a famous historical figure to do or not to do something. Aelius Aristides (second century C.E.), who in the Byzantine period was read alongside Demosthenes as a model of Attic Greek, wrote a number of *suasoriae* on Greek historical topics (*Or.* 5–15). Although some declamations, as D. A. Russell has argued, were not very strict in their use of historical detail and are characterized by "the superficiality of a bad historical novel or film," others show "a real imaginative grasp of the classical world." [47] It is a tribute to the enduring popularity of classical Greek history that the authors of late antiquity looked to it for inspiration for their own creative acts of fiction.

There is one tantalizing passage in our commentaries that is explicitly pitched to a particular audience. At the beginning of his discussion of the tyrant Hermias, Didymus says that he has "decided to speak about this subject at length, to gratify the receptive ears of those who are still curious about such things" (Berol. 9780, col. 4.59–63). Unless these introductory words were taken over from an earlier source,[48] Didymus envisions an audience in the first century B.C. that is interested in the lives of barbarian philosopher-kings from the classical period. This may serve to remind us that an ancient reader's reasons for picking up a commentary cannot necessarily be assumed to be the same as the reasons for which a modern reader might. Certainly this section of the commentary—more evocative of the supermarket tabloids than of anything in a modern scholarly commentary on Demosthenes—could have had an audience far wider than we might otherwise have predicted.

Future research on the texts examined in this study may find new ways to connect our commentaries with ancient readers who used them for a variety of purposes not discussed here. These commentaries and the results of this study can also be used to illuminate such topics as the history of ancient scholarship, the history of lexicography, oratory and its ancient reception, Greek and Roman education, postclassical an-

---

47. Russell, *Greek Declamation,* 109; see also 113–28.
48. See notes on cols. 4.48–6.62, with bibliography.

tiquity's understanding and appropriation of its classical past, the relationship between ancient historical scholarship and ancient historiography,[49] and the history of how classical texts were made accessible for
ancient readers. A number of interesting possible connections remain to
be explored.

49. On which see the recent account of Potter, 102–19.

CHAPTER 3

Didymus

Berol. 9780 is a papyrus of the second century C.E. containing a series of discussions of problems raised by certain passages in Dem. 9–11 and 13. Didymus's selective coverage of these four speeches has provoked scholarly debate over the past century.[1] For a modern commentator, omitting to address every detail of a text may be considered a serious fault. But to explain Berol. 9780's spotty coverage of the four orations we need not resort to condemning this ancient scholar's intelligence, diligence, or scruple. I argue here that the practice of excerption (as defined and discussed above in chapter 1) is the best way to account for the apparent "gaps" in coverage in Berol. 9780.

THE GENRE OF BEROL. 9780

A few years after the original publication of Berol. 9780 in 1904, F. Leo advanced a clever hypothesis to explain why Berol. 9780 does not meet some scholars' expectations as a commentary on Dem. 9–11 and 13: Berol. 9780, he argued, is not a commentary at all. Leo had taken it as a given that Didymus's lost rhetorical commentaries on Demosthenes were

---

1. The most important discussions are D-S[1], xv–xviii; Leo, "Didymos"; S. West, 288–96; Arrighetti, esp. 53–59, 65. Further references to the important contributions of Diels and Schubart and West can be found throughout the notes on Berol. 9780.

the ultimate source of the mainly rhetorical scholia found in the margins of mediaeval manuscripts. It has already been argued in chapter 1 that Leo was mistaken on this point.

Working from this assumption, Leo posited a hard distinction between the ancient genres of the running commentary *(hypomnema)* and the monograph *(syngramma)*. Since he began with the assumption that Didymus's lost commentaries were rhetorical in nature—the logical extension of his belief that they gave rise to the Byzantine scholia—he concluded that Berol. 9780, which contains next to nothing of rhetorical interest, was not a commentary. As part of the argument Leo dismissed as irrelevant the two nonrhetorical comments (fragments 5 and 20 in Harpocration) that are explicitly attributed to Didymus's *hypomnemata* on Demosthenes.[2] Instead, he argued, Berol. 9780 must be a monograph *(syngramma)* "on" (περὶ) a particular topic, applying a model from his area of expertise, ancient biographies.[3] Unfortunately, however, the model does not work, as was first shown by S. West.[4] Leo mounted his argument on the title from the end of the roll,[5] which declares the contents to be part of Didymus's *On Demosthenes* (περὶ Δημοσθένους). Leo suggested that the word "on" (περί) clinches Berol. 9780's status as a monograph rather than a commentary.

Leo's conclusion has had far-reaching effect. A. Momigliano saw in Berol. 9780 "a great many biographical details" about the orator and even posited an entire ancient scholarly tradition of "historical interpretations of selected passages from one classical author."[6] In addition, with specific reference to Berol. 9780, E. G. Turner warned his readers not to draw any mistaken conclusions: "Indeed, the discussion in papyri of particular passages from the same author has at times led to the works in question being mistaken by the moderns for hypomnemata, which they may appear to resemble in form."[7] R. Pfeiffer endorsed the distinction of "running commentary vs. περὶ literature" throughout his influential *History of Classical Scholarship from the Beginnings to the*

2. Leo, "Didymos," 260.
3. He had recently completed an authoritative study of this topic. See Leo, *Biographie*.
4. S. West, 290–91; followed by Arrighetti, 53–56, and Osborne, 12–14.
5. Wilcken, "Die Subskription des Didymus-Papyrus," 325; Gudeman, "Scholien," 698–99; Momigliano, *Greek Biography*, 70–71; Pfeiffer, *Classical Scholarship*, 278 (also 29, 213, 218); Turner, *Greek Papyri*, 113–14. The view that Berol. 9780 is a monograph is also followed by Reynolds and Wilson, 10, 18.
6. Momigliano, *Greek Biography*, 70–71.
7. Turner, *Greek Papyri*, 113–14.

End of the Hellenistic Age.[8] Against these formulations, however, several scholars have convincingly argued that in antiquity a rigid distinction between the genres of the *hypomnema* and the *syngramma*—as formulated by Leo and others—did not exist.[9]

The title at the end of the Berol. 9780 reads ΔΙΔΥΜΟΥ ΠΕΡΙ ΔΗΜΟ-ΣΘΕΝΟΥΣ ΚΗ ΦΙΛΙΠΠΙΚΩΝ Γ. This is followed by four lines containing ordinal numbers to represent orations 9, 10, 11, and 12 (sic) and the first few words of each oration. A literal translation of the title as it appears on the papyrus is "Didymus's *On Demosthenes*, Twenty-Eight, of the *Philippics*, Third." The absence of an overstroke on the numeral ΚΗ indicates that it is a cardinal numeral (twenty-eight) rather than an ordinal (twenty-eighth). If correct, the cardinal "twenty-eight" could mean something like "in twenty-eight books" or "on twenty-eight speeches."[10] But if an overstroke has accidentally been omitted, the numeral should be taken as an ordinal meaning "twenty-eighth" or "book twenty-eight."[11] Both choices pose certain interesting problems of interpretation, in particular the relationship between Berol. 9780 and the rest of Didymus's lost commentaries on Demosthenes.[12]

Nevertheless, even if the title *On Demosthenes* says something significant about the genre of the work, it need not have been created by

8. Pfeiffer, *Classical Scholarship*, 278 (also 29, 213, 218).

9. See S. West, 291 with n. 2; Arrighetti, 53–56; West's view on this is discussed with approval by Osborne, 12–14. Arrighetti discusses at length the variety of such texts that exist from antiquity, and the difficulty of imposing precise definitions on them. There is an excellent discussion of *hypomnema* in Skydsgaard, 107–11; it is partially in response to Börner (215–26), who denies identity between Greek *hypomnemata* and Latin *commentarii*. None of this is meant to imply that the terms *syngramma* and *hypomnema* are meaningless. Where a distinction between the two is made or implied in ancient literature, *syngrammata* seem to have been regarded as more polished literary efforts intended for public distribution, while *hypomnemata* were more spare, perhaps simply in the form of "notes," and in some cases were regarded as rough drafts not meant for the public eye; see Potter, 29–35.

10. Both possibilities are considered by D-S[1], xviii. The twenty-eight speeches, according to D-S[1], xxv–xxvi, could be our orations 1–31, omitting 12 *(Letter of Philip)* and the two speeches *Against Aristogeiton* (25 and 26), leaving the speeches that were most important for understanding Demosthenes' life and politics. This view is followed by Sealey, *Demosthenes*, 228.

11. This is the interpretation of Wilcken ("Die Subskription des Didymus-Papyrus"), who explicitly declined to speculate further as to the consequences of his interpretation.

12. Our only other reference to Didymus's commentaries on Demosthenes by "title" and book number is irreconcilable with the title from Berol. 9780: Ammonius refers to a discussion found "in book 11 of the commentaries on the orators" (ἐν ἑνδεκάτῳ ῥητορικῶν ὑπομνημάτων, no. 334, ed. Nickau); see discussion above, p. 23. Apparently, different arrangements of Didymus's commentaries were known in antiquity (see also fragments 5 and 20 in Harpocration [text 2]).

Didymus; it could easily have been added by the person who was making this copy for private use.[13] Someone who has consulted Didymus's commentary, selected items of interest, and copied them out for later consultation and study is not obliged by any ancient scholarly principles that we know of to preserve the work's original title, if in fact it even had one. Modern scholars are no less prone to refer to, say, Pfeiffer's books on classical scholarship, C. D. Adams's book on Demosthenes, or Didymus's commentaries on Demosthenes, without intending for readers to believe that these descriptions were the actual titles of the works in question. It is only the modern practice of using capitalization and italics to distinguish titles from descriptions that tells us that Adams's *Demosthenes and His Influence* is a title and Adams's book on Demosthenes is a description.[14]

This book label is insufficient evidence to support the claims of a rigid distinction between the ancient "commentary" and "monograph." The label need only have indicated that the roll contained something on, about, or pertaining to Demosthenes—a description that can be considered true from any number of perspectives. Whatever the title may have meant to its originator (who was not necessarily Didymus), the contents and organization of Berol. 9780 do not support the view that it is a biographical or historical monograph "on Demosthenes."

DIDYMUS'S REPUTATION IN ANCIENT AND MODERN SCHOLARSHIP

So far we have been addressing the physical and literary "fragments" of Didymus, which report in some form what he said about Demosthenes'

13. According to D-S[1], xi–xii, xv–xxi, the fact that Berol. 9780 was a copy made for private use is indicated by the frequency of abbreviations, the poor quality of the handwriting and spelling, and apparent omissions and abbreviations of source material and sections of the argument. The view that this is a copy for private use is followed by Sealey, *Demosthenes*, 228, who adds that "the copyist may have shortened the explanatory comments of Didymos." Osborne, 14, argues that "the subscription itself was written by someone who was not concerned with the scholarly distinction between σύγγραμμα and ὑπόμνημα, and who found it convenient, for his own purposes, to refer to Didymos' work by the title Περὶ Δημοσθένους instead of the more technical description of ὑπόμνημα εἰς Δημοσθένην." For mistakes due to abbreviation during excerpting, see Mejer, 25–28, on Diogenes Laertius (third century C.E.), who sometimes incorrectly expands his own abbreviations: e.g., Xeno(crates) for Xeno(phanes) and So(lon) for So(crates).

14. Nevertheless, in the translations and notes I have followed standard practice in italicizing the "titles" of ancient books.

speeches. We also have several "testimonia" about Didymus.[15] Here I shall argue that some modern interpretations of Berol. 9780 have been unduly influenced by the low esteem in which certain ancient authors seem to have held Didymus.

The testimonia about Didymus's scholarship are quite colorful. Praising the qualities of his lexicographical studies, Macrobius (fifth century C.E.) calls Didymus "the most learned of all grammarians *(grammatici)*" *(Sat.* 5.18.9) and "the most accomplished of all the *grammatici* who live now or who have ever lived" (5.22.10).[16] This is no small compliment, given that Macrobius represents some of the greatest scholars of his day as being present to hear it. The *Suda* records that Didymus was "nicknamed Bronze Guts because of his perseverance regarding books; for they say he wrote over 3,500 books."[17] This number is almost certainly hyperbole. Nevertheless, the modern response to the *Suda's* description has usually been to believe that Didymus's output was titanic, even if the precise number of rolls is in doubt. For his zeal he is either praised for transmitting the best of Alexandrian scholarship or condemned for treating his subjects superficially. In such a scenario Didymus cannot possibly come out a winner.[18]

One of the most fascinating criticisms of Didymus, however, comes not from a modern scholar but from the pen of the younger Seneca (first century C.E.):

> Didymus the *grammaticus* wrote 4,000 books: I would feel sorry for him if he had only *read* that many superfluous things. In some books he in-

15. A note for the nonclassicist reader: The term "testimonia" is typically used to denote references to details such as an author's life and dates or to the existence of writings from which fragments may or may not survive. For example, if a later scholar mentions in passing that Didymus wrote a commentary on *On the Crown* (Dem. 18), that statement is a testimonium to the existence of said commentary; if the scholar also reports that Didymus made a particular statement in that commentary, the report of that statement is considered a "fragment."

16. Grammaticorum omnium eruditissimus *(Sat.* 5.18.9); grammaticorum omnium quique sint quique fuerint instructissimus *(Sat.* 5.22.10) (ed. Willis).

17. Χαλκέντερος κληθεὶς διὰ τὴν περὶ τὰ βιβλία ἐπιμονήν. φασὶ γὰρ αὐτὸν συγγεγραφέναι ὑπὲρ τὰ ͵ζφ βιβλία. Athenaeus (4.139C) reports that Didymus was also called *Bibliolathas* (Book Forgetter) for the same reason: "Demetrius of Troezen calls this man [sc. Didymus] the 'Book Forgetter' because of the number of books that he published; for there are 3,500 of them" (καλεῖ δὲ τοῦτον Δημήτριος ὁ Τροιζήνιος βιβλιολάθαν διὰ τὸ πλῆθος ὧν ἐκδέδωκε συγγραμμάτων· ἐστὶ γὰρ τρισχίλια πρὸς τοῖς πεντακοσίοις).

18. Daintree, 65, notes similar treatment of late-ancient and mediaeval scholarship by modern scholars: "There are classicists who hold that the only good scribe was the man who copied unthinkingly everything that was set before him, while at the same time despising him for the very stupidity made manifest."

quires about the fatherland of Homer, in others about the true mother of
Aeneas, in others about whether Anacreon was more of a letch or more of
a drunk, in others about whether Sappho was a whore, and in others about
other topics, whose contents you would have to unlearn if you knew them.
(*Ep.* 88.37)[19]

There is a similar passage in Quintilian's characterization of Didymus
(later first century C.E.), which corroborates Seneca's image of a scholar
whose great productivity had harmful consequences:

It is known to have happened to Didymus, than whom no one wrote more
books, that when he objected to someone's account as being false, a book
of his that contained the same account was produced. This happens especially with legendary stories even to certain quite ridiculous and shameful
extremes; as a result the most inferior writers have a great deal of freedom
to lie, to the extent that they safely lie about whole books and authors, as it
occurs to them to do so, because those sources cannot be found that never
existed: for in better-known details they are very frequently caught by careful readers. (1.8.19–21)[20]

Both these passages have figured in modern discussions of Didymus's
abilities as a commentator but probably should not have. There is not a
single word in either passage to suggest that Seneca and Quintilian were
familiar with Didymus's commentaries on Demosthenes. Their relevance
to a discussion of the contents or nature of Berol. 9780 is dubious for
this reason alone. But there is more. Why is Didymus such an object of
scorn for both Seneca and Quintilian?[21] As we see here, Seneca argues
that Didymus's scholarship is trivial and irrelevant, while Quintilian ac-
cuses him of inconsistency and perhaps the use of fabricated sources.
Both testimonia, however, need to be reconsidered in context. Seneca's
attack on Didymus's scholarship comes from a letter in which he discusses how one should properly pursue the liberal arts. Seneca argues
that the purpose of the liberal arts is to inculcate moral virtue in stu-

---

19. Quattuor milia librorum Didymus grammaticus scripsit: misererer si tam multa
supervacua legisset. In his libris de patria Homeri quaeritur, in his de Aeneae matre vera,
in his libidinosior Anacreon an ebriosior vixerit, in his an Sappho publica fuerit, et alia
quae erant dediscenda si scires.

20. Nam Didymo, quo nemo plura scripsit, accidisse compertum est ut, cum historiae
cuidam tamquam vanae repugnaret, ipsius proferretur liber qui eam continebat. Quod
evenit praecipue in fabulosis usque ad deridicula quaedam, quaedam etiam pudenda, unde
improbissimo cuique pleraque fingendi licentia est, adeo ut de libris totis et auctoribus, ut
succurrit, mentiantur tuto, quia inveniri qui numquam fuere non possunt: nam in notiori-
bus frequentissime deprehenduntur a curiosis.

21. I wish to acknowledge Francis Newton for prompting me to pursue this particular line of inquiry.

dents; the liberal arts should therefore include nothing but the "study of wisdom" (*studium . . . sapientiae, Ep.* 88.2). But most scholarship, according to Seneca, does not contribute toward this end. As he so colorfully puts it, why should we care to know where Ulysses' wanderings took him if that does not keep us from wandering (i.e., making mistakes with moral implications) ourselves? (88.7). Granted, as Seneca admits, it is easy to become absorbed in details, but "to want to know more than is sufficient is a kind of immoderation" (88.36).[22] In Seneca's view, this is precisely where Didymus the *grammaticus* has gone wrong. "Why is it," asks Seneca, "that this eager pursuit of the liberal arts makes people annoying, verbose, ill timed, and self-satisfied, and so they do not learn the necessary things, simply because they have learned the superfluous things?" (88.37).[23] His discussion of Didymus—our not-so-innocent "testimonium" from above—immediately answers this rhetorical question.

We find essentially the same opinion expressed in Quintilian. In his handbook for the prospective orator, Quintilian advises him to acquire a good general knowledge of history, but not to become obsessed with tracing down every possible version of an event (1.7.33–35). Why not? As Quintilian argues,

> To follow up whatever any of the most contemptible authors has ever said is a sign of too much misery or empty boasting, and it detracts and ruins intellects that are better left free for other things. For he who combs through every page, even the ones not worth reading, can end up spending his effort even on old wives' tales. But the commentaries of the *grammatici* are full of impediments of this sort, scarcely known well enough to those who composed them. (1.8.18–19)[24]

Quintilian adduces Didymus's dismissal of an account that he had mentioned favorably in one of his earlier books, as the specific example to support this general statement. And the lesson that Quintilian draws from this anecdote? "Not to know some things will be regarded as among the virtues of the *grammaticus* (1.8.21)."[25]

22. Plus scire velle quam sit satis, intemperantiae genus est.
23. Quid quod ista liberalium artium consectatio molestos, verbosos, intempestivos, sibi placentes facit et ideo non discentes necessaria quia supervacua didicerunt?
24. Persequi quidem, quid quis umquam vel contemptissimorum hominum dixerit aut nimiae miseriae aut inanis iactantiae est, et detinet atque obruit ingenia melius aliis vacatura. Nam qui omnes etiam indignas lectione scidas excutit, anilibus quoque fabulis accommodare operam potest: atqui pleni sunt eius modi impedimentis grammaticorum commentarii, vix ipsis qui composuerunt satis noti.
25. Ex quo mihi inter virtutes grammatici habebitur aliqua nescire.

When these two testimonia are reconsidered in their original context, it is clear that Seneca and Quintilian are not specifically criticizing Didymus's abilities as a *grammaticus;* rather, they are impugning the nature of grammatical scholarship in general. Didymus is the perfect foil for their criticism because he was the best-known (and perhaps the best) practitioner of the discipline. This was still true three centuries later in the time of Macrobius, who had one of his characters praise Didymus as the best *grammaticus* of all time. But according to Seneca and Quintilian, the writings of *grammatici* are inimical to the young student's pursuit of a proper education, for they pervert the true meaning of liberal studies by distracting him with their superfluous theories, excessive pursuit of parallels, and downright lies.

This criticism of Didymus is no more objectively trustworthy than the generic criticism of *grammatici* that we find later in the satirist Juvenal (second century C.E.). In *Satire* 7.229–36, the poet ironically instructs parents to take every opportunity to quiz their sons' *grammatici* about minutiae from Vergil:[26]

> But you establish harsh laws: that a grammatical straightedge be applied to your instructor, that he read histories, that he know all authors like his own fingernails and fingers, and—when he happens to be asked while he is headed for the hot tubs or the baths of Phoebus—that he be able to name the nurse of Anchises, to give the name and fatherland of Anchemolus's stepmother, and to say how many years Acestes lived and how many jugs of wine the Sicilians gave to the Phrygians.[27]

It is interesting that these Vergilian brainteasers in Juvenal's satire give the same impression as the alleged list of trivial research topics that Seneca attributes to Didymus: the true mother of Aeneas, whether Anacreon was more of a letch or more of a drunk, and whether Sappho was a whore. The testimonia of Quintilian and Seneca, it seems, are no less biased and thus no more credible than the amusing satire of Juvenal: Didymus the *grammaticus,* for these two champions of rhetoric and the liberal arts, was simply a convenient whipping boy who exemplified the hypereducated pedant.[28]

---

26. Courtney, 378–79, identifies these topics as Vergilian. For an analysis of the poem's themes and structure, see Helmbold and O'Neil.

27. Sed vos saevas inponite leges, / ut praeceptori verborum regula constet, / ut legat historias, auctores noverit omnes / tamquam ungues digitosque suos, ut forte rogatus / dum petit aut thermas aut Phoebi balnea, dicat / nutricem Anchisae, nomen patriamque novercae / Anchemoli, dicat quot Acestes vixerit annis, / quot Siculi Phrygibus vini donaverit urnas (ed. Clausen).

28. On the relationship between Juvenal and Quintilian, see Anderson.

These testimonia from Seneca and Quintilian are at best irrelevant and at worst outright misleading to anyone who hopes to discover why Didymus discusses only some topics and not others in Berol. 9780. Let me be clear on this point: if the purpose of examining ancient scholarship were simply to distinguish the correct from the incorrect, there would indeed be a great deal in Berol. 9780 to criticize. I do not defend Didymus against charges of incompetence per se.[29] Nevertheless, allowing the testimonia about Didymus to dictate how we evaluate the surviving fragments of his work introduces an unacceptable bias into the process and can produce skewed results.

For example, in an important article entitled "Chalcenteric Negligence,"[30] S. West suggested, as had some ancient scholars before her, that Didymus's great scholarly output resulted in—or was itself the result of—negligence. In West's view, Berol. 9780 is a "slapdash and ill-digested" commentary thrown together by an overworked compiler of other people's opinions.[31] Support for such a view can be found in the papyrus. But this scholar's characterization of the text seems to have been influenced as much or more by pejorative ancient testimonia as by her detailed examination of the text: "It is a certain inference from the astronomically high total of Didymus's writings[32] that he must have been a rapid worker; it is not surprising if the result shows signs of haste, inaccuracy, and superficiality."[33] The result, according to West, is "potted scholarship, hurried compilation rather than intelligent reinterpretation, and that is no proper activity for a learned man."[34] The ancient testimonia about Didymus's productivity—taken out of context—suggest that one should find "signs of haste, inaccuracy, and superficiality" in Berol. 9780. West did.

Similarly, L. J. Bliquez argues that Didymus's cross-reference to his own commentary on Dem. 18 is incorrect. In his commentary on oration 11.6, Didymus provides a lemma and then remarks only: "We have

29. As does Osborne.
30. A reference to Didymus's nickname *Chalcenterus* (Bronze Guts); see note 17 in chapter 3 above.
31. S. West, 288.
32. Evidently following Seneca and the *Suda*, S. West, 288 n. 2, comments that Didymus "is variously credited with 3,500 or 4,000 books." She adds that the number "has no doubt been tidily rounded off, but need not, as is often said, be wildly exaggerated," and speculates that such a large number of books might have been produced over a period of 35 years, with the help of "trained slaves acting as research assistants, stenographers, and copyists."
33. S. West, 296.
34. S. West, 296.

shown that the Macedonians paid tribute to the Athenians in the (commentary on) *On the Crown*" (col. 12.35–37). Didymus's commentary on *On the Crown* does not survive, so one might expect him to be given the benefit of the doubt about its contents. Bliquez notes: "In view of the fact that 'Old Brass Guts,' as one of the first absent-minded professors, was notoriously forgetful of what he had included in previous compositions, one suspects that he actually treated the matter of Macedonian [tribute] in his lost commentaries on Dem. III or (Dem.) VII and not in the *[On the Crown]* commentary at all."[35] Again, this portrait of the "notoriously forgetful" Didymus derives, it seems, not so much from a new examination of Didymus's work as from an old trust in Didymus's ancient reputation, a reputation whose credibility and usefulness to us are dubious.

Despite some grim evaluations of his work, the news has not been all bad for Didymus in modern times. Some modern scholars have honored him with the generous assumption that, as scholars, they share a special mental connection with each other. H. Diels and W. Schubart, the first editors of Berol. 9780, suggested that the commentary in Berol. 9780 was excerpted from a lost original commentary.[36] On the face of it this is not an unreasonable suggestion; it could account nicely for the commentary's apparently spotty coverage of the four speeches. They noticed that several items in Harpocration assumed to have been derived from Didymus were not present in the commentary,[37] and that the commentary on Dem. 13 was much shorter than the commentaries on Dem. 10 and 11.[38] Diels and Schubart seem to have assumed that the lost original would reveal a Didymus who commented on the same passages that other ancient and modern scholars found worthy of comment, perhaps with the same (or at least a consistent) depth of coverage.

35. Bliquez, "Didymus Papyrus," 357.
36. D-S[1], xv–xviii, lii–liii; this view is tentatively accepted by Arrighetti, 65. Yunis's recent discussion of Berol. 9780 is problematic, due in part to his nontraditional application of vocabulary from this debate. Observing that Didymus's main interests were in "the body of literature and learned opinion that had been expressed on subjects related, often tangentially, to Demosthenes and Athenian history" (1050), Yunis suggests that "Didymus aimed to *condense* this body of learned opinion into an easily grasped *abridgement*" (1050; emphasis mine). In his new formulation of the question, Yunis apparently intends the term "abridgement" to refer to Didymus's own activities as producer of the text in Berol. 9780, rather than to a subsequent scholar's editing of a now lost commentary by Didymus.
37. D-S[1], xvii.
38. D-S[1], xix.

As S. West astutely pointed out, however, the excerption theory of
Diels and Schubart is untenable, because it is "grounded only on the assumption that Didymus must originally have said more."[39] One might
also say that Diels and Schubart's theory (like that of Bliquez) is grounded
on the assumption that there is a natural, obvious way for commentators of any period to approach a given text. Diels and Schubart suggested that Berol. 9780 was not the original commentary largely because
it omitted discussion of material that was interesting to other ancient
scholars and modern classicists, while Bliquez doubted that Didymus
would have discussed Macedonian tribute payments in places other than
the two that modern scholars might reasonably expect. However, pe-
rusal of any surviving ancient commentary will reveal that ancient scholars more often than not brought to classical texts a set of evaluative criteria and methods that are very different from those of their presumed
modern counterparts. This has been well demonstrated in the case of
ancient textual criticism, whose ancient practitioners did not approach
classical texts with the same values and procedures that modern textual critics employ.[40] The kinship between ancient and modern classical
scholars, encomia to *philologia perennis* notwithstanding,[41] is largely
illusory.[42]

Failure to take into account such differences between the aims and
practices of ancient and modern classical scholars leads Yunis to conclude that "while Didymus adopted the format of a commentary, he used
it not to explain the text or necessarily even to talk about it at all, but to
meander from one literary topic to another, reproducing in condensed
form and with entertaining, illustrative quotations what had by his day
become standard discussions of classical literature."[43] Granted, there are
several discussions in Berol. 9780 whose connection to their target lem-

39. S. West, 290.
40. Zetzel, *Latin Textual Criticism*, 1–9, 232–39; similarly, Slater, "Grammarians."
41. Pfeiffer, *Classical Scholarship*, vii.
42. Similarly, Slater, "Interpreting Scholia," 40, criticizes the common assumption
that ancient scholars had "the same aims and interests" as modern ones. More generally,
see Veyne, 117–29.
43. Yunis, 1055, based on a very selective survey of the contents of Berol. 9780. It is
difficult to see how his characterization of the text might apply—to take but two examples
—to Didymus's discussion of the dates of Athenian aid sent to Oreus and Eretria (col. 1.1–
25) or to his comments on fifth- and fourth-century Athenian revenues (cols. 8.44–9.9),
neither of which is "literary" or contains anything particularly "entertaining." D-S[1], xxxv,
state that Didymus seems more interested at certain points in collecting interesting anecdotes than in commenting on Demosthenes.

mata—in the eyes of modern classical scholars—might seem tenuous at best. But Yunis's statement implies that if Didymus does not comment on the text of Demosthenes in a way that is recognizable by modern standards, Berol. 9780 cannot be a real commentary. This is not very compelling. If Didymus's interests were really topical rather than textual, as suggested, then why does he behave as ancient commentators usually did? That is, why does he introduce each discussion with a lemma from Demosthenes and arrange these discussions and their introductory lemmata in precisely the order in which a reader would normally encounter them in his text of Demosthenes? Yunis's dismissive assessment of the text leaves this important question unaddressed, but the answer is obvious: Berol. 9780 takes the form of a commentary on Demosthenes, because it *is* a commentary on Demosthenes.

BEROL. 9780 AND DIDYMUS'S INTERESTS

S. West aptly criticized Diels and Schubart's theory that Didymus must have written more on Dem. 9–11 and 13 than what is now contained in Berol. 9780. But she also criticizes their theory that Berol. 9780 is a series of excerpts from a lost original commentary for another reason: "It is hard if not impossible to divine any principle of selection on which the hypothetical excerptor might have been operating."[44] This interesting objection stems, it seems, from the quite understandable difficulty of imagining what the lost original might have looked like. Since Didymus is known to have been interested mainly in history, how (one might ask) did the excerptor decide which historical discussions to extract? This would be a good question, except that it assumes that (1) Berol. 9780 adequately represents Didymus's interests and scholarly agenda, and (2) we can somehow—independently of Berol. 9780—"know" that Didymus was interested primarily in the kinds of questions treated in Berol. 9780.

The first assumption is circular. If Berol. 9780 is taken to be the only surviving commentary of Didymus, it cannot be held up as the standard by which to prove that Berol. 9780 is representative of Didymus's work. The second assumption is also untenable. There are currently twenty-four other known fragments of Didymus's commentaries on Demosthe-

---

44. S. West, 289.

nes. These come from lexica (Berol. 5008, Harpocration), commentaries (Berol. 21188), and literary sources (Athenaeus). These twenty-four fragments demonstrate conclusively that Didymus's scholarly interests in Demosthenes included such wide-ranging topics as etymology, proverbial expressions, and the details of life in classical Athens. If we had only these twenty-four other fragments and did not have Berol. 9780, there would be little evidence to suggest that Didymus was interested in detailed analyses of historical matters at all.[45]

But even though the existence of most of these other fragments has been known for almost 150 years, scholars have universally treated Berol. 9780 as Didymus's one surviving (and thus representative) commentary on Demosthenes. On the face of it, there seems to be good reason to do so: the most recent printed text of Berol. 9780 is fifty-four pages long, while the largest of the other fragments is less than six lines long. But this disparity is misleading. In the case of many classical authors, like the tragedian Sophocles or the philosopher Aristotle, a respectable number of writings survive in the mediaeval manuscript tradition. Scholars then use newly discovered papyrus texts and fragments preserved elsewhere in ancient literature to supplement and illuminate the major texts. This is a helpful procedure, one that can tell us a great deal about the authors that we might not otherwise have known.

But such a distinction between "texts" and "other fragments" does not apply to Berol. 9780 and the twenty-four fragments preserved elsewhere, for several reasons. First, Berol. 9780 is but one text, not seven (as with Sophocles) or thirty-some-odd (as with Aristotle). Its status as a "representative" text is called into question for this reason alone. Second, Berol. 9780 is a single chance survival from an ancient trashheap in Egypt.[46] A different random survival might have resulted in a very different impression of Didymus. For this reason the soundest strategy is to consider all the chance survivals—both the papyrus fragments and the literary "fragments"—together as a whole. Third and most important, Berol. 9780 is not a continuous, unified text in the same way that a tragedy or a philosophical treatise is; it consists of twenty-seven

45. This point loses a little of its force if some of the Didymus fragments in Harpocration do not actually come from commentaries on Demosthenes. See the introduction to text 2.

46. Wilson, "History of Scholia," 248, reminds us of the implications of using such texts: "As the surviving papyri come from country districts of Egypt it is far from certain that they are representative of the ancient book trade as a whole, at least in the matter of books catering for the tastes of a highly literate and learned minority of the public."

distinct discussions of individual points from four different orations of
Demosthenes.[47]

This last point is where the known practice of excerption, as defined
and discussed in chapter 1, is most helpful. The history of scholarly texts
in antiquity suggests that such distinct discussions are liable to be copied
out by other scholars who are interested in some kinds of topics but not
others. Thus in the case of Didymus, the distinction between a "main
text" and "other fragments" completely breaks down. The total number
of Didymus's "other fragments"—a loaded and intentionally misleading label—nearly equals the number of individual, distinct discussions
in Berol. 9780. So the only claim that one might possibly make in favor
of the centrality and representativeness of Berol. 9780 is that its individual comments currently happen to appear together in one papyrus roll.
But how meaningful is that? The history of ancient commentaries suggests that it is not very meaningful at all: the "other fragments" of Didymus's commentaries originally came from texts just like Berol. 9780,
where they, too, were once located among a series of other individual,
isolated comments.

EXCURSUS: APPARENT GAPS IN COVERAGE IN BEROL. 9780

Without resorting to an argument based on genre or on ancient testimonia about Didymus the *grammaticus,* how might one explain the
fact that Didymus does not discuss most of the contents of the orations
that he treats in Berol. 9780? We shall pretend for the moment that
Berol. 9780 is substantially the commentary as Didymus wrote it, and
that there is a good reason to expect him to have commented on more
passages than he did. One possible explanation for the apparent gaps in
coverage is that Didymus discussed most topics only the first time that
they occurred,[48] and that he did not routinely repeat, allude to, or cross-
reference his earlier discussions. The scholia to Cicero's *Pro Sestio* suggest that a commentator's treatment of a particular speech might have
been influenced by his treatment of previous speeches in the series. In the
introduction to *Pro Sestio,* a scholiast announces: "We shall pass over

47. Similarly, in discussing the transmission of late-ancient and mediaeval commentaries on Vergil, Daintree criticizes the commonly held assumption that "each commentary
. . . may be regarded as a single, discrete and integrated work of literature whose several
parts share a common history" (71–72).
48. As S. West, 289–90.

many things in the course of the oration that, due to the similarities between the two cases, we have already presented in the commentary on the previous oration. So do not expect us to cover the same topics again, if they should turn up anywhere."[49]

Didymus's approach may have been the same. In his commentary on Dem. 10 (a speech consisting of seventy-six sections in modern editions), Didymus discusses items in sections 1, 17, 32–35, 37–38, 44, and 70. But Dem. 10 contains two long passages that also appear in Dem. 8: Dem. 10.11–27 is found in Dem. 8.38–51, and Dem. 10.55–70 is found in Dem. 8.52–67.[50] Since it stands to reason that Didymus's commentary on Dem. 8 preceded his commentaries on Dem. 9–11 and 13, it is possible that the discussions "missing" from his commentary on Dem. 10 occurred earlier in his (lost) commentary on Dem. 8.[51] But if this is the case, Didymus does not call attention to it.

Similar observations can be made about Didymus's commentaries on orations 11 and 13. In his commentary on Dem. 11 (a speech consisting of twenty-three sections), Didymus comments only on sections 1–2, 4, 16, and 22. He opens by reporting the view that much of the material in Dem. 11 seems to have been taken from other Demosthenic speeches (col. 11.7–10): "But someone might suspect—not far from the mark—that a derivative little speech has been assembled, compiled from certain orations of Demosthenes." Didymus does not attempt to demonstrate which passages of Dem. 11 were copied, and from where, but it is interesting to note that Dem. 11.8–17 is similar to Dem. 2.14–23. So it is again possible that Didymus discussed certain topics only the first time he encountered them, and that he felt no need to treat the same material twice.

In his brief commentary on oration 13 (a speech consisting of thirty-six sections), Didymus comments only on sections 1, 7–8, and 32. As he observes, however, "Nothing is explored in the speech that has not received some discussion in the ones (sc. speeches or commentaries?) before this" (cols. 13.62–14.2); it has plausibly been suggested that this statement accounts for the relative brevity of the commentary on this

49. Multa quidem in orationis cursu praetermittemus quae propter similitudinem causae in commentario proxumae orationis ostendimus: ergo ne expectaveris ut, sicubi inciderit, eadem rursus iteremus (ed. Stangl, p. 136).
50. See Sealey, *Demosthenes*, 232–35, on the relationship between Dem. 8 and 10.
51. The only real evidence for the order of composition of Didymus's commentaries on Demosthenes are two references in Berol. 9780 to earlier commentaries on Dem. 18 (cols. 12.33–37, 12.37–13.12).

speech.[52] It may also be significant that Dem. 13 bears similarities to certain passages of the *Olynthiacs* (Dem. 1–3), which Didymus may already have discussed in other commentaries.[53]

One should hesitate to attribute to lost writings all the "goodies" that one would like to find in the surviving ones, but it is conceivable that a scholar who wrote on the entire corpus of Demosthenes might avoid discussing the same topic twice, except in those places where he felt a cross-reference or a second, abbreviated discussion was in order. The only cross-reference is at col. 12.35–37, where, in commenting on Dem. 11.16, Didymus refers the reader to the parallel discussion in his commentary on Dem. 18. He says that a longer discussion from elsewhere has been abbreviated for the present discussion in col. 12.40–43 and cols. 13.62–14.2. In the first of these, Didymus opens his discussion of Dem. 11.22 by saying: "We have <elsewhere> fully discussed the wounds that Philip had. But at this point we must briefly comment on the subject." In cols. 13.62–14.49, after noting that "nothing is explored in the speech that has not received some discussion in the ones (sc. speeches or commentaries?) before this," Didymus could easily have moved on to the next speech in the corpus. Instead he says: "Nevertheless, the subject of Orgas must be briefly clarified." The lengthy discussion that follows this statement makes one wonder how much longer the implied original treatment of the subject could have been.[54]

BEROL. 9780 AS THE RESULT OF EXCERPTION

If one rejects certain untenable assumptions—namely that there is a meaningful and measurable difference between "commentaries" and "monographs" that can help illuminate the nature or contents of Berol. 9780; that one may accurately evaluate the surviving fragments of Didymus through the lens of decontextualized ancient testimonia; that Didy-

---

52. S. West, 290. According to D-S[1], xix, the relative brevity of the commentary on Dem. 13 indicates that it has been abbreviated.

53. Also noted by S. West, 290. See Trevett for a full discussion of the authenticity of Dem. 13 and its relation to other speeches; also discussed by Sealey, *Demosthenes*, 235–37.

54. Other characterizations of Berol. 9780 variously account for its spotty coverage. Foucart, 39, characterizes the work as *De Demosthenis Philippicis quaestiones selectae*. D-S[2], vii, suggest that "non excerpta habemus ex toto corpore breviata, sed eclogas integras historico maxime gustu selectas"; their implied contrast between *excerpta* and *eclogae integrae* is not entirely clear (snippets vs. large selections?), but I would certainly agree with *historico maxime gustu selectas*.

mus can be evaluated by the same standards as modern commentators, without taking into account the differences between ancient and modern scholarly attitudes and practices; and that Berol. 9780 is the "main text," while everything else is "other fragments"—Berol. 9780's spotty coverage of Dem. 9–11 and 13 may, in fact, be reduced to the status of a nonissue. The burden of proof should be on the scholar who would choose to argue that Berol. 9780 is anything other than what it appears to be: a commentary on Demosthenes whose contents reflect the interests and conscious choices of a rational being, a scholar who may have discussed some topics only the first time that he encountered them, and who may have opted not to discuss certain other topics at all, despite the interest shown in them by other ancient or modern commentators.

On the other hand, given what we know about the volatility of ancient scholarly writings and the interest shown in Didymus by later authors, it would be nothing short of amazing if the only commentary of Didymus that survives also happened to be a commentary unaffected by such a widespread phenomenon as excerption. Let us reconsider Diels and Schubart's theory that Berol. 9780 is an abbreviated version of a lost original commentary, in the light of evidence of which they were perhaps unaware. Given what we now know about excerption in the transmission of the ancient commentaries on Demosthenes, Berol. 9780's spotty coverage of Dem. 9–11 and 13 may be due to excerption from a lost original commentary. First, the evidence to the contrary: No physical evidence of the excerpting process survives. We do not have the requisite original commentary to serve as control. There are no other excerpted copies of the commentary (or of any individual section of the commentary) to show how the excerptor carried out this task. If we possessed two or more commentaries that were derived from the same (lost) original commentary, we could compare them in order to get a better sense of the scope and contents of the lost original.[55] But we do not and cannot.

Nevertheless, there are two compelling reasons to accept the theory that Berol. 9780 is a string of excerpts from a longer original commentary. First, as we see throughout the ancient commentaries on Demosthenes, isolated sections of discussion have often been lifted from their original context, rewritten or refocused, and redeployed in quite different contexts and for quite different purposes. S. West's notion of "nor-

---

55. In the case of Berol. 5008, for example, such parallels have helped to reconstruct part of the history of how commentaries and lexica to Demosthenes were transmitted. See Gibson, "P.Berol.inv. 5008."

mal, common-sense epitomization" simply does not hold up in the face of the surviving textual evidence.[56] In fact, the ancient point-by-point commentary on Demosthenes ideally lent itself to excerption, whether for a special lexicon to a particular speech (Berol. 5008), a general lexicon to the canonical orators (Harpocration), or even another commentary (Berol. 21188). Second, as has already been noted, the fragments of Didymus's commentaries that are found in places other than Berol. 9780 reveal a wide variety of scholarly interests and do not give the impression that Didymus was that much more interested in fourth-century political history than, say, in Athenian festivals or boat-shaped drinking vessels.

That something is "not impossible" does not make it plausible, much less convincing or true. But the phenomenon of excerption can help us create a possible scenario for how the commentary preserved in Berol. 9780, a papyrus from Hermoupolis dating to the second century C.E., was created. Consider, then, a hypothetical historian or scholar living in Hermoupolis in the early second century C.E.[57] Turning up a copy of Didymus's extensive commentary on Dem. 9–11 and 13, he finds a great deal of interesting historical material. The evidence of the Didymus fragments in Harpocration shows that history was not Didymus's sole interest, so it is reasonable to conjecture that other concerns were represented in the lost original commentary. Our Hermoupolite historian rightly feels no need to preserve Didymus for the sake of Didymus. Didymus's commentaries are merely a source of information, not a classical text, and our historian regards them simply as raw material to be used or adapted as needed.[58] As he combs through the point-by-point commentary of Didymus, the physical layout of the commentary—individual lemmata followed by comments and perhaps separated by ticks in the margin *(paragraphoi)*—would aid him in his research. He then

56. S. West, 289; also noted by Arrighetti, 57, 59.
57. The palaeographical date of Berol. 9780 is, of course, not necessarily the date of the excerption (which could have been made at any point after the "publication" of the original commentary); likewise, it is not necessarily the case that the series of excerpts was made at Hermoupolis. These details, however, are much less important than the process of excerption and the possible motivations for someone to carry it out. D-S[1], xvi–xvii, describe the copyist as an uneducated man (based on their examination of errors made in copying) but also admit that the original commentaries of Didymus may already have suffered in transmission before this time.
58. M. L. West, 16–17, also notes the differences in how ancient authors treated texts like ours in comparison with the "sacrosanct literary entities" of classical authors; similarly, Daintree, 71–72. Likewise in the transmission of Latin commentaries on Donatus, according to Zetzel, "Latin Scholia," 353: "Abridgments were the commonest form of the commentary on Donatus, and . . . they were all individual abridgments, not copies of a single, authorized text."

excerpts only those isolated sections of discussion that interest him, perhaps further abbreviating or paraphrasing them as he works. This is not
at all an unusual activity: excerpting during reading was a regular practice for ancient readers, particularly for scholars.[59] The result of our historian's research—an active intellectual process, not mindless compilation—is a series of excerpts from Didymus's commentary on Dem. 9–11
and 13 that emphasize history above all else.[60] Our Hermoupolite historian, an active researcher into fourth-century history or at least the historical circumstances of Demosthenes' orations, can therefore be placed
alongside the other imperial-age scholars who were carefully combing
through Didymus's commentaries and excerpting material to use toward
their own interests.[61]

59. See Mejer, 17–18, with many ancient references; see also Skydsgaard, 107–15,
specifically on the working methods of ancient historians. On excerpting and its effects on
the process of composition, see Mejer, 16–29 (on Diogenes Laertius), and Bloomer, 59–
146 (on Valerius Maximus).

60. There are a few exceptions. The discussion of "hyperbatic phrasing" in cols. 6.66–
7.7 could be seen as a practical aid for the beginning reader of Demosthenes. The etymology of Orgas in cols. 13.62–14.49 may have been retained in toto because—rather than
despite the fact that—it contains a fragment of Androtion covering the same events as the
fragment of Philochorus given earlier in col. 13.25–62. The only other exception is an etymological discussion in col. 11.14–26. Excerption, in this case and others, is carried out
by an idiosyncratic reader, not a computer program. Nevertheless, we may observe that a
general pattern of an interest in history emerges when the contents of Berol. 9780 are
compared to Didymus's other surviving comments on Demosthenes.

61. My purpose in the preceding argument has been not so much to "prove" that
Berol. 9780 is a string of excerpts from a lost commentary—this cannot be done on the
basis of the textual evidence currently available—as to argue that none of the arguments
against excerption is particularly persuasive, and to demonstrate that parallels for the proposed procedure exist.

PART TWO

Texts, Translations, and Notes

THIS PART OF THE BOOK provides Greek texts, English translations, and explanatory notes on the ancient philological and historical commentaries on Demosthenes. A Greek text is given for each text surveyed except for Berol. 9780, whose length and ready availability in a recent edition precluded its inclusion here. A brief introduction to each commentary or lexicon and a bibliographical notice are given before each text. In the explanatory notes, ancient authors cited in the commentaries are identified on first appearance, with brief bibliographical recommendations. The other bibliographical references in the notes are intended to serve several purposes: to point the curious reader to the relevant editions or collections of ancient texts, to help sketch in broad terms the topics of modern debate for which individual comments provide important evidence, to recommend the most recent or fullest treatments of those topics, and to report and weigh particularly noteworthy opinions advanced by other scholars who have studied these texts in detail but for purposes often quite different from mine. Analysis of these commentaries often entails discussing topics and arguments that, though sometimes not my primary interest, cannot and should not be ignored. This is especially true of matters pertaining to the political and military history of the fourth century B.C.

For the translator of fragmentary, subliterary texts such as these, several options are available. Some translators have made admirable attempts to superimpose the apparatus and specialized symbols used in modern editions of Greek texts onto their English translations through the use of such conventions as square brackets (e.g., [abc]) and italics. Ultimately it was decided that, for this particular body of texts, such a method of presentation would be cumbersome, impossible to carry out consistently, confusing or meaningless to those able to read only the English translation, and unnecessary for the rest. Instead, (1) footnotes to the translation of Berol. 9780 draw the reader's attention to places where the Greek text is especially uncertain and susceptible to radically different interpretations depending on the restoration; (2) the introduction to each of the other papyrus texts discusses its physical condition; and (3) the notes following each translation provide further discussion of the most important textual problems.

In the translations, all lemmata (i.e., target words or passages from Demosthenes) are translated, except where a translation would be misleading or otherwise unhelpful to someone reading only the English. Lemmata and other quotations from Demosthenes are presented in sans-serif type. A series of three dots (. . .) stands for short unrestored passages of less than a line in length,[1] and a series of three dashes in parentheses (– – –) for passages of one to three lines in length. Longer unrestored passages are noted in parentheses in the body of the translation: (– – –20 *lines unrestored*– – –). Angle brackets (e.g., <abc>) enclose lengthy or particularly controversial editorial additions made where the scribe is thought to have omitted something. Superfluous words are excluded by braces (e.g., {abc}). Dates, references to explain the commentators' citations of ancient authors, and the translator's expansions of elliptical expressions are placed in parentheses.

The texts included for consideration here are as follows:

1. Texts preserved on papyrus that show by their contents and organization that they are philological and historical commentaries on Demosthenes, or lexica derived from such commentaries: P.Berol.inv. 9780, P.Berol.inv. 5008, P.Berol.inv. 21188, P.Stras.inv. 84, and P.Rain.inv. 7. The longest and most frequently studied text, Didymus's *On Demosthenes* (Berol. 9780), is presented first. Following the fragments of Didymus in Harpocration are two texts that cite Didymus (Berol. 5008 and 21188) and two texts that do not (Stras. 84 and Rain. 7).[2]

2. Comments on Demosthenes that are attributed to Didymus by name in Harpocration's *Lexeis of the Ten Orators*. These fragments are presented immediately following Didymus's commentary on Dem. 9–11 and 13 (P.Berol.inv. 9780).

3. *P.Lond.Lit.* 179, one of the earliest surviving rhetorical commentaries on Demosthenes, is included as an appendix. This final text nicely illustrates some of the differences between the

---

1. Except in the fragments of Didymus's commentaries preserved in Harpocration (text 2), where three dots indicate ellipsis of material in the entry that is not relevant to my purpose.

2. Two papyrus texts that have been called commentaries on Demosthenes are excluded: (1) P.Rain.inv. 1.25 (Pack² 294) is more likely a rhetorical exercise aimed at recasting specific passages in Dem. 19. It contains "fairly banal paraphrases" of passages from Dem. 19, according to Wilcken, in *Archiv*, 270. More precisely stated, the papyrus contains a mixture of quotation and paraphrase from Dem. 19.40, 42, 47, and 51 (on the verso, and with the passages not treated in order) and 19.103, 117, 156, and 158 (on the recto). Recto, line 5, is similar to the Demosthenic scholia ad loc. (Dilts 333). Recto, line 7, contains the word "swiftness" (τῆς ταχυτῆτος), perhaps a reference to the swiftness of Demosthenes' delivery. The word is used in this sense by Dio Chrysostom (τῇ ῥώμῃ καὶ τῇ ταχυτῆτι τῶν λόγων, 33.5; ed. von Arnim). (2) *P.Yale* II 106 is rhetorical in interest and thus falls outside our purview; on this see Hubbell. Furthermore, the citation of Didymus that supposedly occurs in it (according to Gilliam) does not exist, as Stephens, 80, has shown.

ancient rhetorical tradition and the ancient philological and
historical tradition of commentaries on Demosthenes.

Excluded are the hundreds, perhaps thousands, of entries in Harpocration and later lexica that discuss words and phrases in Demosthenes
but do not make explicit reference to commentaries or named commentators in the philological and historical tradition,[3] and whose sheer vol-
ume and complex history of transmission do not easily allow us to assess the agenda of their authors or excerptors in a meaningful way.

---

3. The later lexica referred to here would include Pollux, Hesychius, and Photius, as
well as the *Suda*. Hesychius (fifth century C.E.), who like Harpocration derived many of
his entries from previous lexica (Schultz, 1318), attributes none of his entries to commentaries on Demosthenes. Photius and the *Suda* cite nothing from Didymus's commentaries
on Demosthenes that does not come to them from Harpocration; see Cunningham on the
relationship between these works. On Photius's lexicon and the *Suda* in general, see Wilson, *Scholars,* 90–93, 145–47.

Commentary on Dem. 9-11 and 13 (P.Berol.inv. 9780)

P.Berol.inv. 9780 (Pack[2] 339) is a substantial papyrus roll from Hermoupolis dated to the early second century C.E. The recto contains Didymus's commentaries on Demosthenes' *Third Philippic* (Dem. 9), *Fourth Philippic* (Dem. 10), *Reply to Philip's Letter* (Dem. 11), and *On Organization* (Dem. 13). Toward the end of the second century, an introduction to Stoic ethics by Hierocles (early second century C.E.) was copied on the verso and in the opposite direction. Most of the commentary on Dem. 9 is lost; the extant text begins with the end of the commentary on that speech. The commentaries on Dem. 10, 11, and 13 are preserved almost in their entirety, the most notable exceptions being cols. 1.31–45, 2.3–3.62, 4.16–59, and 5.32–51, which are very poorly preserved. The surviving commentary extends for fifteen columns. The scribe labeled some of the columns with a brief table of contents,[1] probably indicating his intention to consult the text frequently. These column headers read as follows:

Col. 1   (header not restored)

Col. 2   Who are the ones. . . . Concerning the suspicion (that) . . .

---

1. Col. 12a is the one exception: it is a critical comment about a word occurring in the text at col. 12.3, rather than a description of the column's contents. D-S[1], x–xi, mention the possibility that the column headers were written by a different hand from that of the main text.

the Thebans . . . alliance. . . . That . . . is ill disposed. . . .
(ends of each of 4 lines not restored)

Col. 3   (header not restored)

Col. 4   Who it was who was dragged off to the king and informed
him of Philip's preparations against him. What those who
have written about Hermias of Atarneus say about him.

Col. 5   (no header given)

Col. 6   A reconstruing of hyperbatic phrasing.

Col. 7   What the king's recent philanthropy[2] toward the Athenians was.

Col. 8   What the date was when, humbled, they (the Athenians)
were receiving only 130 talents of revenue. Concerning
the Athenians' receiving 400 talents of revenue.

Col. 9   That there are two men named Aristomedes, one from
Pherae, the other an Athenian nicknamed "Brazen."

Col. 10   Dates and cities of the speech. That the speech is by
Anaximenes.

Col. 11   What ὀρρωδεῖν (means). Concerning Nicaea. Concerning
σκορακίζειν and the proverbial expression "to the
crows."

Col. 12   But if (it is) not (νεομένους or ναιωμένους, then it is)
νεμομένους.[3] Concerning Philip's wounds.

Col. 13   That the speech is not one of the Philippics, but is otherwise by Demosthenes.

Col. 14   Concerning Orgas. Why he called the Megarians
"accursed."

Col. 15   (no header given)

At the end of the roll is a title identifying it as the third book of Didymus's commentaries on the *Philippics,* part of a series of commentaries
on twenty-eight speeches of Demosthenes.[4]

2. *Philanthropia* is perhaps in error for "magnanimity" *(philotimia),* given the terms
of Didymus's discussion.
3. Reading εἰ δὲ μὴ for ιδεμη. D-S¹, D-S², and P-S ἰδὲ μὴ does not readily construe.
For this text-critical comment, see notes on cols. 11.52–12.33.
4. Or, alternatively, the twenty-eighth book in a series of commentaries. See pp. 53,
136.

The commentary is written along the fibres of the recto of the papyrus.[5] The height of the papyrus is 30 cm, the width of columns 6–15 is 90 cm, and the width of the entire roll is 134 cm. The undamaged original would have been no more than 25 columns long. Each column consists of approximately 70 lines; the number of letters per line decreases slightly toward the bottoms of columns. Abbreviations are frequently used, both as parts of words and in place of whole words. The scribe used indentation and special punctuation marks to designate lemmata (quotations) and the ends of the commentaries on individual orations.

The contents of Berol. 9780 suggest an author who was interested primarily, but not exclusively, in questions of a historical nature.[6] Didymus identifies important historical persons, places, and events; discusses the dates and authenticity of the speeches; clarifies obscure passages; and discusses the etymology of some of the more unusual words in Dem. 9–11 and 13. He typically supplies a lemma (quotation) from Demosthenes, discusses something suggested by the lemma, and then quotes other sources to corroborate his view. Didymus's commentary consists largely of quotations from classical Greek authors and fourth- and third-century historians, usually with only a spare narrative to connect them.

In the translation of Text 1 (P.Berol.inv. 9780), some special formatting is required since Didymus quotes so extensively from Demosthenes and a variety of other sources. All quotations of Demosthenes appear in san-serif type. All quotations of other authors appear in inset blocks but in the same font as the surrounding text.

The column contents of the papyrus can be summarized as follows:

Col. 1.1–25	Missing lemma (from Dem. 9.57–58?). Athenian aid sent to Oreos in 342/1, to Eretria in 341/0. Citations: Dem. 18.79, Philochorus.
Col. 1.26–53	Lemma from Dem. 10.1. Oration 10 delivered in 341/0, not earlier. Citations: Philochorus.
Col. 1.53–3.62	The peace still in effect in 340/39; compare Dem. 10.17. Some date the speech to 342/1. Citations: Philochorus.

5. This physical description is derived from P-S, iii–vi and xix–xx.
6. This copy may misrepresent the scope and focus of Didymus's lost original commentary, if the argument presented in chapter 3 is correct.

Col. 4.1–47	Subject unknown. Citations: Amphictyonic decree regarding the Megalopolitans and Messenians, Aristotle's *Customs of the Barbarians*.
Col. 4.48–5.63	Lemma from Dem. 10.32. The debate concerning Hermias of Atarneus. The negative portrayal of him. Citations: Theopompus.
Col. 5.64–6.18	The favorable portrayal of Hermias. Citations: Callisthenes.
Col. 6.18–49	Hermias's relationship with Aristotle. Citations: Aristotle's hymn to Hermias, the epigram from Delphi, Theocritus of Chios's response to the epigram (via Bryon).
Col. 6.50–62	Other views on Hermias's arrest and death. Citations: Hermippus, Callisthenes, Anaximenes.
Col. 6.63–66	Lemma from Dem. 10.33. Demosthenes' use of specific, individual examples.
Col. 6.66–7.7	Lemma from Dem. 10.34. Demosthenes' use of "hyperbatic phrasing."
Col. 7.7–8.2	Lemma from Dem. 10.34. The previous restoration (ἐπανόρθωσις) not the failed peace of Antalcidas (392/1), but Conon and Pharnabazus's defeat of the Spartans at Cnidus (394, but described under the year 397/6), or possibly one of several other events. Citations: Philochorus.
Col. 8.2–32	The recent restoration in 344/3, when the Persian king made a peace offer rejected by the Athenians. Citations: Philochorus.
Col. 8.32–44	Lemma from Dem. 10.35. The Theoric Fund.
Col. 8.44–9.9	Lemma from Dem. 10.37. Athenian revenues of 130 talents in 405 B.C. But then 400 talents in the time of Philip. Citations: Dem. 10.38, Theopompus.
Col. 9.9–37	Lemma from Dem. 10.44. On the rich and poor, and the behavior of demagogues.
Col. 9.38–10.10	Lemma from Dem. 10.70. Who is Aristomedes? Not the one from Pherae, but the Athenian

nicknamed "Brazen." Citations: Philip, Theopompus, Anaximenes, Dinarchus, Philemon,
Timocles.

Col. 10.13–11.7   Lemma from Dem. 11.1. Date of the speech is
340/39. Philip's activities at Byzantium, Perinthus, Hieron. Citations: Philochorus, Theopompus.

Col. 11.7–14   Dem. 11 compiled from other speeches; possibly
written by Anaximenes.

Col. 11.14–26   Lemma from Dem. 11.2. Non-Demosthenic language of Dem. 11. Etymology of ὀρρωδεῖν =
ὄρρος (rear end) + ἰδίειν (to sweat). Citations:
Homer, Aristophanes.

Col. 11.26–52   Lemma from Dem. 11.4. Where is Nicaea? Citations: Timosthenes, Philochorus.

Col. 11.52–12.33   Lemma from Dem. 11.11. σκορακίζειν = to go
ἐς κόρακας (to the crows). Origin of the proverbial expression "to the crows." Citations:
Aristophanes, Demon.

Col. 12.33–37   Lemma from Dem. 11.16. Macedonian tribute
payments to Athens. Citations: his own commentary to Dem. 18 *(On the Crown)*.

Col. 12.37–13.12   Lemma from Dem. 11.22. Philip's wounds. Citations: Theopompus, Marsyas of Macedon,
Duris.

Col. 13.14–25   Lemma from Dem. 13.1. This speech not a
Philippic.

Col. 13.25–62   Lemma from Dem. 13.7–8. Some date the speech
after 346, but the date is 349/8. Boundaries
of Orgas (compare Dem. 13.32). Citations:
Philochorus.

Col. 13.62–14.49   Compare Dem. 13.32. Etymology of "Orgas."
Specific and general place-names. Boundaries
of Orgas. Citations: Sophocles, Aeschylus,
Homer, Callimachus, Androtion.

Col. 14.49–15.10   Lemma from Dem. 13.32. Why the Megarians
are called "accursed." Citations: Theopompus.

My translation and notes had essentially been completed when I learned of the dissertation of K. T. Osborne, "The 'Peri Demosthenous' of Didymos Grammatikos" (Ph.D. diss., University of Washington, 1990). I have greatly benefited from Osborne's detailed treatment of Berol. 9780, different as it is from mine. He sets himself the unenviable task of defending Didymus's accuracy and originality, which has been beneficial in countering the common opinion that Didymus is valuable only where he accurately preserves quotations from presumably more intelligent authors; however, despite scoring several points in Didymus's favor,[7] Osborne is occasionally led into the trap of ascribing to Didymus a great deal more intelligence and clarity of thought than is actually suggested by the text as we have it. Second, whenever Didymus quotes a passage from Demosthenes or a historian that figures in a modern historical debate, Osborne takes this as an opportunity to review and comment upon the history of scholarship on these issues. His commentary is thus much more devoted to matters of fourth-century history. My goal is mainly to understand Didymus as commentator: what he was doing, what he was reading, and (to the extent that this is possible) what he was thinking when he read Demosthenes.

Text: Text of Pearson and Stephens (abbreviated "P-S"), incorporating some corrections and suggestions from Rusten, Wankel, Milns, D-S[1], and D-S[2] (this last only where it differs from D-S[1]). Two earlier editions by Diels and Schubart, abbreviated D-S[1] and D-S[2], respectively. Commentaries by Stähelin and Florian (historical fragments only), Foucart, and Osborne. Thirteen selections from the papyrus previously translated by Harding, *End of Peloponnesian War* (see his index).

TRANSLATION OF DIDYMUS'S
COMMENTARY ON ORATIONS 9–11 AND 13

Oration 9

Col. 1.1–25:[8]

(– – –7 *lines unrestored*– – –)

I first <proposed the embassy to the Peloponnese, when he (Philip) first> was creeping into the Peloponnese; then the embassy to Euboea, when he was grasping at

7. Noted throughout, particularly in the notes on Berol. 9780.
8. Only the end of Didymus's commentary on oration 9 survives.

> Euboea; then the military expedition—not an embassy—to Oreus, and one to Eretria,
> when he set up tyrants in those cities. (Dem. 18.79)

Some passages in Philochorus bear witness to these events; for on the subject of the aid sent to Oreus, which he puts under the archonship of Sosigenes (342/1), he says the following:

> And the Athenians made an alliance with the Chalcidians, and with the
> help of the Chalcidians they freed the people of Oreus in the month of
> Scirophorion, under the general Cephisiphon, and Philistides the tyrant
> died. (*FGrH* 328 F159)

On the aid sent to Eretria, the same author again says the following, putting it under the archonship of Nicomachus (341/0):

> In this year the Athenians crossed over to Eretria under the general Pho-
> cion, restored the democracy, and besieged Clitarchus, who previously was
> an opponent and political rival of Plutarchus, but when that man died Cli-
> tarchus became tyrant. But then the Athenians took him by siege and re-
> stored the city to the people. (*FGrH* 328 F160)

Oration 10

Col. 1.26–53:

> Athenian gentlemen, since I consider the things that you are debating as very impor-
> tant and necessary for the city, I shall try to say some things on the subject that I
> consider useful. (Dem. 10.1)

Someone might perhaps perceive the date of the speech from what Philochorus says, putting it under the archonship of Nicomachus (341/0) (*FGrH* 328 F161) (– – –16 *lines unrestored*– – –) with Philistides of Oreus having died in the archonship of Sosigenes (342/1), and Clitarchus of Eretria having fallen in the archonship of Nicomachus. And Philochorus lends credence to the fact that these events, which the oration does not know as having already occurred, happened at the end of the archonship of Nicomachus. Therefore, it is now sufficiently obvious that the speech was written *before* the aforementioned archonship, and not after Nicomachus.[9]

Cols. 1.53–3.62: But the same author, putting it under the archonship of Theophrastus (340/39), the one after Nicomachus, (– – –) the oaths

---

9. The correct restoration of the two previous sentences (col. 1.49–53) is debated. See notes.

concerning the peace with Philip, and the inscription of the peace agreements was still standing in the archonship of Theophrastus (– – –). In
saying the following, Demosthenes is a clear witness that I am speaking
the truth:[10]

> Now, let no man who is knowledgeable and perceptive of these things propose that
> the man who is advising what is best in terms of justice declare war. For this is the
> kind of thing that those of you who want to find someone with whom to go to war
> would do, not the kind of thing that people who want to benefit the state would do.
> (Dem. 10.17)

For he never would have said these things, if the Athenians had already actually broken the peace agreement. And so Philochorus, writing
clearly as follows in book 6, is sufficient proof that the agreements were
broken in the archonship of Theophrastus (340/39), who was archon after Nicomachus:

> When the people had heard the letter, and when Demosthenes had urged
> them to go to war and had proposed a decree, the people voted to tear down
> the inscription which had been put up concerning the peace with Philip and
> the alliance, and to man the ships and wage war. (*FGrH* 328 F55b)

But some say that the speech was composed in the archonship of Sosigenes (342/1) (– – –137 *lines unrestored*).[11]

Col. 4.1–47:

> (– – –) of the Amphictyons, and participating in the Amphictyony, in accor-
> dance with the following decree:[12] "Since the Megalopolitans and the
> Messenians have requested to be inscribed as benefactors of the god and
> of the Amphictyons and to be considered to be Amphictyons, the Amphic-
> tyons voted to reply to them that having referred the matter concerning the
> Amphictyony back to the individual cities, they would take counsel, and
> would reply to them about these things at the next meeting. And they voted
> that they were to be considered benefactors of the god and of the Amphic-
> tyons; and to answer the . . . that the Amphictyons vote to inscribe them
> as benefactors of the god and of the Amphictyons, just as they requested."
> (*Syll.*³ 224)

---

10. Col. 1.60–61, "that I am speaking the truth": Restoring ἀ[ληθεύω] with Wankel,
Blass, "Literarische Texte," and D-S² for P-S ἀ[ποδείξω], "as I will reveal."

11. Little survives of cols. 2 and 3.

12. Col. 4.2, "in accordance with the following decree": Restoring [κατὰ] with
Wankel and D-S¹ for P-S [κ(αὶ) τὸ], "and the decree was as follows."

. . . Aristotle in book 3 of the *Customs,* which is on the customs of the Scythians, says (– – –) to have been addressed by the barbarians (– – – *29 lines unrestored).*

Cols. 4.48–5.63: (– – –) having been deceived by Mentor the Rhodian, and having been dragged off to the king (– – – *19 unrestored lines).* Since those who have handed down accounts about Hermias greatly disagree, I have decided to speak about this subject at length, to gratify the receptive ears of those who are still curious about such things. For example, there are those who represent this man in the best light, but there are others who represent him in the worst light; among these, in addition to other authors, is Theopompus in book 46 of his *On Philip.* For he writes as follows:

> Hermias, who was a eunuch and a Bithynian, started on this road (– – –). Along with Eubulus, he took Assos (– – –) (and) Atarneus and the territory around it. For this man, in his dealings with everyone, committed the cruelest and most wicked acts of all, both against the citizens and the others, for he would destroy one with poison and another with the noose. And when they established him as governor of the land that the Chians and the Mytilenaeans disputed, he acted unlawfully [13] in many ways along with the unpaid troops, and he horribly abused most of the Ionians. For when he was a purchased slave and a money changer, and when disasters befell the Chians, he did not keep still (– – –) to destroy the existing constitutions. He did not get away scot-free, nor did he completely escape notice as being evil and worthless, but when he was dragged off to the king, he endured many outrages to his body, was crucified, and ended his life. (*FGrH* 115 F291)

The same author in his *Letter to Philip* also relates his reputation among the Greeks:

> For he was a eunuch, but nonetheless is elegant and refined, and although a barbarian he practices philosophy with the Platonists, and although once a slave he competes in the festivals with his costly team. Having gotten possession of crags and other insignificant areas, he obtained . . . , and he persuaded the city of the Eleians to proclaim to him the sacred truce . . . , for when that man was celebrating a festival (– – –*20 lines unrestored*– – –) of Plato. At that time, then, Hermias ruled over the people round about, and he invited Coriscus and Erastus and Aristotle and Xenocrates as companions. And so all these men came to Hermias. Later, when others came, he gave the group some land as a gift. (*FGrH* 115 F250)

---

13. Col. 5.8, "he acted unlawfully": Restoring π[αρενόμει] with Rusten for P-S π[αρ-ώινησε], "he mistreated (them)."

And he also says this:

> He purposefully converted the tyranny into a milder rule. And so he held power over all the nearby area up to Assos, when, having completed his education, he assigned the city of the Assians to the aforementioned philosophers. He especially approved of Aristotle beyond all the others, and became very attached to him.[14]

Cols. 5.64–6.18: But Callisthenes, in his book about him, says many other things, including the following:

> Thus not only when he was well out of danger, but also when confronted with it, he conducted himself in the same way, and he gave the greatest contemporary example of *arete* (virtue) in this most marvelous way. For the barbarians, gazing upon him, wondered at his courage. Indeed, although the king knew nothing about him beyond having heard the same rumors, he admired his courage and the steadfastness of his character, and intended altogether to release him, thinking that once he (Hermias) had become his friend, he would be the most useful man in the world to him. But when Bagoas and Mentor opposed him—out of envy and the fear that, once released, he would become more powerful than themselves—the king changed his mind again, . . . he kept him free from mistreatment on account of his *arete*. Such moderation toward their enemies[15] was extremely unusual and completely contrary to the character of barbarians. He (Hermias), when about to die, summoning . . . said nothing else, but took care to send messages to his friends and companions to the effect that he had done nothing shameful or unworthy of philosophy. (*FGrH* 124 F2)

Col. 6.18–49: And his connection by marriage with Aristotle and the paean written for him might seem to bear witness to his *arete*, and it

---

14. Text of col. 5.51–63 (from "of Plato" to "attached to him") from Milns. Col. 5.52: Πλάτ[ωνος 8]. . .[.]ε̣ι̣ς̣ τ(ὴν), P-S, Πλάτ[ωνος τότε μὲν οὖν Ἑρμ]ί̣α̣ς̣ τ(ῶν), Milns. Col. 5.52–53: ἐ̣|στρατήγε̣ι̣ [π(αρ)εκάλεσεν ἐξ Ἀθηνῶν], P-S, ἐ̣|στρατήγει [ὡς δ᾿ ἑταίρους π(αρ)εκάλεσε], Milns. Col. 5.54: [σ(υμ)βιωσομ(έν)ους], P-S, [καὶ Ξενοκράτην], Milns (who follows Foucart). Col. 5.55: [εἰς Ἀσσό]ν, P-S, [ὡς Ἑρμία]ν, Milns. Col. 5.57: [Εὐβούλου δ᾿ ἀποθάνοντος], P-S, [λέγει δὲ κ(αὶ) τοῦτο· ἐπίτηδ]ες, Milns. Col. 5.58: τυραν[νίδ]α μεθεστη[κώς εἶχε] πρ[αο]τέραν, P-S, τυραν[νί]δα μ[ετέ]στη[σεν εἰς πραό]-τεραν, Milns. Col. 5.60: δ[ὴ πάνθ᾿ ὑπερ]θεὶς, P-S, δ[ιαπαιδευ]θεὶς, Milns. Col. 5.61: ἀ[πήιει εἰς], P-S, ἀ[πένειμεν], Milns (who follows Rusten and D-S¹). A translation based on the P-S text would read: "(– – –) of Plato . . . ruled over the . . . round about, and he invited Coriscus and Erastus and Aristotle from Athens to come live with him. And so all these men came to Assos. Later, when others came, he gave the group some land as a gift. When Eubulus died, he succeeded to the tyranny but wielded a milder rule. And so he held power over all the nearby area up to Assos, when, having handed over everything to the aforementioned philosophers, he went off to the city of the Assians. He especially approved of Aristotle beyond all the others and became very attached to him."

15. Col. 6.11, "toward their enemies": Restoring [κατ]ὰ with Rusten for P-S [παρ]ὰ, "from the enemy."

might not be a bad idea to give this text, because it is not easily accessible for most people. The poem runs as follows:

> *Arete,* toilsome for the human race, quarry most beautiful for life: for the sake of your beauty, Maiden, even to die is a sought-for fate in Greece, and to endure raging, unceasing labors. You instill in the heart an immortal fruit better than gold or parents or soft-lidded sleep. For you it was that Heracles the son of Zeus and the sons of Leda,[16] stalking your strength, did endure manifold labors. Through their desire for you, Achilles and Ajax went to the house of Hades. For your loving grace, the man of Atarneus widowed the rays of the sun. The Muses, the daughters of Memory, will glorify him, making him famed for his deeds and immortal, exalting the reverence of Zeus of Hospitality and the prize of true friendship. (Page, *PMG* 842)

And Aristotle is said to have dedicated a monument to him at Delphi, which stands . . . , and he himself composed the following inscription:

> Trangressing the sacred law of the blessed gods in an unholy way, the king of the bow-wielding Persians killed this man, mastering him not openly in the murderous contest of the spear, but with the faithlessness of a deceitful man. (Page, *Ep.Gr.* 622–26)

To which Bryon, in his *On Theocritus,* says that Theocritus of Chios wrote an epigram in response. It is as follows:

> Empty-headed Aristotle built this empty monument for Hermias, the eunuch and slave of Eubulus, who (sc. Aristotle), honoring the lawless nature of his belly, preferred to dwell at the outlet of the Borborus instead of at the Academy. (Page, *Ep.Gr.* 627–30)

Col. 6.50–62: But there are still other versions of both his arrest and his death. For Hermippus in book 2 of his *On Aristotle* says that he died in prison. But others say that he was tortured by the king and crucified, as was said above. Yet others say that he was tortured but did not divulge any of the agreements that he had made with Philip, as Callisthenes says (*FGrH* 124 F3). Moreover, some say that he was arrested in Aeolian Catane; others say elsewhere. And Anaximenes in book 6 of his histories *On Philip*—of which I omit any quotation, for it is not useful— might seem to have set forth the stories about him, as it were, deficiently (*FGrH* 72 F9).[17]

---

16. The Dioscuri, Castor and Pollux.
17. Col. 6.59–60, "deficiently": Restoring ἐν[δεῶς] with Foucart for P-S ἐν[τύπως], "in relief (?)."

Col. 6.63–66:

"Barbarian," and "a common {and} enemy to everyone," and all such descriptions.
(Dem. 10.33)

He also gives specific, individual examples in his narrative, as in the cases
where the Athenians say this sort of thing against a barbarian.

Cols. 6.66–7.7:

For whenever I see someone fearing the man at Susa and Ecbatana and saying that
he is ill disposed toward the city, the man who also previously restored the city's
affairs and now has made an offer to us—but if you did not accept his offers but
voted against them, it is not his fault—and see him saying something different about
this robber of the Greeks who is growing in power at our very door in the middle of
Greece, I am shocked, and I, for my part, fear this man, whoever he may be, since he
does not fear Philip. (Dem. 10.34)

He used "hyperbatic phrasing," which must be reconstrued as follows:
"For whenever I see someone fearing the man at Susa and Ecbatana, but
not speaking about this robber of the Greeks growing in power at our
very door in the middle of Greece, I am shocked and I, for my part, fear
that man, whoever he may be."

Cols. 7.7–8.2: He says that the king at some earlier time restored the
city's affairs, and that he has recently treated the city with magnanimity,
but that the city voted against his offers. And so some say that by the
"previous restoration" he means the Peace that came down in the time
of Antalcidas the Spartan, which in my opinion seems to be incorrect.
For the Athenians not only did not accept this peace proposal, but they
even—completely the opposite—rejected the things that had been offered to them. Philochorus gives an account of this in this manner, naming names, putting it under the archonship of Philocles of Anaphlystus
(392/1):

And the king sent down a peace proposal in the time of Antalcidas, which
the Athenians did not accept, because it was written therein that "the
Greeks inhabiting Asia were all dwelling together in the house of the king."
But at the proposal of Callistratus, they also drove into exile the ambassadors who had made concessions in Sparta and who did not wait for their
trial: Epicrates of Cephisia, Andocides of Cydathenaeum, Cratinus of Sphet-
tus, Eubulides of Eleusis. (FGrH 328 F149a)

Therefore, it is obvious that Demosthenes probably was not reminding
them of this peace, but of some other benefaction, perhaps the one hav-

ing to do with Conon the son of Timotheus, because, using the resources
of Pharnabazus, he defeated the Spartans soundly in the naval battle at
Cnidus. And Philochorus lends credence to these things, for he writes as
follows in book 5, putting it under the archonship of Suniades of Acharnae (397/6):

> Conon, having sailed with many ships from Cyprus, . . . Pharnabazus the
> satrap of Phrygia (– – –4 *lines unrestored*– – –) led forth from Syria (– – –)
> leading the king's ships around Loryma of the Chersonese and from there
> . . . attacking the admiral of the Spartans (sc. Pisander), who had moved to
> Physcus, and he was victorious in the naval battle that ensued, and he took
> fifty triremes captive, and Pisander died. (*FGrH* 328 F144–45)

After this naval battle Conon also rebuilt the Long Walls for the Athenians, against the wishes of the Spartans, as the same author again relates
(*FGrH* 328 F146). I think that it is a very persuasive argument (to say)
that the orator is recalling the king's magnanimity toward the city. For
to say:

> and previously he restored the city's affairs (Dem. 10.34)

is fairly consistent with Conon apparently defeating the Spartans in a
naval battle by using the resources of Pharnabazus.

But in the present passage Demosthenes might possibly be recalling
another peace proposal from the king, one which the Athenians gladly
accepted, of which Philochorus again gives an account: unwilling to
maintain mercenary troops and exhausted by the war[18] for a very long
time, they accepted a peace proposal *resembling* the Peace of the Spartan Antalcidas, at which time they also erected the Altar of Peace (*FGrH*
328 F151). And someone might be able to point out many other bene-
factions of the king to the city, such as the peace proposed before the assembly by Callias, son of Hipponicus, and the monetary contributions
—both individual and public—to the city, of which Demosthenes might
perhaps be reminding them here, as in a summary.

Col. 8.2–32: I think that the above discussion is sufficient on the subject
of the previous restoration of the city's affairs, but the reference to a *recent* one, concerning which he says

> And now he has made an offer—but if you did not accept his offers but voted against
> them, it is not his fault (Dem. 10.34)

---

18. Col. 7.69, "by the war": Emending the τοῦ πολέμου of the papyrus (which is
printed by P-S) to τῶι πολέμωι, with Wankel, who follows Wilamowitz, "Lesefrüchte."

must be explained next. Five years earlier, when Philip sent a peace proposal to Athens in the archonship of Lyciscus (344/3), the Athenians
received the (Persian) king's ambassadors, but they spoke to them more
contemptuously than they should have. For they said that they would
make peace with the king, if he would not attack the Greek cities. Androtion, who . . . , and . . . give an account of these events.[19] But it might
be better to note briefly the words of Philochorus. For this author begins
as follows, putting it under the archonship of Lyciscus (344/3):

> In this year, when the king sent ambassadors to Athens and demanded that
> their ancestral friendship toward him continue, he (?) replied to his ambas-
> sadors at Athens (that the Athenians would) persevere in their friendship for
> the king, if the king would not attack the Greek cities. (FGrH 328 F157 =
> 324 F53 = 72 F28)

Clearly in this passage the king's offer was peaceful and philanthropic,
but the reply from the people was completely the opposite, rather harsh
and rough. And someone might conjecture that the king's magnanimity
toward the Athenian people arose from his suspicion against the Macedonian (sc. Philip), against whom he intended to bring war, because
he had heard from Hermias of Atarneus that war was being prepared
against him.

Col. 8.32–44:

> There is yet another thing that is destroying the city, injuring it by unjust slander and
> unsuitable language, and furthermore it is offering an excuse to those in our state
> who wish to do nothing just. And you will find that this reason has been put forward
> in the case of all those individuals who have failed when something was needed from
> them. (Dem. 10.35)

. . . he is alluding to the Theoric Fund (– – –). He says that . . . slander . . .

Cols. 8.44–9.9:

> There was a time not long ago when no more than 130 talents came into the city as
> revenue. And there was no one of those eligible to finance a warship or to pay the
> special property tax who decided not to do the things that were proper for them
> simply because there was not a surplus of money. (Dem. 10.37)

---

19. Harding, "Political Career," 197–98, argues that the D-S[1] text of col. 8.14–15
(which is followed by P-S) is implausible: [ἀφηγο](ῦν)ται τ[αῦ]τα Ἀνδρο|τίων ὃς κ(αὶ)
τ[ότ' εἶπε, κ(αὶ) Ἀνα]ξιμ(έν)ης, "Androtion, who actually spoke on that occasion, and
Anaximenes give an account of these events."

This date might be when they were beaten and humbled at Aegospotami (405) and when, for a short time, the people were curtailed, since the foreign revenues were cut off. But he will make this clear: [20]

> Later, beneficent fortune made the public revenues great, and 400 rather than only 100 talents came forth, and none of the property owners lost anything. (Dem. 10.38)

Theopompus also, in book 27 of his *On Philip*, bears witness to the fact that the Athenians in the time of Philip had a revenue of 400 talents. In this passage he has Aristophon the demagogue speak with these words:

> You should consider that we would be doing the most uncourageous thing of all, if we accepted the peace proposal after withdrawing from Amphipolis, since we inhabit the greatest city of the Greeks, and we have the most allies, possess 300 triremes, and receive revenues of nearly 400 talents. Since we have these things available, who would not find fault with us if, fearing the power of the Macedonians, we yielded in some way, contrary to what is right? (*FGrH* 115 F166)

Col. 9.9–37:

> But where does this thing rub, and where is it painful? Whenever they (the rich) see some people transferring the practice from public revenues to private ones, when a speaker becomes immediately great and even immortal among you, thanks to his privilege, and the secret vote is different from the open applause. This causes disbelief, this causes anger. (Dem. 10.44)

It is worth examining what the demagogues were doing when they provided assistance for themselves from the multitude but ignored what was good for the city. And the following is apparently what he wants to say: they did not see fit to distribute all these public funds, which actually belonged to the people. But they (the demagogues) devised some tricky schemes against the (allegedly) "unjust," [21] charging that the wealthy were withholding the public resources or managing the public funds improperly or doing wrong in some other way; and rushing to trials and public indictments, they would lead to the assembly and to the court-

---

20. A blank space of about ten lines appears here in the papyrus following col. 8.54. See notes.

21. Col. 9.22–23, "but they (the demagogues) devised some tricky schemes against the (allegedly) 'unjust'": Restoring ἄλ[λας δ᾽ ἐ]μ[η]χανῶντο κ(ατὰ) τῶν οὐ δικ(αί)ω[ν τιν]ὰς | [στ]ρ[οφ]άς with D-S² for P-S ἀλ[λ᾽ ἐπε]μ[η]χανῶντο κ(αὶ) τῶν οὐ δικ(αί)ω[ν ἰδί]ας | [τ]ρ[οφ]ά[ς], "but (the demagogues) schemed at getting the private resources of the 'unjust.'"

house whomever they wished. And the people were ostensibly agitated about these accusations and shouted that the rich were suffering terrible things, but they secretly voted against them and fined them large sums of money. (– – –) these policies provided great security and powers (– – –4 *lines unrestored*).

Cols. 9.38–10.10:

> And yet with all abuse put aside, if someone should say, "Tell me, Aristomedes—for no one is ignorant of such things—why, since you know well that the life of private citizens is secure and free from care and not dangerous, but the life of politicians is liable to blame and perilous." (Dem. 10.70)

There are two men named Aristomedes. One is the man from Pherae who fought against Philip along with the king's generals, the one whom, among others, Philip himself in the *Letter to the Athenians* and Theopompus in book 48 of his *On Philip* discuss (*FGrH* 115 F222), and who, along with Darius, opposed Alexander in Cilicia and escaped to Cyprus, as Anaximenes says in book 9 of his *On Alexander* (*FGrH* 72 F17). But the other Aristomedes, against whom Demosthenes is speaking here, is the Athenian nicknamed "Brazen," concerning whom Dinarchus, among others, in the *Defense of Docimus Concerning the Horse,* says as follows:

> When he,[22] behaving unjustly, was persuaded by Aristomedes "the Brazen" and Chaerestratus his uncle to indict me, at that time he charged me with failing to appear in a case against him (Chaerestratus), even though I was living abroad, and in Thessaly at that!" (Conomis frag. LXXI–II)

And the comic writers mention him, such as Philemon in *The Sculptor:*

> For at the perfumer's I heard from some men that Brazen, a certain thief, was around. But being ignorant of what they were talking about, I asked Aristomedes when I saw him passing by. And he immediately attacked me, kicking at me with his leg, and he struck me with the heel and with the fists, so that I nearly died, until I barely escaped and, without his knowledge, went off elsewhere. (Austin 206)

Timocles in *The Heroes:*

> Hermes, the son of Maia, conducts these affairs however he wishes. He came down gladly, showing favor to Aristomedes the Beautiful, in order that Satyrus might no longer call him a thief. (Austin 222a)

---

22. Col. 9.58, "he": Emending the προήχθης of the papyrus (which is followed by P-S) to προήχθη, with Wankel, who follows D-S[1].

Also in *The Icarians:*

> A: Flute-loving Marsyas—that's Autocles—flayed, naked, standing nailed
> to an oven; and Tereus—that's Aristomedes.
>
> B: Why do you mention Tereus?
>
> A: Because it is necessary to keep close watch over (τηρεῖν) your things
> when this man is nearby. If not, you will become a Procne, and you
> would[23] scratch your head (κνώμενος) and lose it all.
>
> B: What a terrible joke!
>
> A: (To the audience) But, by the gods, please restrain yourselves and don't
> hiss us off the stage! (Austin 222b)

Oration 11

Cols. 10.13–11.5:

> Athenian gentlemen, it has become clear to all of you that Philip did not make peace
> with us, but rather postponed the war. (Dem. 11.1)

The date of the speech is quite clear. For up to this time, Demosthenes'
speeches were about how Philip's intent was to take action against the
Greeks, violating the peace agreement and trangressing the oaths. But
now, since war has obviously broken out, he rather forcefully says that
he knows what they should do to him (sc. Philip) for openly announc-
ing war against them in the *Letter.* Indeed, at the end of the *Letter,* he
(Philip) says:

> Therefore, since you are the aggressors and are still pressing on me, thanks
> to my avoidance of conflict, and are forever busying yourselves, as much as
> you are able, in order to entrap me in a war—me, your former benefactor!
> —I, with justice on my side, shall defend myself against you, opposing you
> by every means. (compare Dem. 12.23)

He (Demosthenes) begins his deliberative speech as follows:

> Athenian gentlemen, it has become clear to all of you that Philip did not make peace
> with us, but rather postponed the war. (Dem. 11.1)

Athens's war against Macedonia has flared up. The other offenses of
Philip during the time when he was pretending to keep the peace goaded
the Athenians on, but mostly his campaigns against Byzantium and Pe-

---

23. Col. 10.10, "would": Accenting ἄν with Wankel (who follows D-S[1]) for P-S ἄν,
"which."

rinthus. He endeavored to win the cities for two reasons: to cut off the Athenians' grain transport, and so that, being foremost in naval power, they might not have coastal cities as bases and places of refuge from the war with him. At that time he carried out an extremely illegal act, stealing the merchants' boats at Hieron—230 of them according to Philochorus, but 180 according to Theopompus—from which he got 700 talents. These events occurred a year earlier, in the archonship of Theophrastus (340/39), who was the one after Nicomachus, just as Philochorus, among other authors, says, as follows:

> And Chares departed to the assembly of the royal generals, leaving behind the ships at Hieron, so that they might bring together all their boats from the Pontus. But when Philip found out that Chares was away, he first attempted to steal the boats by sending[24] (his own) ships. And being unable to accomplish this by force, he led his soldiers across to the headland at Hieron and took charge of the boats. The total was not less than 230. Selecting out the warships, he broke them up and used the lumber for siege machines, and he came into control of grain and leather and money. (*FGrH* 328 F162 = 115 F292)

Col. 11.5–14: This might be the date of the deliberative speech and the end of the *Philippics*. But someone might suspect—not far from the mark—that a derivative little speech (λογίδιον) has been assembled, compiled from certain orations of Demosthenes. And there are those who say that this deliberative speech is by Anaximenes of Lampsacus, because of the fact that it has been inserted in book 7 of his *Philippica* with almost these very words (*FGrH* 72 F11a).[25]

Col. 11.14–26: Some interpreted his words as being rather "vulgar,"[26] since ὀρρωδεῖν, and whatever words there are like it, are hardly Demosthenic:

That we must neither fear (ὀρρωδεῖν) his power nor oppose him in a base manner. (Dem. 11.2)

24. Col. 10.59, "sending": Rejecting P-S's suggestion that there is a gap in the text after the word πέμψας, with Wankel.

25. Greek text of the previous sentence (col. 11.11–12) from Milns, 86. Col. 11.11: τήν, P-S, τῶι, Milns. Col. 11.12: δή, P-S, δή, Milns; ἥν, P-S, <αὐτ>ήν, Milns. The P-S text would be translated as follows: "And there are those who say that this deliberative speech is by Anaximenes of Lampsacus, which is in book 7 of his *Philippica* and is inserted there with almost these very words."

26. Col. 11.14–15, "Some interpreted his words as being rather 'vulgar'": Using my own conjecture of ἔνιοι δ(ὲ) τ(ὰ) ὀνόματ(α) φορτικώτερ<α> ἡρμήνευσαν for P-S ἔνια δ(ὲ) τ(ῶν) ὀνομ[ά]τ(ων) φο[ρτι]κωτέρως ἡρμήνευσαν, "They interpreted some of the words in a rather vulgar way."

Ὀρρωδεῖν means "to fear," and it is formed on the basis of something that happens to those who are afraid. For the word concerns the rear end (ὄρρος) <sweating (ἰδίειν)>, as in "people with sweaty rear ends" (ἴδεδροι). Homer:

> I broke into a sweat (ἴδιον) when I saw him (the old man); my eyes are full of tears. (*Odyssey* 20.204)

And the comic writer Aristophanes in the *Frogs,* when Dionysus was cowering:

> And my anus (πρωκτός) has been sweating for some time now. (line 237)

Col. 11.26–52:

> He is suspected by the Thebans, because, having gotten into the Amphictyonic Council, and holding Nicaea with a garrison. (Dem. 11.4)

Nicaea is a coastal city, twenty stades from Thermopylae, concerning which Timosthenes in book 5 of his *On Harbors* says as follows:

> For someone traveling by boat from Thermopylae, the city of Nicaea is about twenty stades; for someone on foot, about fifty. At most five stades from this lies a sandy headland, up to four stades, with a harbor for a long ship.

And Philochorus says that Philip ordered the Thebans to give this city back to the Locrians. In book 6 he says as follows:

> Philip took control of Elateia and Cytinion and sent to Thebes ambassadors from the Thessalians, Aenianes, Aetolians, Dolopes, and Phthiotians, demanding that they hand over Nicaea—which,[27] contrary to the order of the Amphictyons, had been garrisoned by Philip—to the Locrians; but when he was among the Scythians, the Thebans themselves, kicking out the garrisons, took control, and they told them that <they would send> an embassy on everyone's behalf to discuss it with Philip. (*FGrH* 328 F56b)

But there are other cities named Nicaea, which I do not think it is necessary to discuss here.

---

27. Col. 11.45 or 46, "which": P-S move the relative pronoun ἥν from col. 11.46 (after Ἀμφικτυόν(ων)) to col. 11.45 (after παραδιδόναι). Wankel, 222, suggests that it should not be moved. If one follows Wankel, the word "which" in this translation should be placed after the word "Amphictyons," making the handing over of Nicaea (rather than its garrisoning by Philip) an action that was "contrary to the order of the Amphictyons." See Wankel, 222, for further discussion and bibliography.

Cols. 11.52–12.33:

Moreover, if one of the ordinary people makes a mistake, he gets a punishment suited to his station. But the prominent people are treated especially contemptuously (σκορακίζονται) and are horribly abused when they are the most successful. (Dem. 11.11)

This word is formed from the saying "to the crows" (ἐς κόρα[κα]ς), which we are accustomed to address to those departing with a curse or an insult—wherever they are going. Aristophanes mentions this in the *Birds:*

And prepared to go to the crows. (line 28)

For he means to say "to the birds," but he makes a joke out of the colloquial expression, which Demon says was handed down from the following occasion. He writes as follows:

They say that when the Boeotians had been driven out by the Thracians, they marched to what was then called Aeolis but is now called Thessaly, drove out those who inhabited this land, and took control of it. But since the Aeolians were warring against them and were always destroying their yearly harvests, they sent to Delphi and asked whether they should remain at this place or seek another land. When the god said that "white crows would appear before they would drive the Boeotians from the land," they became confident at the oracle's response . . . they eagerly participated in . . . , which even now the Thessalian people participate in. Then, some of the inebriated young men caught some crows and covered them with chalk—not for any evil purpose—and let them fly, making this a source of fun and laughter. But when the birds were flying around their cities and everyone was marvelling at what had happened—some of them declaring that the oracle had been fulfilled, saying in the local dialect that "something like it" had happened, <and others shouting that something terrible had happened and making an uproar—the frightened young men fled and>[28] settled along the Gulf of Pagasae, whence they say that the people there, from that time forward, were called "Crows." The Aeolians attacked the Boeotians when they were in turmoil, drove them out, and regained the land. And they would send away those who had committed some crime and were to be punished by a lengthy exile to these so-called "Crows," whence this word ἐ[σ]κορακί[ζει]ν is still even now applied to those who have been exiled. (*FGrH* 327 F7)

---

28. The scribe has indicated a lacuna in the text by placing a mark (like our "slash") beside col. 12.22. On this mark, see McNamee, 17–18. P-S conjecture that something like the words contained within the angle brackets are needed to complete the sense of the passage.

Col. 12.33–37:

> And (the Macedonian kings) paid tribute to the Athenians, but our city never (paid tribute) to anyone. (Dem. 11.16)

We have shown that the Macedonians paid tribute to the Athenians in the (commentary on) *On the Crown* (Dem. 18).

Cols. 12.37–13.12:

> But this man (sc. Philip), having rushed forth from Macedonia, loves danger so much that, in trying to increase his power, he has been wounded throughout his entire body while fighting against his enemies. (Dem. 11.22)

We have <elsewhere>[29] fully discussed the wounds that Philip had. But at this point we must briefly comment on the subject. For at the siege of Methone, he was struck by an arrow and lost his right eye when he was examining the siege engines and the so-called "siege sheds," as Theopompus recounts in book 4 of the histories on him; Marsyas the Macedonian also agrees with this account (*FGrH* 115 F52 = 135–36 F16). But Duris—for he must also tell his marvelous tales here —says that Aster ("Star") was the name of the man who hurled the deadly *javelin* at him, although almost everyone who made the campaign with him said that he was wounded by an *arrow* (*FGrH* 76 F36). For (Duris's) story about the flute players is also corroborated by Marsyas, since, in accordance with some divine power, while he (Philip) was holding musical competitions a little before the accident, it so happened that all the performers—Antigenides son of Philoxenus, Chrysogonus son of Stesichorus, and Timotheus son of Oeniades—performed a flute song about the Cyclops (*FGrH* 135–36 F17). That is how they say that he lost his eye, but they say that Pleuratus the Illyrian pursued him (and wounded) his right collarbone in an ambush among the Illyrians, when 150 of his Companions were wounded, and Hippostratus the son of Amyntas died. He received a third wound in the invasion against the Triballoi, when one of those being pursued thrust a spear into his right thigh and maimed him. Alexander might seem to have enjoyed a better fortune than his father with regard to wounds and blows. For although he received ten deadly blows at various times, he remained unmaimed, but Philip's entire body was in terrible shape.

---

29. Col. 12.42, "<elsewhere>": Adopting the conjectural lacuna <καὶ ἄλλοθι> after ἐντελῶς, from D-S².

Oration 12[30]

Col. 13.14–25:

> Athenian gentlemen, concerning the money that we are presently discussing and the
> reasons for which you are holding this assembly, neither of the two alternatives
> seems difficult to me. (Dem. 13.1)

And some include this speech with the *Philippics*, which seems to me
to be incorrect. For there is no mention of Philip in it at all, nor of the
Macedonians, nor of the cities that he took in violation of the treaties
and oaths—Perinthus, Olynthus, Potidaea—rather, the speech is about
the freedom of the Rhodians and Mytilenaeans, neither of which cities
has anything to do with Macedonia.

Col. 13.25–62: And Demosthenes perhaps composed this speech after
the peace with Philip (346), when[31] the Athenians' dealings with the
Macedonians were quiet, but their dealings with Asia were keeping them
very busy. Concerning this state of affairs, he says as follows:

> For if it were sufficient for you to be at peace and you did not busy yourself with how
> any of the Greek states were doing, it would have been a different story. But as it is,
> you have decided to be the foremost state and to set the boundaries of justice for the
> others, and you have neither prepared <nor are you currently preparing> a force to
> supervise and protect these interests, but in the course of your great inactivity and
> absence, the Mytilenaean democracy was destroyed, and in the course of your great
> inactivity the Rhodian democracy was destroyed. (Dem. 13.7–8)

Someone might perceive the date of the speech as being the archonship
of Callimachus (349/8), the one after Apollodorus. Why? Because he
mentions things that the Athenians did to the Megarians with regard to
the sacred Orgas. These things happened during the archonship of Apollodorus (350/49), as Philochorus recounts, writing as follows:

> When the Athenians had had a dispute with the Megarians regarding the
> boundary making for the sacred Orgas, they advanced against Megara with
> Ephialtes as general for the territory and marked boundaries for the sacred
> Orgas. The boundary makers were—with the concession of the Megarians
> —Lacratides the hierophant and Hieroclides the torchbearer, and they con-
> secrated the properties bordering on Orgas, after the god responded that "it
> was more desirable and better for them to let it be and not to farm it." And

---

30. This is our oration 13.
31. Col. 13.27, "when": Or possibly "because" (ἐ[πεὶ]), with Wankel, 222 (who follows D-S¹) for P-S ἐ[ν ὧι].

they marked the boundaries in a circle with markers in accordance with the decree of Philocrates. (*FGrH* 328 F155)

When we have examined this passage, (we can see that) the speech— which contains a recommendation for things needed for war, in preparation for the event that there should actually be a war—might have been composed after this archonship.

Cols. 13.62–14.49: Nothing is explored in the speech that has not received some discussion in the ones (sc. speeches or commentaries?) before this. Nevertheless, the subject of Orgas must be briefly clarified. "Orgas" in common usage means "all wooded land," like ἄλσος; the word is formed from ὀργᾶν (to swell with moisture) and to have a certain ὀρμή (eagerness) for budding. For thus they used to say ὀργᾶν to mean "being in readiness for any sort of ὀρμή," just as today we say that we ὀργάσαι (knead) the clay in preparing it for ointment. Sophocles in the *Shepherds:*

I have mixed up as much clay as is good to ὀργάσαι. (Radt, 4: 510)

And Aeschylus on the corpses in front of the Cadmeia, when they are ready for burial:

The matter was coming to a head (ὤργα); the corpse was already rotting. (Mette frag. 269)

They used to call ὀργάδαι both ἄλματα and ἄλση (groves) after their upward ἄλσις (growth).

There the Trojan ἄλμα (grove) and tombs of Munippus (Lloyd-Jones and Parsons, *Suppl.Hell.* 454)

A similar example is the one given in Homer:

He (Achilles) shot up like an ἔρνος (shoot). (*Iliad* 18.56, 437)

From this both the ὄρπηξ (sapling) and it itself (sc. ἔρνος or ὀργάς?) are formed from ἕρπειν (to creep). So that is all on the subject of ὀργάς in its common usage. But there is an ὀργάς that among the Megarians is specifically called "Orgas," as a proper name: just as Ida is both the one at Ilion and "a wooded place," and Aegialus is "the seashore" and the place called by that name, and Acte is both a place in Attica and "a coastal region,"[32] and Rhion is a place at Molycrion and, in common

32. Col. 14.28, "and Acte is both a place in Attica": Restoring κ(αὶ) <Ἀκτὴ> ἥ τε τῆς Ἀττικῆς with Wankel (who follows D-S¹) for P-S κ(αὶ) ἡ Ἀκτὴ <τῆ>ς Ἀττικῆς.

usage, "the entire top of a mountain," and so on. Demosthenes' present use of the word is in reference to Megarian Orgas, which Callimachus also mentions at some point and says:

> Garlic from Nisaean Orgas (Pfeiffer frag. 495)

Androtion also discusses this Orgas in book 7 of his *Atthis,* where he writes as follows:

> And the Athenians set boundaries for Orgas for the Megarians because of[33] the two goddesses, as they wished. For the Megarians conceded that the boundary makers should be the hierophant Lacratides and the torchbearer Hieroclides. And as they (Lacratides and Hieroclides) defined it, so they (the Megarians) allocated it. And they consecrated the properties bordering on Orgas, however many there were, after they consulted the oracle and the god answered that "it was more desirable and better for them not to farm it." And it was bounded by stone markers all around, as Philocrates proposed. (*FGrH* 324 F30)

Cols. 14.49–15.10:

> For instance, consider the things that you decreed against the accursed Megarians when they cut you off from Orgas, that you should march out, stop them, and not allow it. (Dem. 13.32)

He calls the Megarians "accursed" because they, as well as the Boeotians, were ill disposed toward the Athenians, as Theopompus witnesses in book 26, where he has Philocrates the demagogue speak with these words:

> You should consider that there is no time for arguing; nor are[34] the city's affairs in good shape, but many dangers surround us. For we know that the Boeotians and the Megarians are ill disposed toward us, and of the Peloponnesians some support the Thebans, some the Spartans; and the Chians and the Rhodians and their allies are hostile toward the city, but they are discussing friendship with Philip. (*FGrH* 115 F164)

[The text ends with a subscription giving the author, title, and book number of the work.]

---

33. Col. 14.39, "because of": Rejecting P-S's conjecture of a gap in the text after διά, with Wankel.

34. Col. 14.61, "are": Rejecting P-S's conjecture of a gap in the text (to be filled by <δοκεῖ>), and emending the ἔχειν of the papyrus to ἔχει, with Wankel (who follows in part a conjecture of D-S²).

Didymus'
On Demosthenes.
(Commentaries on) 28 (Speeches)
Book 3 of the *Philippics* (Commentaries)[35]

9th: "Athenian gentlemen, many"
10th: "And considering as important"
11th: "Athenian gentlemen, that Philip"
12th: "Concerning the present"[36]

NOTES ON P.BEROL.INV. 9780

Notes to Col. 1.1–25: Didymus closes his treatment of the *Third Philippic* (Dem. 9), of which only the end survives, with a discussion of the dates of military assistance sent to Oreus and Eretria. The first seven lines are too fragmentary to reconstruct the topic of discussion. For lines 1–5, P-S have distinguished the word "tyrant" (probably Clitarchus or Philistides "became tyrant") and references to "Eretria" and "campaigns" (στρατείας). Since this is near the end of the commentary on Dem. 9, and since Didymus discusses passages in the same order as they appear in Demosthenes, the topic of discussion is most likely Dem. 9.57–58: "It was not only with them (the Olynthians) that this habit achieved all sorts of evils, and nowhere else; but at Eretria, when Plutarchus and the mercenaries were expelled, the people held the city and Porthmus, and some wanted to hand affairs over to you, others to Philip. Hearing these latter ones on many matters—rather, on all of them—the wretched and unfortunate Eretrians were finally persuaded to expel those who were speaking to their benefit. And of course their ally Philip, sending Hipponicus and a thousand mercenaries, destroyed the walls of Porthmus and set up three tyrants—Hipparchus, Automedon, and Clitarchus." Prior to 9.57 Demosthenes has been discussing how the fate of Olynthus, destroyed by Philip in 348, resulted from strife between the supporters of Philip and the patriots. See Hammond and Griffith, 321–28, on this event. Osborne, 58–59, prefers Dem. 9.63 or 65ff. as the subject of discussion, sections of the speech where Oreus and Eretria are mentioned together.

---

35. This is one of several possible interpretations of the title. See pp. 51–54 and notes on the text.
36. This is item 13 in the modern corpus of Demosthenes. Didymus does not comment on our item 12, the *Letter of Philip.*

P-S suggest restoring col. 1.6–8 with something like the following: "The speech *On Behalf of Ctesiphon* (Dem. 18) narrates more exactly than these words the alliance, narrating all the affairs of Philip" (see their notes ad loc.). The alliance mentioned here (συμμαχικὰ) is most likely the one mentioned in the first quotation from Philochorus (*FGrH* 328 159). Line 8 opens with a quotation from Dem. 18.79. Osborne, 84, sees this passage, which "places the expedition to Euboia in the context of some of Demosthenes' other diplomatic activity during the years between the peace of Philokrates (346) and the battle of Chaironeia (338)," as Didymus's attempt to give the reader "sufficient information for a complete understanding of the historical and biographical background to the Demosthenic speeches."

Since the passage from Dem. 18 does not contain the specific chronological and other information that he needs, Didymus cites Philochorus (*FGrH* 328 F159–160) on the date of the Athenian aid sent to the Euboean cities of Oreus (342/1, the archonship of Sosigenes) and Eretria (341/0, the archonship of Nicomachus). Philochorus (c. 340–260) was the last of the Atthidographers, fourth- and third-century historians who wrote on the history of Attica. His *Atthis* in seventeen books survives only in quotations from such authors as Didymus, and he was Didymus's main source for chronological arguments. On Philochorus, see Harding, *Androtion;* Stähelin, 56–71, on the fragments of Philochorus in Berol. 9780. Both the Philochorus passages cited here are dated by archon years. On the aid sent to Oreus, the scholia to Aeschines 3.85 say that the Athenian forces liberated Oreus and "killed the tyrant Philistides when Sosigenes was archon at Athens, in the month of Scirophorion, the nineteenth year of Philip's kingship" (ed. Baiter and Sauppe). (Aeschines was an Athenian orator and contemporary of Demosthenes.) The imperial-age historian Charax (*FGrH* 103 F19) mentions the killing of Philistides and the liberation of Oreus but gives no date, and he includes the Megarians in the relief effort. Neither passage derives directly from Philochorus, according to Jacoby (*FGrH* 3bI, p. 535). On the aid sent to Eretria, the scholia to Aeschines 3.103 (ed. Baiter and Sauppe) give the same date, but there is no mention of Clitarchus's political opponent Plutarchus. The spare account of Diodorus 16.74 is entirely in agreement with that of Philochorus. On the first-century universal historian Diodorus see Sacks.

Modern controversy about these events centers on how much time passed between the two operations (no month is given for the aid sent to Eretria, only a year), whether these apparently separate operations were really part of the same campaign (a question closely related to the former one), and what the military aims of Athens were at this time. For excellent surveys of the relevant ancient sources and modern bibliography on this question, see Brunt, "Euboea"; Cawkwell, "Euboea"; also Hammond and Griffith, 501–4, 545–54.

Dem. 9 exists in two versions, the longer of which is found in manuscripts FAY and the shorter in S (see Sandys, *Demosthenes*, lix–lxvii; Sealey, *Demosthenes*, 232–35), but this does not affect our understanding of Didymus's commentary or his text of Demosthenes. Dionysius of Halicarnassus *First Letter to Ammaeus* 10 gives the date of Dem. 9 as 342/1 (the archonship of Sosigenes). On Dionysius's proposed dates for speeches see Sealey, "Dionysius of Halicarnassus." An excellent historical overview of the speech is found in A. Schaefer, 2: 467–80.

Notes to Col. 1.26–53: Didymus opens his commentary on the *Fourth Philippic* (Dem. 10) by attempting to establish its date. Körte, 388–410, has commented extensively on Didymus's commentary on this speech. Didymus opens with a quotation from the very beginning of Dem. 10 (col. 1.27–29), whose authenticity he never questions. Modern scholars have questioned its authenticity; on this see Sealey, *Demosthenes*, 232–35. The lemma of Dem. 10.1 is not directly relevant to the comments that follow it. It may originally have been used to signal the beginning of the commentary on the new oration, but it would have become superfluous when the copyist added the overstroked *iota* (indicating the "tenth" oration) at col. 1.26. (There is no evidence that Didymus himself ever referred to Demosthenes' speeches by number.)

Didymus then proceeds to discuss a date of 341/0 (the archonship of Nicomachus) for the speech, since "someone might perhaps perceive the date of the speech" ([τοὺς κ]αιρ[οὺ]ς τοῦ λόγου τάχ᾽ ἄν τ[ις σ]υν[ίδοι], col. 1.29) as being 341/0 on the basis of information contained in a particular passage of Philochorus (*FGrH* 328 F161). The quotation beginning at col. 1.30 is almost totally lost; some fifteen lines later the text resumes with a summation of information already learned at the end of the commentary on Dem. 9, regarding the dates of the deaths of Philistides and Clitarchus (col. 1.46–49; see notes on col. 1.1–25). Col. 1.49–53 reads as follows: κ(αὶ) ταῦτα πιστώ[σεται Φιλόχ]ορος | [ὡς σ(υμ)βεβη-κότ᾽] ἐπὶ [τ]έλει τ(ῆς) Νικ[ομάχου ἀρχῆ]ς, ἃ ο[ὔπω] | [γενόμ(εν)᾽ οἶδ᾽ ὁ λ]όγος. οὐκο(ῦν) ὅτι μ[(ὲν) πρότερον γέγ]ραπτ[αι] | [τ(ῆς) προ-ρηθεί]σης ἀρχῆς ὁ λό[γος, μὴ ὅτι μετ]ὰ Νικ[ό]ⱆ[μαχον, ἤδη ἱ]κανῶς ἑώρατα[ι], "And Philochorus lends credence to the fact that these events, which the oration does not know as having already occurred, happened at the end of the archonship of Nicomachus. Therefore, it is now sufficiently obvious that the speech was written *before* the aforementioned archonship, and not after Nicomachus." Wankel, 221, has rightly regarded the restorations of col. 1.47–53 as doubtful, partly because the formula ταῦτα πιστώ[σεται Φιλόχ]ορος in col. 1.49 should, as in col. 7.35, almost immediately introduce a quotation.

The P-S text, as it stands, suggests the following analysis: In col. 1.49–51, Didymus says that "these events" (ταῦτα) happened at the end of 341/0. Which "events" could he mean? The death of Philistides occurred in 342/1 (col. 1.13–18), and the death of Clitarchus (341/0) hardly merits the use of the plural. Furthermore, it is likely that Clitarchus died early in 341/0, for his death is mentioned at the beginning of Philochorus's entry for that year (see Jacoby, *FGrH* 3bII, pp. 432–33). These "events" may have been listed in the lost lines (col. 1.31–46) that immediately preceded this part of the discussion. Whatever they were, if one follows the P-S text, Didymus sees Demosthenes' failure to mention these events—note the highly conjectural clause "which the oration does not know as having already occurred"—as an argument from silence that the speech dates from *before* 341/0. This conclusion does not necessarily follow from the evidence given: it is necessary only that the speech was written *before the end of* that archonship, and so a date of earlier in that year is not necessarily ruled out. But the state of the text is almost certainly to blame for the confusion: most of col. 1.31–46 is missing, and a number of words in lines 50–53 have been partly or even wholly restored. Osborne, 91, conjectures that Didymus "may have been trying to demonstrate that the Athenian expeditions to Euboia in 341 had been completed sometime during Nikomachos's year and that Dem. 10, though delivered subsequent to these events, was spoken prior to the end of the same archonship" (see also P-S ad loc.). The correct date of the speech is 341/0; see for example Cawkwell, "Demosthenes' Policy," 134–36. This is also the date given by Dionysius of Halicarnassus, *First Letter to Ammaeus* 10; on Dionysius's proposed dates for speeches see Sealey, "Dionysius of Halicarnassus."

Notes to Cols. 1.53–3.62: Didymus attempts to rule out a date of 340/39 (the archonship of Theophrastus, col. 1.53–54) for Dem. 10. He employs an argument from silence: οὐ γ(ὰρ) ἂν δήπου ταῦτ' ἔλεγε[ν], εἰ λελυκ[ό]ι[τες τὴν εἰ]ρήν(ην) ἐτύγχανον Ἀθην[αῖο]ι, "For he (Demosthenes) never would have said these things (that he says in Dem. 10.17)

if the Athenians had already actually broken the peace agreement"
(col. 1.66–67). In other words, if the inscription listing the terms of the
peace with Philip (col. 1.56–57) had already been torn down (signifying
the end of the peace agreement) at the time of the delivery of Dem. 10,
then Demosthenes would not have encouraged his audience to maintain
the peace as he does in Dem. 10.17 (quoted in col. 1.61–66). The peace
mentioned here is the Peace of Philocrates of 346, on which see Hammond and Griffith, 329–47. Didymus does not seem as interested in
proving his own date correct (of 341/0? See notes on cols. 8.44–9.9) as
he is in demonstrating that alternate dates are either too early or too
late. He cites Philochorus (*FGrH* 328 F55b, largely restored from Dionysius of Halicarnassus *First Letter to Ammaeus* 11) on the date of the
broken peace agreements (cols. 1.70–2.2). The "letter" mentioned in
the Philochorus passage (col. 1.71) is most likely not the one preserved
as item 12 of the Demosthenic corpus (with Osborne, 96–97; see notes
on col. 11.7–14). In col. 2.2–3 another possible date of 342/1 (the archonship of Sosigenes) is mentioned, attributed only to "some" (ἔνιοι).
This early dating is clearly in conflict with the evidence that Didymus
has already presented. Didymus probably gave this theory no more than
a passing glance. One might compare his treatment of Hermias's arrest
and death, where he appends several other options to the end of his discussion, perhaps simply to let his readers know that other views exist
(see notes on col. 6.50–62).

The text breaks off here. The rest of col. 2 is almost completely lost,
and the column headers survive only in the beginnings of lines. P-S suggest that col. 2.9 concerns Dem. 10.29 and that col. 2.28–30 concerns
Dem. 10.33. For reasons already given above, I do not follow P-S's suggestion that the whole of col. 2.2–39 is concerned with the date of
Dem. 10. There is no reason to believe that Didymus pursued this line
of argument any longer than it would take to reject it with a simple reference to his earlier discussion (cols. 1.26–2.2). Cols. 2.63–3.62 are in
very poor shape. Foucart's reconstruction of the argument of this section
(pp. 56–57) is creative but entirely conjectural.

Notes to Col. 4.1–47: The argument of cols. 2–3 is almost entirely lost.
The text resumes in the middle of a discussion of an unknown topic that
uses an Amphictyonic decree for its evidence. I have no confidence in
any of the various attempts to reconstruct the argument of the lines immediately preceding. See Wankel, 219–20, for further discussion of the
possibilities. The Amphictyonic decree of col. 4.2–13, dated by Pomtow

in *Syll.*[3] 224 (ed. Dittenberger et al.) to c. 345/4, may appear in the context of a quotation from another source; see P-S on οὕ(τως) in col. 3.59. The decree does not seem immediately relevant to any particular passage in Dem. 10. This has led some to suspect that Didymus quoted the wrong decree, when he should have been quoting the one granting Philip membership in the Amphictyonic League, the league of Greek city-states connected with the protection and maintenance of the sanctuary at Delphi. (According to Wankel, 219–20, the view that Didymus quoted the wrong decree here has been erroneously attributed to Pomtow in *Syll.*[3] 224.) On this event see Hammond and Griffith, 450–56. Foucart, 114–17, suggests that the decree relates to Dem. 5 (see P-S on col. 3.43). Osborne, 102–5, suggests that the decree is to be connected with Demosthenes' reference to "benefactors" (εὐεργέται) in Dem. 10.31 (compare εὐεργέτας δ(ὲ) τοῦ θεοῦ κ(αὶ) [τ]ῶν Ἀμ|φικτυόν(ων), col. 4.9–10).

Which passage of Dem. 10 introduced this section of the commentary is unknown, though it must have come from between Dem. 10.17 (quoted in col. 1.61–66) and Dem. 10.32 (presumably quoted prior to col. 4.48), since Didymus always comments on passages in the order in which they occur in Demosthenes. But it is important to note that no new lemma intervenes between the Amphictyonic decree of col. 4.1–13 and the subsequent reference in col. 4.13–15 to Aristotle's *Customs of the Barbarians* (on which see Rose, frags. 604–10). Any adequate explanation of this section of the commentary must show how both the Amphictyonic decree and Aristotle's observations from a book on Scythian customs could be connected with a single lemma from Dem. 10.17–32. Osborne, 106, who also recognizes this point, conjectures that the Aristotle passage may have had something to do with relations between barbarians and the Delphic oracle.

Notes to Cols. 4.48–5.63: In cols. 4.48–6.62, Didymus discusses the life, death, and friendships of Hermias of Atarneus. This first section alludes to a large and continuing debate about the man's life and quotes at length from negative portrayals of him. Dem. 10.32 invites consideration of the man: "Second, the man (sc. Hermias) who did and saw everything that Philip prepared against the king has been dragged off to him . . ." The career of the tyrant Hermias, his intrigues with Philip of Macedon, his death allegedly at the hands of the Persian king, and (most of all) his friendship with Aristotle and the consequences that this relationship had for Aristotle's life, were popular topics of discussion in antiquity. Radically different lines of interpretation emerged, which then, after creative elaboration and editing, produced a variety of biographies of the man. Didymus is aware that a "Hermias problem" exists, and the number of surviving ancient accounts of Hermias corroborate this perception. Düring, 272–83, and Wormell are indispensable guides to this tradition. Wormell argues that Didymus has lifted most if not all of this discussion from the Peripatetic biographer Hermippus (similarly, Milns, 80–81, considers Theophrastus a possibility). Wormell adduces the fact that Didymus introduces the topic twice. If this view is followed, the first introduction (somewhere prior to col. 4.47) is Didymus's own, and the second (at col. 1.59, following a lacuna of nine lines) is the introduction included in the source that he is quoting verbatim. Unless Didymus first sketched out an overview of Hermias's life and then started over again with the more detailed treatment that survives (as Osborne, 22–31, 107–8), Wormell may be correct. However, the burden of proof is upon Düring, 275, to show why "it is not likely that the Hermias episode was much discussed in Didymus' time," especially since (as Osborne, 108–9 and n. 13, and Yunis, 1050–52, point out) several of Didymus's near contemporaries were interested in Hermias: Diodorus 16.52.5–7; Demetrius of Magnesia (in Diogenes Laertius *Life of Aristotle* 5.3); Dionysius of Halicarnassus *First Letter to Ammaeus* 5; and Ovid *Ibis* 319–20. In the absence of more concrete confirmation to the contrary, I shall treat the section as though Didymus was responsible for composing it.

A brief historical background is necessary (cf. Wormell, 57–59). In 348 Aristotle moved to Assos, where he stayed for three years as leader of a new Platonic school founded by Coriscus and Erastus (and Xenocrates, if one accepts Milns's and Foucart's restorations in col. 5.54). According to Plato's *Sixth Letter,* the plan was for Coriscus, Erastus, and Hermias to carry out a practical experiment of Plato's theories on government; should they have any problems, they were to write to Plato about them. Hermias was also very close to Aristotle; Aristotle even married Hermias's niece and adoptive daughter Pythias (note κηδεία, col. 6.18). In 341 Mentor was ordered by the Persian king to make the cities of Asia Minor submit to the Persian empire. Hermias of Atarneus was a prime target, both because of the powerful position of his city (on the mainland directly east of Mytilene) and because of the suspicion that he was plotting with Philip. Mentor besieged Atarneus, tricked Hermias into meeting with him, arrested him, and delivered him up to the Persian king, Artaxerxes. The king tried to no avail to find out Philip's plans against him and subsequently had Hermias executed. This event was representative of a failure in Persian foreign policy. As Wormell, 58, notes,

"The ease with which Hermias was suppressed seems to have blinded Persia to the danger threatening from Macedonia, and to have led her into the fatal mistake of leaving the Greek cities to struggle against Philip unaided." On these events, see Hammond and Griffith, 517–22; on Hermias and Aristotle, see Jaeger, 105–23, 288–90.

Didymus has found a current topic of scholarly disagreement. His goal is apparently to make sense of a topic that had suffered from one-sided treatments (compare 4.53–65), for an audience interested in this sort of topic (col. 4.61–63). He marshals and arranges competing sources, beginning with Theopompus, the fourth-century historian from Chios (on whom see Flower, esp. 85–89; Wormell, 66–74; Florian, 22–31, 50–53). In the selection from his *On Philip* (*FGrH* 115 F291), Theopompus traces the tyrant's career in brief, labeling him a eunuch, a slave, and a Bithynian (cols. 4.68–5.21). This is in stark contrast to the more favorable portrayals by Callisthenes and Aristotle, which are introduced below. See Wormell, 67, on Theopompus's ancient reputation as a "malicious slanderer." Linked with Eubulus and perhaps wrongly accused here of things that only Eubulus did (Wormell, 73), Hermias is said to have behaved as the typical tyrant, "commit[ting] the cruelest and most wicked acts of all, both against the citizens and the others" (ἀπάν[τ(ων) γ(ὰρ) οὗτος ὠμό]τατα κ(αὶ) κακουργότα|τα κ(αὶ) τοῖς [πολίταις κ(αὶ) τοῖς] ἄλλοις διετέλεσε | προσφερό[μενος πᾶσι], col. 5.2–4). But Hermias "did not get away scot-free" (οὐ μὴν ἀθῶιός γε διέφυ|γεν, col. 5.16–17). His "evil and worthless" (ἀσεβῆ κ(αὶ) πονηρὸν, col. 5.17) nature met its appropriate end in torture and crucifixion at the hands of Artaxerxes (col. 5.17–21).

A second selection, from Theopompus's *Letter to Philip* (*FGrH* 115 F250, col. 5.23–63), accounts for Hermias's "reputation among the Greeks" ([π]αρ[ὰ τοῖς] Ἕλλησι | δόξαν, col. 5.22–23). Wormell, 71, says that the purpose of this letter "is clearly to discredit Hermias in Philip's eyes. . . . Theopompus is speaking of Hermias' reputation among the Greeks, and in order to disparage it he introduces into each favourable statement a contrasting and damaging qualification." Hermias is "elegant and refined" (χαρίεις κ(αὶ) φιλ[όκαλ]ος, col. 5.24), a fan of Platonic philosophy, and an athletic competitor—but also a eunuch, a barbarian, and a former slave. There follows a fragmentary discussion of Hermias's rise to power (col. 5.27–51).

The text resumes somewhat more securely at col. 5.52–54 with the first mention of Hermias's relationship to Aristotle. Here is a translation based on the P-S text: "(– – –) of Plato . . . ruled over the . . . round about, and he invited Coriscus and Erastus and Aristotle from Athens to come live with him. And so all these men came to Assos. Later, when others came, he gave the group some land as a gift. When Eubulus died, he succeeded to the tyranny but wielded a milder rule. And so he held power over all the nearby area up to Assos, when, having handed over everything to the aforementioned philosophers, he went off to the city of the Assians. He especially approved of Aristotle beyond all the others, and became very attached to him." The differences between the Greek texts of P-S and Milns are given in a footnote to the translation ad loc. The most significant improvements offered by Milns include the following: (1) The substitution of a break between the two quotations in col. 5.57 ("And he also says this")—a reading that is corroborated by the *paragraphoi* before and after that line—in place of a reference to Eubulus's death (see Milns, 74–75, for further discussion). Rusten's suggestion of [ὀλίγωι δ᾿ ὕστερόν φησι], "a bit later he says," is also possible. (2) The substitution of a reference to Hermias's completed education (δ[ιαπαιδευ]θείς) in col. 5.60, in place of P-S's [πάνθ᾿ ὑπερ]θείς, "having handed over everything." (3) The rejection of certain suggestions of P-S in favor of those of Rusten, Foucart, and D-S[1]. Overall, the sequence of events envisioned by Milns flows more clearly and logically than the one in P-S.

Coriscus and Erastus (col. 5.53–54) are minor Platonists not well known outside of the Hermias story. Xenocrates was to head the Academy from 339 to 314. The main attraction of this story in antiquity might have been the fact that these emigrant Platonists associated themselves with a sort of philosopher-king who had overcome his innate handicaps to become a model of *arete*. Didymus does not mention that Demosthenes knows about Hermias's arrest but not his death, although he tends to fasten upon such details in order to pin down questions of chronology.

Notes to Cols. 5.64–6.18: This section features the favorable portrayals of Hermias. Keeping with his intention to provide a more balanced account than those of his predecessors, Didymus next quotes from the overwhelmingly positive portrayal of Callisthenes (cols. 5.56–6.18). Callisthenes was a fourth-century historian who wrote about the years 386–356 and discussed Alexander the Great's career down to 330. On his writings, see Pearson, *Lost Histories*, 22–49, esp. 27. He studied under Aristotle and according to Wormell, 75, was probably associated with the philosophers at Assos. The quoted passage emphasizes Hermias's Greek characteristic of *arete*, which the barbarians so greatly ad-

mired that Artaxerxes almost decided to let him go (col. 6.7–10). None
of the features of Theopompus's negative portrayal appears here. This
passage nicely fills out Theopompus's earlier statements about the relationship of Hermias with Aristotle (compare col. 5.52–63), and the two
passages together naturally lead in to the hymn of Aristotle. Wormell,
76–77, interprets this section as an encomium that was written to introduce the hymn.

Two of Rusten's suggestions should be noted here: (1) In col. 6.13–
14, Rusten replaces the P-S text φιλι|.[8]ον [ἐπικαλ]εσάμ(εν)ος with
Φιλί|π[που ἄγγελ]ον [μετακαλ]εσάμ(εν)ος, "summoning a messenger
of Philip." Following Jaeger, 117, Rusten links this section with "the
genre 'last words of the philosophers,'" suggesting that Hermias summoned a messenger from Philip to witness them (268–69). That a dy-
ing man would "summon" (even this word is not securely restored) a
messenger from far-off strikes me as unlikely; as also Wankel, 219.
(2) In col. 6.8–9, Rusten suggests replacing the P-S text †δικασωνδ(ε)
| τῶν γιγνομ(έν)ων παρ[. . .]ωι† κακοπαθιῶν with αἰκισμῶν δ(ὲ) | τῶν
γιγνομ(έν)ων παρ' [αὐτ]ῶι κακοπαθιῶν <τ'>, "the maltreatment and
suffering that are customary at the king's hands" (his translation). Here
Rusten, 268, replaces the obviously corrupt δικασωνδ(ε) of col. 6.8 with
αἰκισμῶν δ(έ), "the *vox propria* for mutilation of a corpse." This is an
interesting conjecture that makes some sense of an otherwise nonsensi-
cal bit of Greek, but it must remain speculative.

Notes to Col. 6.18–49: This section discusses Hermias's relationship
with Aristotle. As an introduction to Aristotle's hymn to Arete, Didymus says that "it might not be a bad idea to give this text, because it is
not easily accessible for most people," κοὐκ ἂν [ἔ]χ[ο]ι φαύλως αὐτὸν
ἀναγρά[ψαι δι]ὰ τὸ μὴ πολλοῖς | πρὸ χειρὸς (εἶναι) (col. 6.20–22). It
is interesting to see the learned commentator recognize that his readers
might be interested in having large quotations of relevant but hard-
to-find source material presented to them in a convenient format. Ancient and modern readers, beginning with Athenaeus in the second century C.E. (XV 696A–697B), have been quick to argue that Aristotle's
hymn is not really a *paean*. Athenaeus instead calls the hymn a *scolion*
(drinking song) and gives examples of both types of poem in order to dif-
ferentiate them.

Aristotle's hymn is addressed to a personified Arete (col. 6.22), which
is appropriate given the emphasis on Hermias's *arete* in Callisthenes
(compare cols. 5.66–6.18). Hermias's pursuit of *arete* is compared to

that of Greek mythological heroes (col. 6.28–31). Wormell, 61, says that "the form and phrasing of the poem show that it was composed to be sung by a choir." The hymn is quoted by Athenaeus (XV 696B-D) and by Diogenes Laertius (*Life of Aristotle* 5.7–8). Diogenes Laertius (ed. Long) refers to it both as a hymn (5.7) and a paean (5.4). For further discussion of the poem and its various sources, see Renehan; Gercke; Page, *Poetae*, 444–45, no. 842. See also Jaeger, 108–9, 117–19.

The hymn's reference to Zeus of Hospitality (Διὸς Ξενίου, col. 6.35) suggests that Aristotle regarded Hermias's death as a breach of the guest-host relationship *(xenia)* between Hermias and the Persian king (possibly by proxy for Mentor; see Wormell, 58). The poem inscribed on Aristotle's monument to Hermias at Delphi (col. 6.39–43) also mentions the Persian king's violation of "the sacred law of the blessed gods" (μακάρων θέμιν ἁγνήν, col. 6.40). This poem is also quoted by Diogenes Laertius 5.6 (printed in Page, *Epigrammata,* 622–26). The harsh reply of Theocritus the Chian (6.46–49) includes the jibe that Aristotle "sold out" for the sake of patronage and chose to live in Macedonia—represented by the reference to Borboros, a river near Pella, according to Plutarch *Moralia* 603c *(On Exile)* (ed. Paton et al.)—rather than at the Academy. This reply is also quoted by Diogenes Laertius 5.11 as well as Plutarch *Moralia* 603c. Runia, 533–34, questions Plutarch's identification of Borborus as a river in Macedonia, suggesting that the author is simply guessing from context. Didymus was reading Theocritus of Chios at second hand in a work by Bryon (compare col. 6.43–46). Little else is known about these two fourth-century authors (see Wormell, 74–75). The insult does not really seem to the point—would Aristotle's move to the Ionian coast not be more relevant in this context?—unless one takes "Borboros" as a pun for "barbaros" (sc. Hermias), and "dwell[ing] at the outlet of" as an allusion to a sexual relationship between the two men. Wormell, 75 n.34, vaguely refers to the "obscene double meaning in the last line," while Düring, 277, rejects this view, saying that the last line is simply "a metaphor for 'the shameful and dirty relationship with Hermias as opposed to the serene atmosphere of the Academy.'" Wormell, 74, suggests that Theocritus's attack on Aristotle is really aimed at Alexander and was "composed sometime after the Macedonian occupation of Chios in 332." However, adducing relevant parallels to "filth" (βόρβορος) and the "uncontrollable nature of the belly" (τὴν ἀκρατῆ γαστρὸς φύσιν) in Plato's *Phaedo, Republic,* and *Timaeus,* Runia, 532, more convincingly argues that the epigram is meant to suggest that Aristotle's "move from the serenity of the Academy to the filth

of Asia Minor [was] also a renunciation of the philosophical principles
to which the followers of Plato were meant to subscribe." This text is
printed also in Lloyd-Jones and Parsons, 738, and Page, *Epigrammata*,
627–30.

Notes to Col. 6.50–62: This section discusses various views of Hermias's arrest and death. Didymus concludes the discussion of Hermias
by appending various bits of information that he was unable to connect
with the main line of his argument but was nevertheless unwilling to
omit. The Hermias problem was not discussed exclusively in works specifically devoted to Hermias (as with Callisthenes); a biography of Aristotle would also have been a natural place to find this sort of information. Didymus cites the biography of Aristotle written by Hermippus
(col. 6.51–53), the third-century biographer who was used as a source
by both Plutarch and Diogenes Laertius. As regards Hermias's death,
Didymus notes that there are some works that essentially agree with
Theopompus (compare col. 5.18–21) and others that agree with Callisthenes (compare cols. 5.71–6.18). There is also a question where Hermias was arrested (col. 6.57–59). Didymus's "Aeolian Catane" must
be Stephanus of Byzantium's "Catanae (plural) facing Lesbos" (ἔστι καὶ
ἄλλη κατέναντι τῆς Λέσβου πληθυντικῶς λεγομένη, ed. Meineke); see
Rigsby.

Finally Didymus mentions the existence of and immediately rejects
the value of an account by Anaximenes, a fourth-century historian and
rhetorician from Lampsacus: "And Anaximenes in book 6 of his histories *On Philip*—of which I omit any quotation, for it is not useful
—might seem to have set forth the stories about him, as it were, deficiently" (δόξ[ειε] δ' ἂν ἐν[δεῶς τὰ] περὶ αὐτὸν διατεθεικ[έν]αι Ἀνα-
ξιμένης ἐν τῆι ἕκτηι τ(ῶν) Περὶ Φ[ίλιπ]πον ἱ|στοριῶν, οὗ τὴν ἐκ-
λογ(ὴν) παρίημι. ο[ὐ γ(ὰρ) ὄφε]λος, col. 6.59–62). On Anaximenes, see
Pearson, *Lost Histories*, 243–46. Didymus cannot have rejected Anaximenes as useless on the grounds that his account is derivative (an objection that Didymus never raises about any author) or too repetitive of
another account. In such cases it is likely that Didymus would simply
have included Anaximenes among the other nameless authorities tacked
on at the end of this section of the commentary. It is conceivable, though
not possible to prove, that Didymus is here anticipating the response of
a particular scholarly audience that would expect him to consult and
cite Anaximenes; Didymus shows that he has done so but says that this
source was so worthless (for whatever reason) that he could not use

it (col. 6.62). Whether Foucart's proposed restoration ἐν‖[δεῶς] ("deficiently") in col. 6.59–60 is correct or not, the context certainly demands
something pejorative. See also notes on col. 11.7–14.

Notes to Col. 6.63–66: In Dem. 10.33, the orator generalizes about the
audience's predilection for name-calling, which he believes is distracting
them from the true danger posed by Philip. Didymus says that Demosthenes sometimes "gives specific, individual examples in his narrative"
(ταῦτα ἰδίαι προσιστ[ορεῖ], col. 6.64) to illustrate his points.

Notes to Cols. 6.66–7.7: This is the only remark in Berol. 9780 that
shows any interest in or knowledge of rhetoric (D-S[1], xv, prefer to regard it as an interest in grammar). Didymus elucidates Demosthenes'
use of "hyperbatic phrasing" (ὑπερβάτωι τῆι φράσει, col. 7.1–2) by "(re)-
construing" (καταστατέον, col. 7.2; note also κ(ατά)στασις, col. 6a) a
quotation from Dem. 10.34. The term κατάστασις in ancient rhetoric
could mean an "exposition of facts slanted to the speaker's advantage"
(Heath, 260), but that is not the usage here. What has Didymus done
to the text, and what is "hyperbatic phrasing"? One should not be misled or sidetracked by the trivial differences between the two texts, listed
below:

Dem. 10.34 (from cols. 6.66–7.1)	Reconstrued (col. 7.2–7)
τινὰ ἴδω	τιν' ἴδω
Ἐγβατάνοις	ἐν Ἐγβατάνοις
ἐν ταῖς θύραις	ἐπὶ ταῖς θύραις
αὐξομ(έν)ου	αὐξανομ(έν)ου
ἄλλο τι	μηδὲ

Didymus's intention is to get at the essence of Dem. 10.34 by eliminat-
ing extraneous, "hyperbatic" phrases and clauses that might distract
a reader from the main line of Demosthenes' thought. To demonstrate
what he is doing, the passages that have been eliminated by the so-
called κατάστασις of col. 7.2–7 are underlined in the following text of
Dem. 10.34 (taken from cols. 6.66–7.1): Ἐγὼ γ(ὰρ) ὅταν τι|νὰ ἴδω τὸν
μ(ὲν) ἐν Σούσοις κ(αὶ) Ἐγβατάνοις δεδοικότα | κ(αὶ) κακόνουν (εἶναι)
τῆι πόλει φάσκοντα, ὃς κ(αὶ) πρότε|ρον σ(υν)επηνώρθωσε τὰ τ(ῆς)
πόλεως πράγματα κ(αὶ) | ν(ῦν) ἐπηγγέλλετο, εἰ δ(ὲ) μὴ 'δ(έ)χεσθε
ὑμεῖς ἀλλ' ἀ|πεψηφίζεσθε οὐ τά γ' ἐκείνου αἴτια ὑπὲρ δ(ὲ) | τοῦ ἐν

ταῖς θύραις ἐγγὺς οὐ(τωσ)ὶ ἐν μέσηι τῆι Ἑλλά|δι αὐξομ(έν)ου ληιστοῦ
τ(ῶν) Ἑλλήν(ων) ἄλλο τι λέγοντα, θαυ|μάζω, κ(αὶ) δ(έ)δοικα τοῦτον,
ὅστις ἂν ἦι ποτε, ἔγωγε, | ἐπειδὴ οὐχ οὗτος Φίλιππον.

The peculiar expression "hyperbatic phrasing" occurs in only two
other places in Greek literature: Photius's commentary on 1 *Corinthians*
(ed. Staab, p. 548, line 27) and the scholia to Apollonius of Rhodes's
Argonautica (ed. Wendel, p. 236, line 20). Neither illuminates this particular passage, and neither demonstrates how one might correct for hyperbatic phrasing. Though Demosthenes frequently uses hyperbaton,
there is no mention of it elsewhere in the ancient philological and historical commentaries on Demosthenes or in the scholia to Demosthenes, which focus predominantly on rhetorical aspects of the speeches.
Roughly contemporary parallels to Didymus's analysis here are found in
Dionysius of Halicarnassus *On Demosthenes* 9 and *On Literary Composition* 7–9, where he studies the effects of rearranging select passages
from Demosthenes' orations 9, 18, and 21. On these treatises, see Bonner, 61–78. The most useful discussion of hyperbaton in Demosthenes
is found in Longinus *On Sublimity* 22.1–4 (ed. Russell), where the focus is on its emotional effect on the audience. (He does not use the term
"hyperbatic phrasing.")

Notes to Cols. 7.7–8.2: Didymus discusses several possible meanings
for Demosthenes' reference to a "previous restoration" (πρότερον μ(έν)
ποτ' ἐπανορθῶσαι, col. 7.8; πρότερον συνεπηνώρθωσε, Dem. 10.34).
In Didymus's view, one of these meanings is incorrect (col. 7.11–28),
one is correct (col. 7.28–62), and a cluster of other possibilities is apparently not as convincing but still worth mentioning (cols. 7.62–8.2).
In col. 8.2–32, he moves on to discuss the "recent restoration" mentioned in this passage.

The first interpretation Didymus ascribes only to anonymous authorities (ἔνιοι, col. 7.12), an interpretation "that in my opinion seems to be
incorrect" (οὐ[κ ὀρθῶς ὅσα γο(ῦν)] ἐμοὶ δ[οκεῖ], col. 7.14). The first interpretation of the "previous restoration" is a failed Peace of Antalcidas
(on which see Xenophon *Hellenica* 4.8.12–15). Antalcidas (or Antialci-
das) was the Spartan general who convinced Persia to ally with Sparta
and who later, in 386, made Athens and its allies submit to the Peace of
Antalcidas (Xenophon *Hellenica* 5.1.32–36). Didymus uses Philochorus
(*FGrH* 328 F149a) to date the failed peace to 392/1 (col. 7.19–28). According to Bruce, esp. 273–74 and 278–79, Didymus misunderstood

his secondary sources on the peace, thinking they were referring to 392/1 when they really meant 387/6 (followed by S. West, 294–95; Devoto, 200; Harris, "Chalcenteric Negligence," 37; against which Osborne, 139–47). Osborne, 141, who does not translate, apparently understands αὐτοῖς ὀνό|μασι in col. 7.17–18 to mean that Philochorus's account is "in the same (or nearly the same) words (as the words of the anonymous authorities cited above in col. 7.11–14)." I do not think this is correct. I have translated the phrase as "naming names" (lit., "with the actual names," based on the intensive use of αὐτός), a reference to the list of named individuals that follows. For Epicrates and his condemnation, see Dem. 19.276–77; see Florian, 1–10; Bruce, passim. Badian, "King's Peace," 27–33, argues that Philochorus's account is essentially correct, but that Didymus has made improper use of his source. Col. 7.18–28 has recently been discussed by Keen, who argues that although Didymus has abbreviated the Philochorus passage, it may still be used as evidence for the Peace of 392/1.

Before proceeding to the second possible interpretation, Didymus reminds the reader in a different way why the first one is unlikely. After all, "it is not likely that Demosthenes would have reminded them of this (failed) peace" (οὐκοῦν ὅτι μ(ὲν) οὐκ εἰκός (ἐστι) | [τ]ὸν [Δ]ημοσθένη ταύτης αὐτοὺς ὑπομιμνή|[σκ]ειν τῆς εἰρήν(ης) ἑόραται, col. 7.28–30). The Demosthenic context calls for "some other benefaction" (ἑ[τ]έρας δ(έ) τινος εὐ|[εργ]εσίας, col. 7.30–31), namely, a successful example of how the Persian king "previously restored the city's affairs" (compare col. 6.68–69). Didymus thinks that the story of Conon fits the bill, since the "resources of Pharnabazus" (col. 7.32–33) could qualify, by extension, as help given by the Persian king. "Magnanimity" or *philotimia* (compare col. 7.10 φιλοτιμηθῆναι), here referring to the king's bestowal of gifts on the city, is behavior that is encouraged and controlled for the good of the community, rewarded by the local deme or the polis, and recognized publicly through honorific decrees; see Whitehead, "Competitive Outlay and Community Profit," and id., *Demes of Attica*, 241–43. According to Didymus, "it is a very persuasive argument" (λό|γον δ[έ] τινα κ(αὶ) πάνυ πιθανὸν ἔχειν, col. 7.54–55) that Demosthenes is recalling these events, and his reference to a previous restoration "is fairly consistent with" (συνω|δόν πώς, col. 7.59–60) Pharnabazus's assistance to Conon. Conon's famous naval victory occurred in 394, though Philochorus apparently described it under the year 397/6. The chronology and details of these events are notorious problems. The account of Diodorus (14.81.4–5) is used to restore the fragmentary account of Philochorus (*FGrH* 328 F144–45), which covers several years. Either Philochorus had a series of short entries for the years 397/6 to 394/3, or he did not treat the story of Conon in an annalistic fashion, or it is impossible to reconcile Philochorus's account with that of Diodorus (see Jacoby, *FGrH* 3b1, pp. 513–14). Parallel discussions for these events are found in Diodorus 14.79–85; and Xenophon *Hellenica* 4.3.10–13 and 4.8.9–10. See Devoto for further discussion.

Col. 7.38 refers to Pharnabazus, the satrap of Phrygia who appears in both Xenophon and Diodorus. According to Diodorus 14.81.4–5, after Conon put two Athenians in charge of the fleet, he "sailed on to Cilicia, and having gone from there to Thapsacus of Syria, he sailed down the Euphrates River to Babylon. And there, meeting the king, he promised that he would beat the Spartans in a sea battle, if the king would provide him with money and the other things in accordance with his plan." The rest of Philochorus's fragmentary account is best explained by Diodorus 14.83.4–7: "Conon the Athenian and Pharnabazus were in charge of the royal expedition, and they were spending time at Loryma of the Chersonese (compare col. 7.45–46) with more than ninety triremes. Upon learning that the enemy fleet was at Cnidus, they prepared things for a sea battle. Pisander, the Spartan admiral, sailed out from Cnidus with eighty-five triremes and put in at Physcus of the Chersonese (compare col. 7.48). Having sailed out from there he fell in with the king's expedition (compare col. 7.46–48), and attacking the frontmost ships (compare col. 7.48–49), he was victorious; but when the Persians came to help with their triremes arranged close together, and when all the allies fled toward land, he turned his own ship toward them, considering an ignoble retreat to be shameful and unworthy of Sparta. And having fought brilliantly and having killed many of the enemy (compare col. 7.50–51), he was finally killed while fighting in a manner worthy of his country. And pursuing the Spartans as far as the land, the men with Conon captured fifty of the triremes (compare col. 7.49–50). Most of the men, plunging into the sea, fled toward land, and about five hundred of them were captured. The remaining triremes came safely to Cnidus." The account of Xenophon *Hellenica* 4.3.11–12 is similar but not helpful in restoring Philochorus's account. He gives basically the same story, but he omits specific geographical and numerical references that would help to illuminate Philochorus (and Didymus).

Following the excerpt(s) from Philochorus, Didymus refers in pass-

ing to an event after the battle at Cnidus, namely, Conon's rebuilding of
the Long Walls (col. 7.52–53), which had been dismantled at the end
of the Peloponnesian War. This event is not important to his argument,
however, and he does not quote the available account of Philochorus
(*FGrH* 328 F146; see col. 7.53–54). The story is corroborated by Diodorus 14.85.2–3 and Xenophon *Hellenica* 4.8.9–10. Didymus closes
by repeating the relevant section from Dem. 10.34 and arguing that
Pharnabazus's aid to Conon in the battle against the Spartans at Cnidus
is the event to which Demosthenes is alluding with his reference to the
king's "previous restoration" (col. 7.54–62).

Having rejected one explanation and fully embraced a second, Didymus now appends a grab bag of other possibilities. He does not find the
first option very convincing—the language seems tentative, and he only
summarizes Philochorus rather than quoting him (*FGrH* 328 F151)—
but he apparently includes it because it explains how the anonymous
view presented in col. 7.7–28 could understandably have gone astray
(col. 7.62–68). Demosthenes is not referring to the failed Peace of Antalcidas, Didymus might say, but he could be referring to "a peace proposal *resembling* the Peace of the Spartan Antalcidas" (π(αρα)πλήσιον
αὐ|τὴν τῆι τοῦ Λάκωνος Ἀνταλκίδου, col. 7.66–67). The proponent of
the anonymous interpretation mentioned above, Didymus might say,
was fooled by the similarity between the two peace proposals. There is
otherwise no reason for mentioning any peace proposal of Antalcidas
at this point, whether failed or successful. Osborne, 154, understands
col. 7.66–67 to mean "a peace negotiated, at least in part" by Antalcidas; this could constitute a "resemblance," but Didymus is not so explicit. This peace proposal of 375/4 is discussed in Xenophon *Hellenica*
6.2.1 and Diodorus 15.38.1–2. Neither author corroborates Didymus's
observation that this peace was similar to the failed Peace of Antalcidas,
and neither mentions that the Altar of Peace was erected at this time
(compare col. 7.70–71). In a discussion of the military prowess of Timotheus the son of Conon, Isocrates 15.109–10 (ed. Benseler) mentions
annual sacrifices made in connection with a certain peace treaty, and
Nepos's biography of Timotheus (2.2; ed. P. K. Marshall) says that "then
for the first time an Altar to Peace was publicly established, and a feast
was instituted for the goddess" *(tum primum arae Paci publice sint fac-
tae eique deae pulvinar sit institutum).* Both authors date these honors
to 375/4, shortly after Timotheus's victories over the Spartans. Yet some
have thought that Isocrates and Nepos really meant the peace of 372/1.

Didymus does not supply the archon year, but the peace to which he refers in col. 7.62–71 closely corresponds to the peace treaty discussed by Xenophon and Diodorus, which can be dated securely to 375/4 (Jacoby, *FGrH* 3b1, pp. 522–26). Reflecting on cols. 7.7–8.32 as a whole, Robertson, 14, concludes that Didymus confuses "the Spartan peace mission of 392, the Peace imposed by Sparta in 386, and the Peace of 375; as a result he reduces these three events to two, thoroughly conflating the second and the third. From Philochorus's account of the Peace of 375 Didymus remembered only the altar of Peace; all the other details which he gives, including the King's sponsorship, belong to the Peace of 386."

Didymus then says that "someone might be able to point out many other benefactions of the king to the city" (πολλὰς δ᾽ ἂν κ(αὶ) ἄλλας τις ἔχοι παρα[δ]ε[ι]κνύναι τοῦ βασιλέως εἰς τὴν πόλιν εὐερ|γεσίας, col. 7.71–73) that would account for Demosthenes' reference to a "previous restoration." He is not explicit about the things of which Demosthenes may be "reminding | them here, as in a summary" (ὡς ἐν | κεφαλαίωι τὰ νῦν ὑπομιμνήσκοι, col. 8.1–2), but the sense of it seems to be that Demosthenes' reference to a particular "restoration" by the king would likely conjure up other instances of royal benefactions in the contemporary audience's mind, such as the Peace of Callias (c. 450); on which see Meiggs, 129–51, 487–95. Another is a list of unspecified contributions to the city of money "both individual and public" (χρη|μάτ[ω]ν ἐπιδόσεις ἰδίαι κ(αὶ) κοινῆι, col. 7.74–75). The precise meaning of this last is left unclear. Osborne, 157–59, interprets cols. 7.74–8.2 as a list of examples that Demosthenes could have used but chose not to. However, there is no indication in the Greek that Demosthenes' choices took place in past time. Rather, Didymus seems to use the potential optative here, in conjunction with τάχ᾽ ἂν (col. 8.1), to indicate his lack of conviction about or interest in this particular point: Demosthenes "may perhaps be reminding them (of other such benefactions) here," or he may not be.

Notes to Col. 8.2–32: Didymus now turns from the previous restoration to the question of the recent one. He knows of only one plausible candidate, but as he begins to narrate the story, he errs with a reference to the archonship of Lysiscus (344/3) as being "five years earlier" (πρὸ | τοίν(υν) ἐτῶν πέντε τοῦδε, col. 8.7–8). Since he has already dated Dem. 10 to 341/0, the archonship of Lysiscus was four years earlier (Körte, 396). Didymus's evidence again comes from his favorite Atthidographer, Philochorus (*FGrH* 328 F157, col. 8.18–23). (This selection is also listed as 324 F53 and 72 F28, since col. 8.14–15 has been restored to say that the account appears in Androtion and Anaximenes.) The exact date of these events and the question whether Philip's embassy and the Persian king's embassy arrived at the same time have been debated. See Jacoby, *FGrH* 3b1, pp. 531–33; Hammond and Griffith, 489–95; Cawkwell, "Demosthenes' Policy," 121–34; Lehmann-Haupt. For the Persian king's aims at this time, see Diodorus 16.44.1: "The (Persian) king, placing great importance on defeating Egypt because of his earlier defeat, sent ambassadors to the greatest of the cities in Greece, asking them to join up with the Persians against the Egyptians." If one follows the P-S text of col. 8.14–15, Didymus seems to be rejecting the account of an eyewitness participant (Androtion, the fourth-century Athenian politican, student of Isocrates, and Atthidographer) in favor of the later account of Philochorus. Harding, "Political Career," 197–98, has no confidence in these restorations originally proposed by D-S[1]; see also Cawkwell, "Demosthenes' Policy," 131 n.1; Harris, "Chalcenteric Negligence," 38 n.7; Harding, *Androtion*, 178–80.

Didymus raises the possibility that "someone might conjecture" (στοχάσαιτο δ' ἄν τις, col. 8.26) that the recent restoration could have something to do with Hermias's informing the king about Philip's plans (col. 8.26–32). But this is an especially poor piece of reasoning, as Harris, "Chalcenteric Negligence," 38, argues. At the time when Dem. 10 was delivered (341/0), Hermias had been only recently arrested, but the Persian ambassadors had been received in 344/3. In addition, Didymus here says that Hermias may have told the king about Philip's plans, while earlier (cols. 4.48–6.62) he implies that he did not, since he does not openly disagree with the reported view of Callisthenes. But Osborne, 172–73, objects that "there is no reason why this information about Philip must have been obtained *after* the arrest." See also cols. 4.48–6.62 and the notes, and Jaeger, 119–21.

Notes to Col. 8.32–44: Dem. 10.35 mentions "another thing that is destroying the city." Didymus correctly identifies this as an allusion to the Theoric Fund ([τὸ θεωρι]κὸν αἰνίτ[τ]ε[τ]αι, col. 8.39), as is clear from Dem. 10.36, which Didymus for some reason does not quote. The Theoric Fund was the fourth-century fund administered by an individual or a board, whose nominal intention was to allow poorer Athenian citizens to attend dramatic performances. It was at least politically inexpedient to suggest in peacetime that this fund be used for military purposes; some sources say that this was punishable by death. Since Demosthenes here takes a different attitude to the Theoric Fund from the one that he espouses elsewhere (Dem. 1.19–20, 3.10–11), some have consequently doubted the authenticity of this speech. On the Theoric Fund, see Cawkwell, "Eubulus"; Sealey, *Demosthenes,* 256–58; Buchanan, chaps. 3–4. On the authenticity of Dem. 10, see Sealey, *Demosthenes,* 232–35.

Notes to Cols. 8.44–9.9: Didymus's concern here is Athenian revenues in the fourth century. Part of Dem. 10.35 had already been quoted (col. 8.32–38). Didymus now quotes part of Dem. 10.37 (col. 8.44–49). He is interested in this passage for one reason only: the date to which Demosthenes is referring by the expression "there was a time not long ago." Didymus says that "this date might be when" (εἴη ἂν οὗτος ὁ κ(αι)|ρὸς ἐν ὧι, col. 8.49–50) the Athenians were defeated at Aegospotami (405), the event that marked the end of the Athenian empire (Xenophon *Hellenica* 2.1). Following col. 8.54 there intervenes a lacuna of about ten lines. S. West, 293–94, suggests that Didymus left the large space here hoping later to find an appropriate passage to quote from Philochorus. But even if Didymus had done this, there is no reason for the copyist of Berol. 9780 to preserve the lacuna. D-S¹, xvii, more plausibly conjecture that our copyist, faced with a faulty or lacunose text, left space open in hopes of finding another exemplar later.

To corroborate Dem. 10.38 (quoted in col. 8.55–58), Didymus quotes from a speech delivered by Aristophon and recorded in book 27 of Theopompus's *On Philip* (FGrH 115 F166, cols. 8.64–9.9). Aristophon was an Athenian politician whose career extended from 403/2 down to the 340s, and who is best known for his opposition to other prominent figures on matters of fiscal and foreign policy. The subject of the speech here was the Peace of Philocrates, a peace proposal sent by the Athenians to Philip in 346, and one that Aristophon opposed. Didymus is not interested in the Peace of Philocrates or the conclusion of the Sacred War. His purpose in citing Theopompus is simply to show that Athenian revenue "in the time of Philip" (col. 8.60–61) was 400 talents. On the Peace of Philocrates, see Hammond and Griffith, 329–47; Cawkwell, "Euboea," 91–113, 207–9; Sealey, *Demosthenes,* 143–59, 319–30.

Notes to Col. 9.9–37: Dem. 10.38–42 had discussed the Theoric Fund from the point of view of the poor; now 10.43–45 shows why the rich are upset about it. Didymus paraphrases and attempts thereby to clarify Demosthenes' statement. Textual problems in col. 9.22–23 cause some difficulty. P-S give ἀλ[λ' ἐπε]μ[η]χανῶντο κ(αὶ) τῶν οὐ δικ(αί)ω[ν ἰδί]ας | [τ]ρ[οφ]ά[ς], "but they (the demagogues) schemed at getting the private resources of the unjust," which Wankel, 221, labels "unverständlich." I have adopted the text of D-S² here, but their τῶν οὐ δικ(αί)ω[ν] is still not completely satisfactory. The passage in Demosthenes and the remainder of the explanation in Didymus suggest that the only people who could properly be called "unjust" in this context are the demagogues themselves. If the "unjust" may be taken as extreme ellipsis for "(rich people whom they portrayed as) unjust," then either version of the Greek text could work: the demagogues "devised some tricky schemes against the (allegedly) 'unjust,'" or they "schemed at getting the private resources of the (allegedly) 'unjust.'" This is one of the few occasions when Didymus explains a passage of Demosthenes without resorting to other scholars' opinions or extra-Demosthenic evidence. D-S¹, xv, regard this paraphrase as a reflection of Didymus's grammatical interests.

Notes to Cols. 9.38–10.10: Didymus's purpose here is to identify the obscure man addressed by name at Dem. 10.70. This section of the speech is a bit puzzling because "the *Philippics* habitually refer to the Athenian opponents of Demosthenes in general terms without naming them" (Sealey, *Demosthenes*, 233). Sealey adduces Plutarch *Moralia* 810c–d *(Precepts of Statecraft)* (ed. Hubert et al.): "The *Philippics* are free from all mockery and buffoonery" (καθαρεύουσι καὶ σκώμματος καὶ βωμολοχίας ἁπάσης). The S and A manuscripts of Demosthenes give "Aristodemos" here; it is easy to understand how metathesis and the relative unfamiliarity of the name Aristomedes could lead to this mistake (*RE* lists thirty-six of the former and only five of the latter). An Aristodemos is known from Dem. 18 and 19 as an actor and member of the first embassy to Philip.

Didymus begins by dismissing the identification of Aristomedes as "the man from Pherae who fought against Philip along with the king's generals" and "who, along with Darius (Darius III, c. 380–330), opposed Alexander in Cilicia and escaped to Cyprus" (col. 9.43–52). Philip, Theopompus, and Anaximenes are cited as sources here. Didymus claims (col. 9.46–47) that Philip mentions this Aristomedes in the *Letter to the Athenians,* but Aristomedes does not appear in the text preserved by this name as item 12 in the Demosthenic corpus. Didymus is either mistaken about his source, or he knows of a different letter. It may be relevant in this connection that Didymus does not comment on our oration 12 (see notes on col. 13.14–25). Foucart, 93–94, suggests that Didymus had access to the genuine letter of Philip and that ours is spurious. This Aristomedes is known mainly through Arrian *Anabasis* 2.13.1–2 (ed. Roos), an account of the aftermath of the battle of Issus in 333. According to Arrian, Darius and four thousand Persians and foreign mercenaries fled across the Euphrates to Thapsacus. Aristomedes (Ἀριστομήδης ὁ Φεραῖος), along with Amyntas, Thymondas, Bianor, and eight thousand of their soldiers, deserted to Tripolis. The parallel treatments of Diodorus 17.48.2–5 and Curtius 4.1.27–33 omit mention of Aristomedes by name. On these events see Badian, "Harpalus," esp. 25–26.

Didymus then turns to discuss the correct Aristomedes (cols. 9.52–10.11). It is certain that he has the right man, a well-known thief who is nicknamed "Brazen." In Dem. 10.73, Demosthenes calls Aristomedes a thief, and in 13.20 he mentions his nickname "Brazen." Didymus does not adduce either of these passages as evidence. Both the nickname and his reputation of being a thief appear together in Plutarch's *Life of Demosthenes* 11.4–6. The nickname "Brazen" may refer to the coin called a *chalkous*. A combination of the name of this coin with the reputation for thievery led Page, *Papyri*, 238–39, to conjecture that Aristomedes was the kind of man who would try to steal even the smallest coin from someone. Plutarch, on the other hand, understands it to refer to his audacity in theft, representing Demosthenes as saying to his audience: "But you, Athenian gentlemen, should not be amazed at the thefts that occur, when we have brazen thieves but clay walls." Aristomedes' popularity as a character from the comic stage provided Demosthenes with a convenient butt for a joke about Athens's noble ancestry (Dem. 10.73). Davies, 64–68, no. 2108, argues against identifying our Aristomedes with the trierarch of 356/5 and son of the famous statesman Aristophon.

Didymus provides four pieces of evidence about the correct Aristomedes: a quotation from Dinarchus, one from Philemon, and two from two different plays of Timocles. The Dinarchus quotation (col. 9.56–61, frag. LXXI–LXXII no. 4, ed. Conomis) attests only to the nickname "Brazen." Nothing is known about the circumstances of this oration and next to nothing about the people involved. Worthington, 81, suggests that it was delivered in the late 340s or in the 330s. The other three fragments of the oration are collected in Conomis, 132–33. A Docimus served as trierarch in 342/1; see Kirchner, "Dokimos," 1274. There are at least three possibilities for Chaerestratus; see Kirchner, "Chaires-tratos," 2029. The τῶι μ(έν) of col. 9.59 is in reference to Chaerestra-tus, according to Wankel, 221 (who follows D-S², 55).

The second piece of evidence is a selection from Philemon's *Sculp-tor* (col. 9.63–70), a Middle or New Comedy of unknown date. Ed-monds, 3A: 23, suggests a possible date of 326; Körte, 237, reports the view of R. J. T. Wagner that it dates from 341. This is the only extant fragment. The joke here is that the unknown speaker, who fears running into "Brazen" the thief, inadvertently asks the thief himself (Aristome-des) who the thief is. The text is included as fragment 206 in Austin; also given in Page, *Papyri,* 238–39. Compare the famous story in Plutarch's *Life of Aristides* 7.5–6, in which a man desiring to have Aristides ostra-cized asks Aristides himself to inscribe his name on the man's ostracon.

The third and fourth selections are from plays of Timocles. The selec-tion from *Heroes* (cols. 9.71–10.3) further corroborates Aristomedes' reputation as a thief. The fragment also indicates that Aristomedes was portrayed elsewhere as a thief on the comic stage, if Satyrus is the comic actor from Olynthus praised by Demosthenes at Dem. 19.192. The other fragments of the play suggest that it also emphasized the rivalry of De-mosthenes and Aeschines (Edmonds, 2: 610–11). Edmonds, 2: 612, suggests that Charon is the speaker here and that Hermes is helping him conduct souls to the underworld, among them the soul of Aris-tomedes. In the selection from *Icarians* (the deme or the Aegean island?) (col. 10.4–11), two bad puns are exchanged (most likely) between two characters. Autocles is equated to Marsyas, while Aristomedes is equated to Tereus (col. 10.4–6). Autocles may be the same person as Autoclides, the protagonist of a parody of Aeschylus's *Eumenides* called *Orestauto-clides* (see Constantinides, 59). Marsyas was the satyr who picked up the flute and learned to play after Athena had discarded it, and who later was flayed alive by Apollo after losing to him in a flute contest; see Frazer's notes to Apollodorus 1.4.2. Page, *Papyri,* 240–41, suggests that Autocles may be bald ("flayed") and known for his flings with flute girls (thus "flute-loving"). The peculiar reference to his being nailed to an oven (καμί|νωι προσπεπατταλευμ(έν)ον, col. 10.5–6) is paralleled by Aristophanes fragment 592 (= Pollux 7.108, πρὸ δὲ τῶν καμίνων τοῖς χαλκεῦσιν ἔθος ἦν γελοῖά τινα καταρτᾶν ἢ ἐπιπλάττειν ἐπὶ φθόνου ἀποτροπῇ · ἐκαλεῖτο δὲ βασκάνια), and so the point of the remark, ac-cording to Page, is "that Autocles is good for nothing but to be a dummy or mascot, such as you commonly saw erected on the furnace in a

foundry." Tereus married Procne (mentioned in col. 10.9) and had a son
Itys by her. After Tereus raped and cut out Procne's sister Philomela's
tongue, the two conspired to serve up Itys as a feast for his father Tereus.
Upon discovering this, Tereus chased the two women, and all three were
changed into birds. See Frazer's notes to Apollodorus 3.8. The mythological references are simply convenient vehicles for proferring a couple
of very poor jokes. The texts of both Timocles fragments are included as
Austin 222a-b and are also in Page, *Papyri*, 240–43. Other fragments
of *Heroes* and *Icarians* are assembled in Edmonds, 2: 610–12 and 613–
17, respectively. Platnauer, 177, dates both plays to 342. The best discussion of *Icarians* is that of Constantinides; but see also Körte, 410–
16, on the two fragments of Timocles.

Notes to Cols. 10.13–11.5: Didymus uses a version of Philip's letter
(similar to item 12 in the Demosthenic corpus) to pin down the date of
Dem. 11. See notes on cols. 9.38–10.10. The two versions of the letter
incorporate the same basic ideas but differ in the order of presentation,
choice of words, and omission or inclusion of several phrases. On this
letter and the authenticity of Dem. 11 and 12, see Sealey, *Demosthenes*,
239–40; Pohlenz. At col. 10.31, Didymus labels Dem. 11 as a deliberative speech *(symboule)*. The *symbouleutikoi logoi* as a formal group normally include Dem. 12–16, while the *Philippics* comprise orations 1–
11. Although Dem. 11 is of a deliberative nature, Didymus still groups
it with the *Philippics*. Didymus then discusses the historical background
to the oration, attributing the breakdown of the peace between Philip
and Athens mainly to Philip's attacks on Byzantium and Perinthus (col.
10.34–39). See Hammond and Griffith, 563–64, 566–81; A. Schaefer,
2: 497–516. There is an inconsistency in Didymus's dates. In cols. 1.53–
2.2, Didymus dated the letter of Philip and the subsequent breaking of
the peace to 340/39. In col. 10.34–52, he also dates the end of the peace
to 340/39. So far, no problem. But his statement that Philip's theft of
the boats "occurred a year earlier (than Dem. 11), in the archonship of
Theophrastus" (ταῦτα δὴ | [πέρ]υσι διαπεπρᾶχθαι ἐπὶ Θεοφράστου,
col. 10.50–51) implies that Dem. 11 was delivered in 339/38, *after* the
peace was broken (see S. West, 292): that is impossible.

Philip found this venture quite profitable. While Chares, a famous
fourth-century Athenian soldier and leader of mercenary troops, was
away meeting with the Persian commanders (Philochorus's "royal generals," col. 10.55) about attacking Philip, Philip tried and failed to cap-
ture the boats by sea and then marched his soldiers by land to attack the

boats at Hieron (cols. 10.57–11.1). It is interesting that Demosthenes does not mention this offense in the current speech, although some years later in *On the Crown* he would point to it as the cause of the outbreak of war with Philip (see Dem. 18.73, 139). See also Justin 9.1.1–2, 5–6. Justin (ed. Seel) considers Philip's theft of the ships as an act of war motivated by greed: "When Philip had come into Greece, annoyed by the plundering of a few cities and calculating in his mind, on the basis of the loot of small cities, how great the wealth of all of them would be, he decided to make war on all of Greece." Justin gives 170 as the number of ships, contrary to both Philochorus and Theopompus. See Jacoby, *FGrH* 3b suppl. vol. 1, pp. 537–39.

Notes to Col. 11.5–14: Didymus here discusses the date of Dem. 11, its place in the corpus, and its authenticity. Didymus's date for the speech (340/39) and his statement that Dem. 11 is the end (πέρας) of the *Philippics* is corroborated by Dionysius of Halicarnassus *First Letter to Ammaeus* 10. Scholars have generally accepted Didymus's tentative claim— note especially the cautious "not far from the mark" (οὐκ ἀπὸ | σκοποῦ, col. 11.7–8)—that oration 11 is not what it appears to be. This is the only place in the extant commentaries where Didymus discusses the authenticity of one of Demosthenes' speeches. Didymus says that it is "a derivative little speech" (τὸ λογίδιον, col. 11.8) that has been "compiled from certain orations of Demosthenes" (ἔκ τινων Δημοσθένους πραγματ<ει>ῶν ἐ|πισυντεθέν, col. 11.9–10). In other words, Dem. 11 is not entirely an original speech, since its compiler has lifted portions of it from elsewhere in Demosthenes. Didymus does not attempt to demonstrate which passages have been copied, and from where. See Sealey, *Demosthenes*, 239–40, on the authenticity of Dem. 11.

Didymus goes on to add the separate comment that "there are those who say that this deliberative speech is by Anaximenes of Lampsacus, because of the fact that it has been inserted in book 7 of his *Philippica* with almost these very words" ((εἰσὶν) οἵ φασιν Ἀναξιμ(έν)ους | (εἶναι) τοῦ Λαμψακηνοῦ τὴν συμβουλήν, τῶι | δὴ ἐν τῆι ἑβδόμηι τῶ[ν Φιλιπ- π]ικ(ῶν) <αὐτ>ὴν ὀλίγου δεῖν γρ[ά]μμασιν α[ὐτοῖς ἐ]ντετ[ά]]χθαι, col. 11.10–14, text from Milns). The phrase "because of the fact that it has been inserted"—substituting τῶι for P-S τὴν at the end of line 11, creating the articular infinitive τῶι ἐντετάχθαι, which Milns, 86 n. 33, takes as a causal dative—directly connects this theory of authorship with its justification. The P-S text's τὴν at the end of col. 11.11 is problematic (with Wankel, 221–22) and removes any causality from Didymus's statement: "There are those who say that this deliberative speech is by Anaximenes of Lampsacus, *which is* in book 7 of his *Philippica (and) which is* inserted there with almost these very words (τὴν συμβουλήν, τὴν | δὴ ἐν τῆι ἑβδόμηι τῶ[ν Φιλιππ]ικ(ῶν), ἣν ὀλίγου δεῖν . . .). From this or similar readings, some scholars have taken Didymus's statement as true but have faulted him for not checking into the matter for himself (S. West, 293–94, is the classic treatment). However, Didymus was perfectly capable of checking his references to Anaximenes at col. 6.59–62 and col. 9.51–52, so the argument that he refused to or was unable to at this point loses a good deal of its force. Whether Milns's conjectures are correct or not, Didymus is simply reporting an existing view and the evidence for it here, and it is not justifiable to say more about what he did or did not read for himself.

Notes to Col. 11.14–26: This section contains an etymological discussion probably intended to contribute to the question of the speech's authenticity. The P-S text of col. 11.14–15 cannot be correct: "They interpreted some of the words in a rather vulgar way" (ἔνια δ(ὲ) τ(ῶν) ὀνομ[ά]τ(ων) φο[ρτι]κωτέρως | ἡρμήνευσαν, col. 11.14–15). Something like ἔνιοι δὲ τὰ ὀνόματα φορτικώτερα ἡρμήνευσαν, "some interpreted his words (as being) rather vulgar," must be closer to the original sense. The "some" (col. 11.14) may be the same as the "they" of col. 11.10—that is, those who say that the speech is by Anaximenes. Col. 11.5–26, then, seems to comprise three explanations for the appearance of Dem. 11: it may be a patchwork job, it may be by Anaximenes, or it may be spurious on grounds of "vulgar" language (with Osborne, 20–22). It is possible that "vulgar" existed as a categorical descriptive term in earlier criticism of Demosthenes—note the catchall phrase "and whatever words there are like it" (col. 11.16–17)—that was used to evaluate the authenticity of a speech (see Lossau, 78–79). Interestingly enough, it is possible that the term "vulgar" may ultimately derive from Demosthenes' contemporary opponent Aeschines. In *On Demosthenes* 57 (cf. 55), Dionysius of Halicarnassus claims not to understand Aeschines' charge that Demosthenes uses "vulgar" words, saying that he "cannot find any other vulgar and distasteful (φορτικὰ καὶ ἀηδῆ) words in any of Demosthenes' orations." (Aeschines did not label Demosthenes' language as "vulgar" in any extant speech, but he did make reference to his "abominable and unpersuasive words," τὰ μιαρὰ καὶ ἀπίθανα ῥήματα, in 3.166.) On the possible role of Aeschines in early Demosthenic criticism, see Lossau, 9–21. It is important to note that Didymus himself does not explicitly say that the occurrence of the word ὀρρωδεῖν has some bearing on the authenticity question; he does not seem to have a strong opinion about it. In *On Demosthenes* 57, Dionysius says that the presence of vulgar words in spurious speeches is quite another matter, which might suggest that in his mind the question of authenticity was separate from the question of "vulgar" language. Weil, *Harangues,* in his commentary on Dem. 11.2, notes that the only other occurrence of the word ὀρρωδεῖν in Demosthenes is in an interpolation at Dem. 9.65 in manuscripts LBY (see his app. crit. ad loc.). Didymus also discussed this etymology in his commentary on Aristophanes (see frag. 10 in Schmidt, 249). Ofenloch identifies col. 11.7–17 as frag. 140 of Caecilius, an influential literary critic of the first century.

The subsequent discussion—fairly coherent as ancient etymologies go, but ultimately erroneous—is aimed at demonstrating that ὀρρωδεῖν "is formed on the basis of something that happens to those who are afraid"; to wit, their rear ends sweat. The word ἴδεδροι (people with sweaty rear ends) in col. 11.22, which Didymus no doubt understands as derived from ἰδίειν and ἕδρα, does not occur elsewhere. Neither of the quoted passages shows how the alleged compound ὀρρωδεῖν was formed from ὄρρος and ἰδίειν. The first passage (*Odyssey* 20.204), spoken by the cowherd Philoetius, demonstrates Didymus's point that people who are afraid do indeed sweat, although Philoetius does not specify the origin of his sweat as being his rear end (col. 11.22–23). The selection from Aristophanes (*Frogs* 237), from Dionysus's reply to the frog chorus, is a better parallel in that it provides πρωκτός, more or less a synonym for ὄρρος, as the subject of ἰδίει (col. 11.25–26), but these passages are still far from conclusive proof of Didymus's proposed etymology for ὀρρωδεῖν. On the etymology of this word, see Boisacq, 82–83, 717; Chantraine, 3: 827. On other ancient discussions of this etymology, see Lossau, 99–106.

Notes to Col. 11.26–52: Didymus's aim in this section is to distinguish the correct Nicaea from other cities by the same name, lest the reader be confused (compare col. 11.51–52). Didymus relies on a quotation of a geographical work by Timosthenes (col. 11.32–37), written in the years 270–240, which was available in antiquity in its original ten-book form, in an epitome, or in the collection known as the *Stadiasmon epidrome.* The scholiast to Aeschines 2.132 says that Nicaea is by the sea, forty stades from Thermopylae (as opposed to Timosthenes' twenty). On Timosthenes, see Gisinger. The fragments are collected in Wagner.

The second part of this discussion (col. 11.40–51) gives Philochorus's account of how "Philip ordered the Thebans to give this city back to the Locrians" (col. 11.38–39); on which see Hammond and Griffith, 543–44, 592. Didymus does not give a date for this event and cites Philochorus only by book number (col. 11.39–40). He was apparently not concerned with a date here, but only with the proper identification of a historically important city. This also accounts for his closing statement that "there are other cities named Nicaea, which I do not think it is necessary to discuss here" (περὶ ὧν οὐ|κ οἶμαι ἀ[να]γκ[αῖον] νῦν λέγειν, col. 11.51–52). A convenient selection from Philochorus, with whose writings Didymus was already intimately familiar, was impossible to pass up. Another version of the same section of Philochorus (*FGrH* 328 F56a) is given in Dionysius of Halicarnassus *First Letter to Ammaeus* 11, which dates these events to 339/8; on Dionysius' dates see Sealey, "Dionysius of Halicarnassus." This version says that the Athenians sent ambassadors at the same time as Philip sent his and that the result was an Athenian-Theban alliance. Jacoby (*FGrH* 3b suppl. vol. 1, p. 332) characterizes F56a as "careless," judging that Didymus does a better job than Dionysius of remaining true to Philochorus.

Notes to Cols. 11.52–12.33: To illustrate his derivation of the word σκορακίζειν from the expression ἐς κόρακας, Didymus quotes from Aristophanes' *Birds* and a collection of proverbs by Demon. Col. 11.61–62 gives part of Aristophanes' exchange between Euelpides and Pisthetaerus, where Euelpides uses the colloquial expression "to the ravens" in a literal sense. As Didymus correctly points out, Euelpides "makes a joke out of the colloquial expression" ([χα]ριεντίζεται δ(ὲ) εἰς τὴν παροιμίαν, col. 11.63). To illustrate the origin of the proverb, Didymus appends a lengthy discussion from the fourth-century proverb-collector Demon (cols. 11.65–12.33), perhaps drawn from his own research into proverbs (see fragments in Schmidt, 396–98). See Foucart, 146–48, on Boeotian mythical history. For a collection and examination of ancient thought on crows/ravens, see Thompson, 91–95. Thompson compares Greek references to white ravens to the Latin "black swan" *(cygnus niger)*, in the sense that both refer to "an unheard of thing" (94). Similar derivations of this expression are given in Zenobius 3.87 (ed. Leutsch and Schneidewin, 1: 78–79), and Pausanias Atticista 218 (ed. Erbse). In general on proverbs and the genre of paroemiography in antiquity, see the two articles by Rupprecht. Other fragments of Greek works on proverbs are collected in Leutsch and Schneidewin. Weil, *Harangues,* in his comments on Dem. 11.11, suggests that the author of this speech may have been influenced by misreading σκορακισμούς (instances of contemptuous treatment) for κορδακισμούς (licentious dances) in Dem. 2.18, since the verb σκορακίζειν does not occur elsewhere in the Demosthenic corpus.

At the top of col. 12, a scribe drew a siglum resembling a reverse lunate *sigma* (the so-called "antisigma"), a common symbol in literary papyri used, among other purposes, to designate an error and its correction (McNamee, 14–15). This antisigma is apparently followed by the words ἰδὲ μὴ νεμομένους. The editors take the word ἰδὲ as an aorist imperative meaning "see!" (see their *index verborum*), but it is unclear how the following word, μή, should be construed. To my knowledge no one has explained the phrase as a whole; P-S note only: "Quaerit librarius de l.3." The comment is directed at col. 12.3 (a second antisigma appears in the margin to the left of this line), where, according to P-S ad loc., the scribe apparently first wrote νεομένους, then ναιωμένους. P-S follow the apparent correction in the column header and print νεμομένους. I would suggest that the words ἰδὲ μὴ have been divided incorrectly, and that the correct reading is ι δὲ μή for εἰ δὲ μή, "but if not" or "otherwise." In documentary papyri, iotacism regularly occurs in the word εἰ: In *P.Lond.* III 988.9 (third century C.E.), εἰ δ' οὐ<ν> is written as ιδου. Iotacism of the word εἰ in the phrase εἰ δὲ μὴ occurs in four documentary papyri: *P.Graux* II 27.15 (third century C.E.); *P.Muench* III 58.3 (second century B.C.) and 120.12 (second century C.E.); and *P.Oxy.* LIX 4000.22 (fourth century C.E.). If this suggestion is correct, the text of col. 12a should read as follows: (antisigma) εἰ δὲ μή, νεμομένους. The author of this critical remark observes the difficulty with the word νεμομένους/ναιωμένους and notes: "but if (it is) not (νεομένους/ναιωμένους, then it is) νεμομένους." For ει written as ι, see Mayser, vol. 1, pt. 1, 60–65; Gignac, 1: 189–90. For the independent or elliptical use of εἰ δὲ μή, see Smyth 2346d. I have previously published my view on this scribal remark; see Gibson, "Didymus Papyrus."

Notes to Col. 12.33–37: In response to Dem. 11.16, Didymus notes briefly: "We have shown (δ(ε)δη|λώκαμεν) that the Macedonians paid tribute to the Athenians in the (commentary on) *On the Crown.*" Didymus probably wrote his commentary to Dem. 18 *(On the Crown)* before the commentaries on the *Philippics;* see Foucart, 29. He uses Dem. 18

in his commentary to Dem. 9 (see col. 1.1–25), and he is most likely alluding to his commentary on Dem. 18 when he says: "We have <else-
where> fully discussed the wounds that Philip had. But at this point we
must briefly comment on the subject" (col. 12.40–43). Nevertheless,
since there is no passage in Dem. 18 that would obviously invite commentary on Macedonian tribute payments, Didymus has been accused of
being mistaken about where he discussed this topic (see Bliquez, "Didymus Papyrus," who prefers Dem. 3 or 7). In his comments on Dem. 11.16,
Weil, *Harangues,* adduces relevant discussions from Dem. 3.24 (where
Perdiccas II is referred to as a subject of Athens) and Dem. 7.12 (another
claim that the Macedonians paid tribute to Athens). It has also need-
lessly been suggested that Didymus is referring to a different text of *On
the Crown* (S. West, 290). But since Didymus's commentary to Dem. 18
is not extant, there is no reason not to give Didymus the benefit of
the doubt. Osborne, 202–3, suggests that Didymus could have discussed this topic in commenting on Dem. 18.152. Didymus changes
Demosthenes' reference to "Macedonian kings" to the more vague
"Macedonians" (col. 12.35). For a detailed discussion of the evidence
provided by the tribute lists regarding Athenian and Macedonian control of northern Thrace, see Edson; and the detailed response of Meritt
et al., 3: 214–23.

Notes to Cols. 12.37–13.12: Didymus is probably summarizing (νυνὶ
δ' εἰς βρα|χὺ ὑπομνηστέον, col. 12.42–43) his research into Philip's
wounds from his commentary on Dem. 18.67, where Demosthenes mentions injuries to Philip's eye, collarbone, hand, and leg (with Osborne,
203). According to Riginos, this passage in Demosthenes generated
many, sometimes elaborate, ancient discussions of Philip's wounds; see
her article for a detailed examination of this tradition. Three of Philip's
injuries are mentioned and discussed: the loss of his eye at Methone
(col. 12.43–62), an injury to his right collarbone in a battle with the
Illyrians in 345 (cols. 12.64–13.2; see Hammond and Griffith, 469–74;
Florian, 34–37), and a wound in the right thigh received at the hands of
the Triballoi in 339 (col. 13.3–7; see Hammond and Griffith, 581–84;
A. Schaefer, 2: 517–22; Florian, 38–42). Didymus discussed the Illyrians and Triballoi in his commentary on Aristophanes (frag. 47 in
Schmidt, 256). Theopompus (*FGrH* 115 F152) and Marsyas of Macedon (*FGrH* 135–36 F16) are listed as sources for the loss of the eye due
to an arrow; this event is also mentioned at Diodorus 16.34.5. On Marsyas, see Heckel, esp. 454–56; Pearson, *Lost Histories,* 253–54. Mar-

syas of Pella and Marsyas of Philippi are treated jointly as nos. 135–36 in *FGrH*. In *How to Write History* 38–39 (ed. MacLeod), Lucian says that the historian should not be concerned "that Philip had his eye put out by Aster of Amphipolis, the archer at Olynthus." The name Aster and the story about the flute contest partially confirm the report of Duris (which Didymus does not believe, perhaps for this very reason; see Osborne, 205–6, and Yunis, 1053), but Lucian calls him an archer (with Theopompus and Marsyas, and against Duris's view of his having used a javelin) and places him at Olynthus rather than at Methone (against Theopompus and Marsyas; Duris's view is not made explicit). In his characterization of Duris as a teller of "marvellous tales" (note τερατ[ε]ύσε[σθαι], col. 12.51), Didymus is the first ancient scholar known to have complained about the quality of the fourth-century Duris's *Macedonian History* (Kebric, 13), but Duris's reputation varied among his other ancient readers (Kebric, 10–18). On his *Macedonian History* and its influence, see Kebric, 36–67. Plutarch's biography of Demosthenes refers to both Marsyas and Duris. The Hippostratus who died in Philip's Illyrian campaign of 344/3 (col. 13.2; compare Diodorus 16.69) may have been the brother of Philip's wife Cleopatra or the father of Alexander's admiral Hegelochus, or both (Heckel, 456). On Philip's "Companions" (τῶν ἑταίρ(ων), col. 13.1), see Hammond and Griffith, 408–10.

Notes to Col. 13.14–25: The aim of this section is to argue that Dem. 13 is not a *Philippic*. The scribe has labeled this speech as the "twelfth" oration, but it appears in the modern corpus as oration 13 *(On Organization)*. It is important to note that this numbering cannot be ascribed with any confidence to Didymus, who never refers to Demosthenes' orations by number. The more usual practice in antiquity was to refer to a speech by title (e.g., *Against Neaera*), by its number within a series (e.g., "the seventh of the *Philippics*"), and/or by the opening words of the speech (as in the closing title of Berol. 9780). Didymus never comments on our item 12 *(Letter of Philip)*, but if he himself rejected it as spurious, he never says as much. Two of the four important manuscripts of Demosthenes (F and Y) include the *Letter of Philip* as item 12 (Sealey, *Demosthenes*, 239–40). The authenticity of Dem. 12 has been doubted because it seems superficially to be the letter that occasioned the reply given in Dem. 11 *(Reply to Philip's Letter)*; since Dem. 11 is most likely not by Demosthenes—see notes on col. 11.7–14, and Sealey, *Demosthenes*, 239—item 12 has been found guilty by association. However, as some have argued, a careful comparison of the political situations described in Dem. 11 and 12 suggests that the letter preserved as our Dem. 12, though it may in fact be an authentic letter of Philip, cannot be the letter that occasioned the reply contained in our Dem. 11. See Sealey, *Demosthenes*, 240, for further discussion and bibliography.

The point that Didymus wishes to make in this section is that Dem. 13 is not a *Philippic:* "And some include this speech with the *Philippics*, which seems to me to be incorrect" (κ(αὶ) τοῦτον ἔνιοι | τὸν λό[γ]ον εἰς τοὺς Φιλιππικο(ὺς) παρεί|ρουσιν · [ο]ὺκ ὀρθῶς ὅσα γο(ῦν) ἐμοὶ δοκεῖ, col. 13.16–18). The term "Philippic" was normally applied to orations 1–11, and above Didymus called oration 11 the "end" (πέρας, col. 11.6) of the *Philippics*. Practically speaking, this was little more than a clerical or bibliographical problem: where should this speech be filed? The distinction between groups of speeches arose from the limitations imposed by ancient writing materials. Rolls of greater than fifty feet would have been difficult to read, much less to consult as a reference tool, so single-roll editions of a prolific author such as Demosthenes would have been impossible. One could, however, place all the *Philippics* together in the same labeled container. See Goldstein, 267–68. Libanius, in his hypothesis (introduction) to Dem. 13 (ed. Foerster), says that the speech is a deliberative speech, not a *Philippic*. Didymus, however, approaches this as a theoretical question, probing the implications of assigning the title *Philippic* to a particular speech. He judges that our Dem. 13 should be excluded: it has nothing to do with Philip, his activities, or Macedonia (col. 13.18–22). The most recent study of the authenticity of Dem. 13 is Trevett, who argues for its genuineness and dates it to the late 350s.

Notes to Col. 13.25–62: Didymus discusses two possible dates for Dem. 13: post-346 and 349/8. From his reading of Dem. 13.7–8 (col. 13.31–40), Didymus concludes that the speech may have been composed after peace was made with Philip (the Peace of Philocrates in 346 —see Hammond and Griffith, 329–47), observing that the Macedonians were not mentioned in it: "And Demosthenes perhaps (μήποτε, col. 13.25) composed this speech after the peace with Philip (346), when the Athenians' dealings with the Macedonians were quiet, but their dealings with Asia were keeping them very busy." His argument would then run as follows: If the Macedonians are not mentioned, they must not currently pose a threat, and so this speech would most likely have been delivered after 346 when peace was made with Philip. On the fall of

Mytilene and Rhodes, see A. Schaefer, 1: 471–87. The use of μήποτε here, meaning "perhaps," has been misunderstood by Osborne, 221–25, as a negative, which resulted in his misinterpretation of col. 13.25–62; see fragments 15 and 19 from Harpocration for parallel usages. Foucart, 98–99, and Lossau, 87–90, interpret the word correctly. Lossau, 88–89, argues that Didymus has found two proposals for the date of the speech. One has a terminus post quem of 346 (col. 13.25–27). Didymus reports this view but does not himself subscribe to it. He then moves on to report his own view that the speech was delivered in 349. "Why?" he asks (col. 13.42). "Because he mentions things that the Athenians did to the Megarians with regard to the sacred Orgas," he answers (col. 13.42–44). Contrary to his usual practice, however, Didymus does not quote the relevant lemma from Dem. 13.32: "Therefore, from these things such are the affairs of the city that if someone read aloud your decrees and then went through your deeds in detail, nobody would believe the former and the latter to be by the same people. For instance, consider the things that you decreed against the accursed Megarians when they were cutting you off from Orgas, that you should march out, prevent them, and not give way." Didymus quotes part of this passage below in col. 14.49–52, but for a different purpose.

   "Someone might perceive the date of the speech" (χρόνον δ(ὲ) τοῦ λό[γ]ου συν[ί]]δοι τις ἂν, col. 13.40–42) as being 349/8 because, according to Didymus, Demosthenes' mention of the Megarians and Orgas is in reference to something that happened in 350/49, so Dem. 13 must have been delivered in the next year. The fragment of Philochorus (*FGrH* 328 F155, col. 13.47–58) provided Didymus with the date of 350/49 for the affair at Orgas. S. West, 292, notes correctly that the Philochorus passage gives only a terminus post quem for the date of the speech. Likewise, Jacoby characterizes Didymus's reasoning as "rather crude and probably mistaken" (*FGrH* 3b suppl. vol. 2, p. 424). Orgas was an area between Megara and Athens that was to be left uncultivated and untouched, as it was dedicated to the goddesses Demeter and Persephone. Athens had passed a decree to fix new borders for Orgas (*IG II*^{2} 204) in 352/1. "After the god was consulted," explains Connor, "Charinus' Megarian Decree," 237, "the Megarians must have been ordered out of the orgas. They refused, apparently with state backing, and gradually the relations between the two states so deteriorated that Athens resorted to military action." On the "general for the territory," see the Aristotelian *Athenian Constitution* 61. Lacratides the hierophant of Eleusis is mentioned in Isaeus 7.9 (perhaps delivered in 355), where he is referred to as "only recently having become the hierophant" (Λα-κρατείδη τῷ νῦν ἱεροφάντῃ γεγενημένῳ, ed. Thalheim). See also below on cols. 13.62–14.49 on the parallel passage from Androtion (*FGrH* 324 F30). For epigraphical and artistic evidence regarding the hierophant, see Clinton, 10–46, esp. 17–18. On the torchbearer *(daidouchos)*, see Clinton, 47–68, esp. 50. An unconvincing attempt has been made by Connor, "Charinus' Megarian Decree," to associate the affair at Orgas with a mid-fifth century Athenian-Megarian dispute mentioned in Plutarch's *Life of Pericles*. See Bliquez, "Anthemocritus"; Cawkwell, "Anthemocritus"; Harding, *Androtion*, 125–27; also Connor, "Charinus' Megarian Decree Again."

Notes to Cols. 13.62–14.49: In this section Didymus discusses the etymology of the word "Orgas." He opens with the tantalizingly brief statement that "nothing is explored in the speech that has not received some discussion in the ones (sc. speeches or commentaries?) before this" (ζητεῖται δ' ἐν τῶι λόγωι | οὐδὲν ὅτι μὴ λόγου τινὸς ἐν τοῖς πρὸ τοῦ | τέτευχεν, cols. 13.62–14.2). This could be Didymus's justification for the brevity of the commentary on Dem. 13: "All the important topics have already been covered by Demosthenes in orations 1–11 or by me in my commentaries on orations 1–11." A different view is offered by Osborne, 226, who interprets Didymus as "remark[ing] on the fact that Dem[osthenes] does not make any direct requests of the δῆμος in [this speech] because he had been unsuccessful hitherto in persuading the Athenians to follow his plans." This is most likely incorrect. In the next sentence Didymus says: "Nevertheless, the subject of Orgas must be briefly clarified" (col. 14.1–2). This statement seems somewhat apologetic: "Although all the important topics have already been covered in my commentaries on orations 1–11, it is necessary to review some of my earlier discussion of Orgas."

Didymus's etymological study of the word "Orgas" has the advantage of including a greater number of illustrative parallels than the two previous etymological discussions (compare cols. 11.14–26 and 11.52–12.33). The study demonstrates fairly well that the word "Orgas" is related to a cluster of nouns and verbs connoting growth and moisture (on its etymology, see Boisacq, 710; Chantraine, 3: 816). The first part of his study includes several quotations from Greek poetry. The quotation of Sophocles (col. 14.11–12) is included in Radt, 4: 510. The second quotation (col. 14.14–15) has been assigned to Aeschylus's *Eleusinians* and is included as fragment 269 in Mette. The author of the next fragment (col. 14.17–18) may be Euphorion, the third-century author of epigrams, epyllia, and catalogue poems (on whom see Skutsch); the fragment is included in Lloyd-Jones and Parsons, 454. The next selection is from *Iliad* 18.56 or 437 (col. 14.19–20), where Thetis bewails her fate for having given birth to a son who was destined to die young.

The subject of the second section of this discussion is how proper names are often taken from prominent geographical features in the area (col. 14.23–35). For example, Didymus says that Ida "is both the one at Ilion and 'a wooded place'" (ἥ τ' ἐν Ἰλί[ω]ι κ(αὶ) τὸ | δενδρῶδες χωρίον, col. 14.25–26). In his commentaries on Homer he gave a different treatment of this word (frag. 7 in Schmidt, 180–81): "Didymus calls all mountains 'Idas' from the fact that it is possible to look down on (καθορᾶν) everything from them"; or, more to the etymological point, "It should be known that, according to Didymus, Ida is not only the one at Troy, but every mountain, from the fact that it is possible to see (ἰδεῖν) things all around it." A line of Callimachus (col. 14.34–35; frag. 495, ed. Pfeiffer) seems merely decorative; Osborne, 232, suggests that it is included "in order to show that the area had a reputation for fertility and for the produce which was grown there."

Finally, Didymus presents Androtion's account of the affair at Orgas (*FGrH* 324 F30, = *Syll.*³ 204.55, col. 14.37–49). Why does Didymus quote this passage, when he has so recently quoted the derivative one by Philochorus (*FGrH* 328 F155) at col. 13.47–58? He does not say. S. West, 293, sees this as a sign of Didymus's negligence. In her view the quotation of Androtion contains nothing new and "merely shows that [Philochorus] has reproduced his source with scrupulous fidelity. Didymus has evidently looked up his lexicographical files and reproduced the information which he found there without dovetailing it to its present context" (compare also Jacoby, *FGrH* 3b suppl. vol. 1, p. 142). Osborne, 236, argues that the "variations in detail [between the accounts of Androtion and Philochorus] are sufficient to show that Did[ymus] chose to quote Androtion at this point in the commentary because, as compared with Philochorus, this extract placed greater emphasis on the religious import of the Orgas and minimized the controversy between Athens and Megara." Ingenious, if true, but one would prefer Didymus to say or at least imply as much. It seems more likely that Didymus came across a second treatment of Orgas too late to revise his earlier discussion; given the unenviable circumstances of ancient research and writing, the fact that Didymus does not "dovetail" the two accounts is not too surprising.

Notes to Cols. 14.49–15.10: This is a fairly weak explanation of why Demosthenes called the Boeotians and Megarians "accursed" (καταράτους, col. 14.52) in Dem. 13.32. The subsequent quotation from Theopompus (*FGrH* 115 F164, cols. 14.58–15.10) merely attests to the fact that the Boeotians and Megarians did not like the Athenians (δυσ|νόως εἶχον αὐτοὶ κ(αὶ) Βοιωτοὶ πρὸς | Ἀθηναίους, col. 14.53–55). It does not use the specific epithet "accursed" (καταράτους) and does not show why Demosthenes used this specific epithet for them. See notes on cols. 13.25–62 and 13.62–14.49 on the Athenian-Megarian controversy over Orgas.

Notes to the closing title: Berol. 9780 ends with the title: Διδύμου | περὶ Δημοσθένους | ΚΗ | Φιλιππικῶν Γ̄. Literally translated as it appears in the papyrus, this says: "Of Didymus | On Demosthenes | 28 | Of the *Philippics*, 3d." I have expanded the title, rendering it as follows: "Didymus's *On Demosthenes*. Commentaries on 28 Speeches. Book 3 of the *Philippics* Commentaries." But various interpretations have been proposed. Some have argued that the title indicates that this work is a "treatise" rather than a "commentary" (see pp. 51–54 above). Others have pointed to the absence of an overstroke on the numeral 28 as indicating that it is a cardinal (28) rather than an ordinal (28th). D-S[1] accepted the numeral as a cardinal, suggesting that Berol. 9780 is the third and final roll of the *Philippics* portion of a set of commentaries on 28 speeches (D-S[1], xxi–xxix). On this interpretation, the first roll contained the commentaries to Dem. 1–4, and the second contained the commentaries to Dem. 5–8. This view is followed by Sealey, *Demosthenes*, 228. On the other hand, Leo, "Didymos," 393–94, interprets the numeral as meaning book 28. Wilcken, "Die Subskription des Didymus-Papyrus," also suggests that the numeral should be understood as an ordinal, but he explicitly declined to speculate on the significance of this interpretation. There is only one other ancient catalogue-type reference for Didymus's commentaries, a reference to "book 11 of the commentaries on the orators" (Schmidt, 321); this evidence does not illuminate the meaning of the title here. Below the title are four lines giving the numbers and opening words of orations 9–11 and 13. Identification of speeches by their first few words is also seen throughout Dionysius of Halicarnassus *First Letter to Ammaeus*.

Didymus Fragments in Harpocration

This section contains a text, translation, and notes on the fragments of Didymus's commentaries on Demosthenes that are attributed to Didymus by name in Harpocration's *Lexeis of the Ten Orators*. Harpocration's lexicon contains about 1,300 entries on words and phrases found mainly in the Attic orators. Bibliographical references in the lexicon suggest a post-Augustan date. The palaeographical dates of two surviving ancient papyri (*P.Ryl.* 532 and *P.Merton* 30), together with biographical information from *P.Oxy.* 2912 and the *Suda,* suggest that it was written before the end of the second century C.E. A date of composition in the second century C.E. seems secure.[1] An epitome of the lexicon was made before the year 850. Our MSS of the fuller recension all date from after 1300. Absolute alphabetization, from first letter to last, is the general rule. The entries that are out of order—fewer than 10 percent of all entries—are the result of some problems in the transmission of the text and the incomplete application of alphabetization in certain sections.[2]

Harpocration cites Didymus as his source thirty-five times in the lexicon, often summarizing Didymus's position without reproducing his argument (see especially fragments 4 and 5). Two of these citations are in entries not aimed at any particular author (A 196, Θ 16). Fourteen oth-

---

1. See Keaney ed., ix–xi; Hemmerdinger, 107; Turner, "Roman Oxyrhynchus," 91–92.
2. Keaney, "Alphabetization."

ers are in entries on words or phrases found in the orators Aeschines (Θ 34, Κ 80, Ξ 4, Π 2), Dinarchus (M 11), Hyperides (E 35, O 25, Π 124), Lycurgus (Π 96, T 19), and Lysias (Δ 23). Harpocration uses the remaining twenty-one citations of Didymus to define words and phrases in Demosthenes. Three of these citations are explicitly said to come from Didymus's commentaries on Demosthenes (fragments 5, 20, and probably 9). Three could come either from commentaries on Demosthenes or from commentaries on other orators named in the entry (fragments 10, 14, and 15). Eleven other citations of Didymus are keyed so closely to specific passages in Demosthenes that it is difficult to imagine them being derived from anything but his commentaries on Demosthenes (fragments 1–4, 6, 13, 16, 19, 21, and perhaps 7 and 17). Harpocration's remaining four citations of Didymus, by contrast, seem less directly connected to the passages of Demosthenes in question (fragments 8, 11, 12, and 18). In these four cases, it is conceivable that Harpocration took information from a work of Didymus having nothing to do with Demosthenes and reapplied it to passages in Demosthenes in which those same words occur. Parallels for this procedure in Harpocration are found, for example, in his entries for ξηραλοιφεῖν (Ξ 4) and δερμηστής (Δ 23): in the first, Harpocration discusses a word in Aeschines but cites Didymus's lexicon to tragedy (λέξις τραγική) (Schmidt, frag. 1); in the second, he discusses a word in Lysias but cites Didymus's lexicon of difficult words (ἀπορουμένη λέξις) (Schmidt, frag. 1).

Although no other entries in Harpocration contain information explicitly attributed to Demosthenic commentaries or to known commentators, it is possible that some of the entries on Demosthenes whose sources are not named are actually drawn from Didymus,[3] other philological and historical commentators, or lexicographers who drew on them. Harpocration's working methods are still something of a mystery. Though he had access to an impressive array of primary source material —the index to Keaney's edition lists 177 named sources—it is impossible to say which of these sources he consulted directly, and which he simply found mentioned in earlier lexica or commentaries. To complicate matters further, alphabetization of his unalphabetized source lexica has removed some of the evidence of how he compiled his lexicon.[4]

3. D-S[1], xvii; see Florian, 83–85, on Harpocration's knowledge of Anaximenes.
4. Keaney, "Alphabetization."

Text: From Keaney's edition. The entries are presented here in the order in which their lemmata occur in Demosthenes. Previously, P-S, 55–61, reprinted these fragments of Didymus from Schmidt, 310–17, who took his text from Bekker's edition of Harpocration. Schmidt omits fragment 16 and includes fragment 11 as part of Didymus's lexicon on comedy (frag. 18, p. 40). Two words are accidentally omitted from fragment 20 as printed in P-S.

TEXT AND TRANSLATION OF THE
DIDYMUS FRAGMENTS IN HARPOCRATION

1. **Πολύστρατος** (Π 84)· . . . ἄλλος δ' ἂν εἴη Πολύστρατος οὗ μνημονεύει Δημοσθένης ἐν τοῖς Φιλιππικοῖς, λέγων αὐτόν ποτε ἐν Κορίνθῳ ξενικὸν τρέφειν. μήποτε μέντοι ἐνταῦθα δεῖ γράφειν Πολύτροπον ἀντὶ τοῦ Πολυστράτου· παρὰ μηδενὶ γάρ φησιν ὁ Δίδυμος εὑρηκέναι τὸν Πολύστρατον ἡγησάμενον τοῦ ἐν Κορίνθῳ ξενικοῦ. τὸν Πολύτροπον μὲν οὖν ἐν τῇ ῇ τῶν Ἑλληνικῶν Ξενοφῶντος εὗρον· ἀλλ' οὔτε τὸ ξενικὸν τοῦτο ἔφησεν ὁ Ξενοφῶν τρέφεσθαι ὑπ' Ἀθηναίων οὔτε αὐτὸς Ἀθηναῖος ἦν ὁ Πολύτροπος.

Polystratus: [A discussion of two other men named "Polystratus" precedes our fragment.] Another would be the Polystratus whom Demosthenes mentions in the *Philippics* (4.24), saying that he once maintained a mercenary force at Corinth. However, one should perhaps write "Polytropus" there instead of "Polystratus." For Didymus says that he could not find a Polystratus in charge of a mercenary force at Corinth anywhere. I have found a Polytropus in book 8 (sic) of Xenophon's *Hellenica* (6.5.11). But neither did Xenophon say that this mercenary force was maintained by the Athenians, nor was Polytropus himself an Athenian.

2. **Περὶ τῆς ἐν Δελφοῖς σκιᾶς** (Π 54)· Δημοσθένης Φιλιππικοῖς. Δίδυμός φησι τὴν περὶ ὄνου σκιᾶς παροιμίαν παραπεποιῆσθαι ὑπὸ τοῦ ῥήτορος λέγοντος περὶ τῆς ἐν Δελφοῖς σκιᾶς, λέγεσθαι δ' αὐτὴν ἐπὶ τοῖς περὶ τῶν μηδενὸς ἀξίων μαχομένοις.

About the shadow at Delphi: Demosthenes in the *Philippics* (5.25). Didymus says that the proverbial expression "about the shadow of an ass" was adapted by the orator when he says "about the shadow at Delphi," and that the expression was directed at those who were fighting about things that were worth nothing. (See notes on Berol. 21188 [text 4].)

3. Ἑωλοκρασία (E 178)· Δημοσθένης ἐν τῷ Ὑπὲρ Κτησιφῶντος, "αἴτιος δ᾽ οὗτος ὥσπερ ἑωλοκρασίαν τινά μου τῆς πονηρίας τῆς αὑτοῦ κατασκεδάσας." Δίδυμος δέ· "οὗτος ἐχθὲς καὶ πρώην ἃ ἐκέρασε πράγματα, τήμερόν μου καταχεῖ καὶ ἐμὲ πρᾶξαί φησιν."

Mixture of dregs of wine: Demosthenes in *For Ctesiphon* (18.50): "But that man is to blame, as he has splashed on me the mixture-of-dregs-of-wine of his own wickedness." Didymus: "This man pours on me today the things that he mixed up yesterday and the day before and says that I did them."

4. Οἰκίσκῳ (O 7)· ἀντὶ τοῦ μικρῷ τινι οἴκῳ Δημοσθένης ἐν τῷ Ὑπὲρ Κτησιφῶντος. ἐκάλουν δὲ οἱ Ἀττικοὶ τὸ ὑφ᾽ ἡμῶν λεγόμενον ὀρνιθο-τροφεῖον οἰκίσκον· Ἀριστοφάνης Πελαργοῖς, Μεταγένης Αὔραις. ἐκ τούτων δ᾽ ἔοικε πλανώμενος ὁ Δίδυμος καὶ τὸ Δημοσθενικὸν ἐξηγεῖσθαι.

Oikiskos: Instead of "a small house," Demosthenes in *For Ctesiphon* (18.97). The people of Attica used to call what we call a "bird coop" an *oikiskos:* Aristophanes in the *Pelargoi,* Metagenes in the *Aurai.* From these examples, Didymus seems to have offered a misleading interpretation of the Demosthenic usage of this word.

5. Ἔνθρυπτα (E 55)· Δημοσθένης ἐν τῷ Ὑπὲρ Κτησιφῶντος. Δίδυμος ὁ γραμματικὸς ἐν τῷ ὑπομνήματι τοῦ λόγου εἰπὼν ὡς τὰ ἔνθρυπτα ἐκκείμενον καὶ γνώριμον ἀπ᾽ αὐτῆς ἔχει τῆς φωνῆς τὸ σημαινόμενον, περιεργότερόν τινα ἐκτίθεται ἐξήγησιν ἀμάρτυρον . . .

Crumb cakes: Demosthenes in *For Ctesiphon* (18.260). When Didymus the scholar, in his commentary on this speech, says that "crumb cakes" has a meaning that is clear and recognizable from the sound itself, he proposes an explanation that is overwrought and without a parallel . . .

6. Ἐσπαθᾶτο (E 143)· Δημοσθένης ἐν τῷ Κατ᾽ Αἰσχίνου. Δίδυμός φησιν ἀντὶ τοῦ ἀπώλλυτο, παρὰ τὴν σπάθην, σπάθη δέ ἐστι ξίφος . . .

It was "bladed": Demosthenes in *Against Aeschines* (19.43). Didymus says that this word is used instead of "it was destroyed," from the *spathe;* the *spathe* is a kind of sword . . .

7. Παρασκήνια (Π 29)· Δημοσθένης ἐν τῷ Κατὰ Μειδίου. ἔοικε παρασκήνια καλεῖσθαι, ὡς καὶ Θεόφραστος ἐν κ̄ Νόμων ὑποσημαίνει, ὁ παρὰ τὴν σκηνὴν ἀποδεδειγμένος τόπος ταῖς εἰς τὸν ἀγῶνα παρα-

σκευαῖς. ὁ δὲ Δίδυμος τὰς ἑκατέρωθεν τῆς ὀρχήστρας εἰσόδους οὕτω φησὶ καλεῖσθαι.

Parascenia: Demosthenes in *Against Meidias* (21.17). As Theophrastus indicates in book 20 of the *Laws*, the place beside the stage (παρὰ τὴν σκηνὴν) that was designated for the props for the play seems to have been called the *parascenia*. But Didymus says that the entrances to either side of the orchestra were called by this name.

8. **Κυμβίον** (K 92)· Δημοσθένης ἐν τῷ Κατὰ Μειδίου. εἶδός τι ἐκπώματος τὸ κυμβίον. φησὶ δὲ Δίδυμος ἐπίμηκες αὐτὸ εἶναι καὶ στενὸν καὶ τῷ σχήματι παρόμοιον τῷ πλοίῳ ὃ καλεῖται κυμβίον.

Cymbion: Demosthenes in *Against Meidias* (21.133). A *cymbion* is a kind of drinking cup. Didymus says that it is oblong and narrow and shaped like the boat that is called a *cymbion*.

9. **Δεκατεύειν** (Δ 16)· Δημοσθένης Κατ' Ἀνδροτίωνος: "οὐ γὰρ αὐτοὺς δεκατεύοντες," ἀντὶ τοῦ τὴν δεκάτην εἰσπραττόμενοι καὶ οἷον λαφυραγωγοῦντες· τὰ γὰρ ἐκ τῶν πολέμων ληφθέντα ἐδεκάτευον τοῖς θεοῖς. Δημοσθένους δ' ἐν τῷ Κατὰ Μέδοντος περί τινος παρθένου λέγοντος οὕτως: "οὐ δεκατεῦσαι ταύτην οὐδὲ μυῆσαι," Δίδυμος ὁ γραμματικὸς περὶ τούτου βιβλίον γράψας φησὶν ὅτι τὸ δεκατεῦσαι Λυσίας ἐν τῷ Περὶ τῆς Φρυνίχου θυγατρὸς ἀρκτεῦσαι εἴρηκεν. δεκατεῦσαι μέντοι, φησίν, ἐλέγετο κυρίως τὸ καθιερῶσαι, ἐπειδήπερ ἔθος ἦν Ἑλληνικὸν τὰς δεκάτας τῶν περιγινομένων τοῖς θεοῖς καθιεροῦν...

To pay a tithe: Demosthenes in *Against Androtion* (22.77): "For not by tithing themselves," instead of "collecting the tithe," and, as it were, "plundering." For they used to dedicate a tenth of the sums seized in wars to the gods. When Demosthenes says as follows about a certain young woman in *Against Medon,* namely, that "she has neither paid her tithe nor celebrated the mysteries," Didymus the scholar in his book on the subject/speech says that Lysias, in *Concerning the Daughter of Phrynichus,* said that "to pay a tithe" means "to act the she-bear." However, he says that " to pay a tithe" properly means "to dedicate," since it was a Greek custom to dedicate a tenth of the surplus to the gods . . .

10. **Ὁ κάτωθεν νόμος** (O 14)· Δημοσθένης ἐν τῷ Κατ' Ἀριστοκράτους. Δίδυμος: "ἤτοι," φησί, "τὴν ἡλιαίαν λέγει ὁ ῥήτωρ διὰ τὸ τῶν δικαστηρίων τὰ μὲν ἄνω τὰ δὲ κάτω ὀνομάζεσθαι, ἢ διὰ τὸ σχῆμα τῆς ἐν τοῖς ἄξοσι γραφῆς βουστροφηδὸν γεγραμμένης ἢ τὸν ἀπὸ τῶν

εὐωνύμων ἀρχομένον νόμον κάτωθεν ὀνομάζει ὁ Δημοσθένης· ὅτι
γάρ," φησί, "βουστροφηδὸν ἦσαν οἱ ἄξονες καὶ οἱ κύρβεις γεγραμμένοι δεδήλωκεν Εὐφορίων ἐν τῷ Ἀπολλοδώρῳ. ἢ ἐπεί," φησί, "τοὺς
ἄξονας καὶ τοὺς κύρβεις ἄνωθεν ἐκ τῆς ἀκροπόλεως εἰς τὸ βουλευτήριον καὶ τὴν ἀγορὰν μετέστησεν Ἐφιάλτης, ὥς φησιν Ἀναξιμένης
ἐν Φιλιππικοῖς."

The law (from) below: Demosthenes in *Against Aristocrates* (23.28).
Didymus says: "Either the orator means the Heliaea because the courts
were called upper and lower, or because the writing on the *axones* was
boustrophedon, in which a law that begins from the left Demosthenes
calls 'from below.' For Euphorion in *Apollodorus* made it clear that
the *axones* and the *cyrbeis* were written boustrophedon. Or because
Ephialtes moved the *axones* and the *cyrbeis* from the Acropolis down to
the Bouleuterion and the Agora, as Anaximenes says in the *Philippica*"
(*FGrH* 72 F13). (See notes on Berol. 5008 [text 3].)

11. **Ποδοκάκκη** (Π 76)· Δημοσθένης Κατὰ Τιμοκράτους. τὸ ξύλον τὸ
ἐν τῷ δεσμωτηρίῳ οὕτως ἐκαλεῖτο, ἤτοι παρεμβεβλημένου τοῦ ἑτέρου
κ, ποδῶν τις κάκωσις οὖσα, ἢ κατὰ συγκοπήν, ὥς φησι Δίδυμος, οἷον
ποδοκατοχή. Λυσίας δ' ἐν τῷ Κατὰ Θεομνήστου, εἰ γνήσιος, ἐξηγεῖ-
ται τοὔνομα· φησὶ γάρ: "ἡ ποδοκάκκη αὐτό ἐστιν ὃ νῦν καλεῖται ἐν
τῷ ξύλῳ δεδέσθαι."

Podokakke: Demosthenes in *Against Timocrates* (24.105). The
wooden stock *(xylon)* in the prison was called by this name—either the
second *kappa* being superfluous, because it is an evil for the feet, or
as Didymus says, it is a syncopated form of *podokatoche* (foot posses-
sor). Lysias in *Against Theomnestus* (10.16), if it is genuine, explains the
word: "The *podokakke* is the same thing as what is now called being
bound in the 'wooden stock' *(xylon)*."

12. **Ὅσιον** (Ο 38)· . . . ὅτι δὲ τὰ ὅσια τὰ δημόσια δηλοῖ Δημοσθένης
ἐν τῷ Κατὰ Τιμοκράτους σαφῶς διδάσκει περὶ τούτων: "καὶ τὰ μὲν
ἱερά, τὰς δεκάτας τῆς θεοῦ καὶ τὰς πεντηκοστὰς τῶν ἄλλων θεῶν,
σεσυληκότες," καὶ μετ' ὀλίγα, "τὰ δὲ ὅσια ἃ ἐγίνετο ἡμέτερα κεκλο-
φότες." Δίδυμος δέ: "διχῶς," φησίν, "ἔλεγον τὸ ὅσιον, τό τε ἱερὸν καὶ
τὸ ἰδιωτικόν."

Hosion: . . . Demosthenes in *Against Timocrates* (24.120) clearly
instructs about the fact that "profane things" *(hosia)* means "public
things" *(demosia)*, both where he says: "Having pillaged the sacred things
(hiera)—the tithes of the goddess and the one-fiftieth of the other gods," and a

bit later, "And having stolen the profane things *(hosia)*, which were ours." Didymus says: "They used to say 'profane' *(hosion)* in two ways: 'sacred' *(hieron)* and 'private' *(idiotikon)*."

13. **Φαρμακός** (Φ 5)· . . . Δημοσθένους δ' ἐν τῷ Κατ' Ἀριστογείτονος λέγοντος, "οὗτος οὖν αὐτὸν ἐξαιρήσεται ὁ φαρμακός;" Δίδυμος προπερισπᾶν ἀξιοῖ τοὔνομα. ἀλλ' ἡμεῖς οὐχ εὕρομεν οὕτω που τὴν χρῆσιν.

Scapegoat: . . . Where Demosthenes in *Against Aristogeiton* (25.80) says: "And so will this man beg him off, this scapegoat?" Didymus would have us accent the word with a circumflex on the penult. But I do not find this usage anywhere.

14. **Προστασία** (Π 106)· Δημοσθένης ἐν τῷ Κατὰ Ὀνήτορος: "ταῦτα οὐχ ὁμολογουμένη προστασία;" ἀντὶ τοῦ βοήθεια προϊσταμένου τινὸς καὶ ἐπικουροῦντος τῷ ἀδικουμένῳ. Αἰσχίνης ἐν τῷ Περὶ τῆς πρεσβείας: "ὡς δεῖ τὰ τῆς Ἀθηναίων ἀκροπόλεως προπύλαια μετενεγκεῖν εἰς τὴν προστασίαν τῆς Καδμείας." Δίδυμος τὴν προστασίαν φησὶ κεῖσθαι ἀντὶ τῆς προστάσεως, τουτέστι τῆς ὑπ' ἐνίων προστάδος καλουμένης.

Prostasia: Demosthenes in *Against Onetor* (30.30): "Is this not admittedly a façade *(prostasia)?*" is used instead of "(is this not admittedly) the assistance of someone who is protecting and helping someone who is being wronged?" Aeschines in *On the Embassy* (2.105): "That it is necessary to transfer the Propylaea of the Athenian Acropolis to the *prostasia* (entrance) of the Cadmeia." Didymus says that *prostasia* appears here in place of *prostasis,* namely, the thing called by some a *prostas* (vestibule).

15. **Πρόπεμπτα** (Π 99)· Λυσίας ἐν τῷ Πρὸς τὴν Μιξιδήμου γραφήν, εἰ γνήσιος, καὶ Δημοσθένης ἐν τῷ Περὶ τοῦ Ἁγνίου κλήρου. Δίδυμος: "μήποτε," φησίν, "ἄλλα τινά ἐστιν ἐπιτίμια τὰ πρὸ τῆς καταβολῆς· εἰσὶ γὰρ οἳ τὰ πέμπτα τῶν τιμημάτων παρακαταβάλλεσθαί φασιν, ὡς Λυσίας ἐν τῷ Κατὰ Ἀπολλοδώρου ὑποσημαίνει. εἰ μὴ ἄρα πρόπεμπτα ὡς Δημοσθένης πρὸ ἡμερῶν πέντε· ταῖς γὰρ μεγάλαις δίκαις οὐκ ἥρκει μία ἡμέρα πρὸς τὴν κρίσιν."

Propempta: Lysias in *Against the Indictment of Meixidemus,* if it is genuine, and Demosthenes in *Concerning the Estate of Hagnias* (43.75). Didymus says: "This is perhaps some other payment that comes before the deposit. For there are those who say that one-fifth of the disputed sum is laid down as a deposit, as Lysias indicates in *Against Apollodorus*. Unless the word *propempta* means 'five days earlier,' as in Demosthenes. For a single day was not enough notice for a trial in the most important cases."

16. Ἐπὶ διετὲς ἡβῆσαι (E 94)· Δημοσθένης ἐν τῷ Κατὰ Στεφάνου. Δίδυμός φησιν ἀντὶ τοῦ ἐὰν ιϛ ἐτῶν γένωνται· τὸ γὰρ ἡβῆσαι μέχρι ιδ ἐστιν. ἀλλ' οἱ ἔφηβοι παρ' Ἀθηναίοις ὀκτωκαιδεκαετεῖς γίνονται, καὶ μένουσιν ἐν τοῖς ἐφήβοις ἔτη β, ἔπειτα τῷ ληξιαρχικῷ ἐγγράφονται γραμματείῳ, καθά φησιν Ὑπερείδης ἐν τῷ Πρὸς Χάρητα ἐπιτροπικῷ· "ἐπεὶ δὲ ἐνεγράφην ἐγὼ καὶ ὁ νόμος ἀπέδωκε τὴν κομιδὴν τῶν καταλειφθέντων τῇ μητρί, ὃς κελεύει κυρίους εἶναι τῆς ἐπικλήρου καὶ τῆς οὐσίας ἁπάσης τοὺς παῖδας, ἐπειδὰν ἐπὶ διετὲς ἡβῶσιν."

Two years after *hebe*: Demosthenes in *Against Stephanus* (46.20). Didymus says: "This is used instead of 'if they are sixteen years old.' For *hebe* extends to age fourteen." But the Athenian ephebes are eighteen years old, and they remain in this state for two years (i.e., ages 18–20), whereupon they are enrolled in the deme register, as Hyperides says in the guardianship speech *Against Chares*: "Since I was enrolled, and the law gave (me) the supervision of what was left to my mother, the law that bids sons to be in charge of the heiress and all the property, whenever they are two years past *hebe*."

17. Λυκιουργεῖς (Λ 31)· Δημοσθένης ἐν τῷ Πρὸς Τιμόθεον. Δίδυμός φησι τὰς ὑπὸ Λυκίου κατεσκευασμένας φιάλας τοῦ Μύρωνος υἱοῦ οὕτως εἰρῆσθαι. ἀγνοεῖν δὲ ἔοικεν ὁ γραμματικὸς ὅτι τὸν τοιοῦτον σχηματισμὸν ἀπὸ κυρίων ὀνομάτων οὐκ ἄν τις εὕροι γινόμενον, μᾶλλον δὲ ἀπὸ πόλεων καὶ ἐθνῶν· "κλίνη Μιλησιουργής" Κριτίας φησὶν ἐν τῇ Λακεδαιμονίων πολιτείᾳ. μήποτ' οὖν γραπτέον καὶ παρ' Ἡροδότῳ ἐν τῇ ζ, ἀντὶ τοῦ προβόλους δύο Λυκοεργέας, Λυκιεργέας, ἵνα ὥσπερ παρὰ τῷ Δημοσθένει οὕτως ὀνομάζηται τὰ ἐν Λυκίᾳ εἰργασμένα.

Lycian-made: Demosthenes in *Against Timotheus* (49.31). Didymus says that the cups made by Lycius, son of Myron, were called by this name. But the scholar apparently does not know that one would not find such a form made from individuals' names, but rather from the names of cities or peoples. Critias mentions a "Milesian-made bed" in the *Spartan Constitution*. So perhaps one should write also in Herodotus, book 7, "two Λυκιεργέας spears" instead of "two Λυκοεργέας spears," so thereby to indicate things produced in Lycia, just as in the passage from Demosthenes.

18. **Περίστοιχοι** (Π 63)· Δημοσθένης ἐν τῷ Πρὸς Νικόστρατον περὶ τῶν Ἀρεθουσίου ἀνδραπόδων: "φυτευτήρια ἐλαῶν περιστοίχων κατέκλασεν." Δίδυμος δέ τι γένος ἐλαιῶν περιστοίχους καλεῖ, ἃς Φιλόχορος στοιχάδας προσηγόρευσε . . .

Peristoichoi: Demosthenes in *Against Nicostratus* (53.15), concerning the slaves of Arethusius: "He broke down the nurseries of olive trees that were set round in rows *(peristoichoi)*." Didymus calls a certain variety of olive trees *peristoichoi*, which Philochorus called *stoichades* . . . (*FGrH* 328 F180)

19. **Ἐξένιζε** (Ε 66)· Δημοσθένης ἐν τῇ Πρὸς Εὐβουλίδην ἐφέσει: "διαβεβλήκασι γάρ μου τὸν πατέρα ὡς ἐξένιζε." μήποτε ἀντὶ τοῦ ξένος ἦν, καὶ οὐχ ὡς Δίδυμός φησιν, ἀντὶ τοῦ οὐκ Ἀττικῶς διελέγετο, ἀλλὰ ξενικῶς.

He foreignized: Demosthenes in the appeal speech *Against Eubulides* (57.18–19): "For they have slandered my father, saying that he foreignized." This is probably instead of "he was a foreigner," and not, as Didymus says, instead of "he spoke foreign-ly rather than Attic-ly."

20. **Γαμηλία** (Γ 2)· Δημοσθένης ἐν τῇ Πρὸς Εὐβουλίδην ἐφέσει, καὶ Ἰσαῖος. καὶ Δίδυμος ὁ γραμματικὸς ἐν μὲν τοῖς Ἰσαίου ὑπομνήμασί φησιν εἶναι γαμηλίαν τὴν τοῖς φράτορσιν ἐπὶ γάμοις διδομένην, παρατιθέμενος λέξιν Φανοδήμου, ἐν ᾗ οὐδὲν τοιοῦτον γέγραπται. ἐν δὲ τοῖς εἰς Δημοσθένην ὁ αὐτὸς πάλιν γαμηλίαν φησὶν εἶναι τὴν εἰς τοὺς φράτορας εἰσαγωγὴν τῶν γυναικῶν, οὐδεμίαν ἀπόδειξιν τῆς ἐξηγήσεως παραθέμενος.

Wedding feast: Demosthenes in the appeal speech *Against Eubulides* (57.43, 69), and Isaeus (3.76, 3.79, 8.18, 8.20). And Didymus the scholar in his *Commentaries on Isaeus* says that a wedding feast was given at weddings to one's fellow clansmen, adducing an expression of Phanodemus, in which no such thing is written. In the *Commentaries on Demosthenes*, the same author again says that a wedding feast is the introduction of wives to the clansmen, but he gives no evidence for this interpretation.

21. **Πωλῶσι** (Π 131)· Δημοσθένης ἐν τῷ Κατὰ Νεαίρας: "ἢ ἐν τῇ ἀγορᾷ πωλῶσί τι ἀποπεφασμένως." Δίδυμός φησιν ἀντὶ τοῦ πορνεύ-

ὡσι φανερῶς· πωλεῖν γὰρ τὸ παρέχειν ἑαυτὴν τοῖς βουλομένοις, ὅθεν
καὶ τὸ πορνεύειν, ὅπερ ἐστὶ περνάναι . . .

They sell: Demosthenes in *Against Neaera* (59.67): "Or they openly sell
something in the Agora." Didymus says that this is instead of "they publicly
prostitute themselves." For *polein* (to sell) means for a woman to *par-
echein* (offer) herself to those who want her, whence also the word *por-
neuein* (to prostitute), which means *pernanai* (to sell) . . .

NOTES ON THE DIDYMUS FRAGMENTS IN HARPOCRATION

1. Harpocration says that "Polystratus" in Dem. 4.24 may be in error for "Polytropus." He appears to have drawn this conclusion from
reading Didymus (note the explanatory γάρ), who said that he could not
find any other reference to a Polystratus who had been in charge of a
mercenary force at Corinth. Harpocration takes the lack of a parallel for
"Polystratus" as an opportunity to suggest a correction to the text of
Demosthenes. The relationship between his conclusion and Didymus's
unreported conclusions is not clear; it is important to note that Harpocration does not expressly attribute the suggested correction to Didymus. Harpocration found someone with the superficially similar name
Polytropus in Xenophon *Hellenica* 6.5.11, which mentions "the mercenary force gathered at Corinth, which Polytropus commanded." In
Xenophon, this Polytropus is said to be in charge of a mercenary force
at Corinth, as the context of Dem. 4.24 demands: "I hear that at an
earlier time Athens maintained a mercenary force at Corinth, whose
commanders were Polystratus, Iphicrates, Chabrias, and others." Parke,
Greek Mercenary Soldiers, 50 n. 4, incorrectly understands "Polytropus" to be a suggestion of Didymus that Harpocration rejects; Pritchett,
119 n. 17, understands it correctly.

Polystratus is not mentioned outside of Demosthenes. He is most
likely the same Polystratus who was rewarded for his service under
Iphicrates in the Corinthian War (Dem. 20.84). Dem. 20.84 implies that
Polystratus was a subordinate and not an Athenian citizen; Parke, *Greek
Mercenary Soldiers,* 50; Harding, *Androtion,* 170–71. He may have
helped gather or may even have been a commander of one of the original parts of the mercenary force raised by Conon and later commanded
by Iphicrates; Parke, *Greek Mercenary Soldiers,* 50. See also the notes
on μόραν in Berol. 5008. He may have been a Thracian mercenary commander, according to Harding, *Androtion,* 170. On the Corinthian War,
see Cartledge, 218–26, 360–68. On mercenaries in the service of Ath-

ens in the fourth century, see Parke, *Greek Mercenary Soldiers*, 48–57; Pritchett, 59–125, esp. 117–25.

Little else is known about Polytropus. According to Diodorus 16.52, he was the leader of a Spartan-sponsored force to Arcadia in 344/3. H. Schaefer, 1839, suggests that he may have been a Spartan.

2. This fragment is discussed along with its parallel in the notes on Berol. 21188 (text 4).

3. Didymus explains ἑωλοκρασία in Dem. 18.50 with a paraphrase designed to emphasize the etymology of the word. Didymus apparently understands ἑωλοκρασία as being derived from ἕωλος (yesterday's) and κρασία (mixture), although he does not make the point explicit. If Harpocration has abbreviated Didymus's treatment of the etymology, he does not say enough to show conclusively that he understands how Didymus's paraphrase works. It is interesting to note that Didymus sticks with Demosthenes' wine metaphor. Κεράννυμι is a verb commonly associated with the preparation of wine for drinking, and καταχέω can be used of pouring anything.

4. Harpocration says that οἰκίσκῳ in Dem. 18.97 should be understood as "a small house" rather than (as Didymus argued) a "bird coop." Harpocration acknowledges that the Athenians formerly used the word to mean a "bird coop" (ὀρνιθοτροφεῖον), as in the comic poets Aristophanes (see under frag. 446 in vol. 3.2 of Kassel and Austin: τί δὲ τὸν ὀρνίθειον οἰκίσκον φέρεις;) and Metagenes (frag. 5 in vol. 7 of Kassel and Austin). Several other fragments of Aristophanes' *Pelargoi* are known, but these reveal nothing about the play's plot or characters (Kassel and Austin, frags. 444–45, 447–57). Four other fragments of Metagenes' *Aurai* survive (Kassel and Austin, frags. 1–4), but again, little is known about the play. But despite these parallels, Harpocration argues that Didymus is mistaken to interpret the word as meaning "bird coop" in Dem. 18.97. It is interesting that Harpocration not only documents his predecessor's alleged mistake but even mentions the evidence that he misapplied on the way to making the alleged mistake.

But is Didymus actually mistaken? Citing Aristophanes as his authority, Pollux 9.39 says that the word οἰκίσκος can refer to a birdcage (ὀρνίθειον) and a partridge cage (περδικικόν). Likewise, Aelian *Historia Animalium* 3.40 (ed. Hercher) says that a bird shut in a cage (καθειρ-γμένη . . . ἐν οἰκίσκῳ) won't sing (note 8.24: ἐν οἰκίσκῳ . . . καθεῖρξεν).

This verb καθείργνυμι is the same one used in Dem. 18.97, κἂν ἐν οἰκίσκῳ τις αὐτὸν καθείρξας τηρῇ. In addition, Demosthenes is known to have borrowed from poetry in orations 18 and 19; see S. Perlman, "Quotations." Nevertheless, the meaning "birdcage" does not seem to be in keeping with the tone of this section of Dem. 18. Harpocration's interpretation is the correct one.

5. According to Harpocration, Didymus believed that the sound of the word ἔνθρυπτα somehow conveys its meaning. This is the only fragment of the ancient philological and historical commentaries on Demosthenes in which an author connects the meaning of a word with its sound. Some ancient literary critics were interested in what Russell, *Criticism,* 111, calls "the 'mimetic' use of language," which "was discussed in ancient theory in connection both with word-groupings (figures and arrangement) and with individual words and sounds." Though this must be the field in which Didymus is working here, Harpocration's entry is not very revealing. It is not even entirely certain what Harpocration means by the word's "clear and recognizable" meaning, though he does go on to mention crumb cakes made from pastry (τὰ ἐκ πεμμάτων) and crumbled foods (τὰ ἐνθρυβόμενα βρώματα) used in sacrifices to Apollo. Two fragments of Didymus's lexicon to comedy show a similar interest in cakes: βόρακες (frag. 25 in Schmidt, 44) and πέλανος (frag. 17 in Schmidt, 40).

6. Didymus explains the etymology and meaning of the verb ἐσπαθᾶτο, which he correctly says derives from the noun σπάθη; for the etymology see Boisacq, 888–89. But he chooses the wrong meaning of σπάθη for the context. The meanings of σπάθη range from any sort of blade to the one used specifically in weaving. The previous sentence in Dem. 19.43 (from before the lemma) ends with the word ἀπολοῦνται, which may account for Didymus's statement that Demosthenes used the verb ἐσπαθᾶτο instead of ἀπώλλυτο. Whatever the reason, Didymus equates ἐσπαθᾶτο with ἀπώλλυτο (it was destroyed), and σπάθη with ξίφος (sword). If we may expand here, this suggests that Didymus understands the verb ἐσπαθᾶτο to mean "it was destroyed with a sword." Harpocration's interpretation of the word is different: "Perhaps it is a metaphor from weavers, for they use a *spathe.* And Aristophanes in the *Clouds* (line 55): 'Woman, you use the *spathe* too much.'" Dover's explanation of this line is useful here: "Excessive use of the blade packs the thread too tight and is therefore extravagant. Hence σπαθᾶν is used

metaphorically of extravagance. . . . If the old man holds up part of his himation to show us that it is threadbare (because he is now impoverished), the joke is that his wife's metaphorical λίαν σπαθᾶν has had the opposite result from literal λίαν σπαθᾶν" (Dover, 101). A similar view is reported by the scholia to Dem. 19.43 (Dilts 115c), which also cites the Aristophanes passage as its authority: "It was woven, it was constructed, or it was lavish, from the act of putting a lot of woof in the warp for clothing" (ὑφαίνετο, κατεσκευάζετο ἢ ἐπεδαψιλεύετο, ἀπὸ τοῦ σπαθᾶν καὶ πολλὴν κρόκην ἐμβάλλειν τῇ ἐσθῆτι; similarly, the B scholia to Demosthenes ad loc., ed. Baiter and Sauppe). Demosthenes' usage of this word is better explained by Harpocration and the scholiast than by Didymus.

7. Harpocration pits Didymus against Theophrastus on the meaning and location of the theatre's *parascenia*. According to Haigh (146 n. 2), Meidias in the target passage was guilty of "preventing [Demosthenes'] dithyrambic chorus from making its appearance. Probably he nailed up the doors out of the side-wings into the *parodoi*." Haigh apparently sides with Didymus; also Weil, *Plaidoyers*, ad loc. So also the scholiast to Dem. 21.17 (Dilts 76), who glosses τὰ παρασκήνια φράττων as "blocking off the entrances next to the *skene*" (ἀποφράττων τὰς ἐπὶ τῆς σκηνῆς εἰσόδους; similarly, the B scholia to Demosthenes ad loc., ed. Baiter and Sauppe). The scholiast goes on to explain that the chorus would then have to enter through the outside entrance, which would make the audience ridicule Demosthenes. The fragment of Theophrastus is not included in the editions of Wimmer or Link and Schneider, but it appears as fragment 16 in Szegedy-Maszak and fragment 24 in Hager.

8. Didymus describes the *cymbion* as a cup shaped like the boat of the same name. Athenaeus, Hesychius, the *Suda*, Eustathius's commentary on the *Iliad*, the scholia to Lucian, and Macrobius all know of a boat called a *cymbion*. Athenaeus 11.481F gives the same explanation as Harpocration and likewise attributes it to Didymus. Hesychius (ed. Latte) says that a *cymbion* is "a kind of drinking cup and a kind of boat" (εἶδος ποτηρίου καὶ πλοίου). The entry for the word in the *Suda*, the scholia to Lucian (ed. Rabe, no. 77, sect. 2, line 3), and Eustathius (ed. Van der Valk, vol. 2, p. 152, line 19; also vol. 4, p. 155, line 31) use almost the same words as Didymus. According to Macrobius *Saturnalia* 5.21.1–19 (ed. Willis), *cymbia* are rarely mentioned in Greek and Latin authors (5.21.2, 7–8), but they are part of a group of four kinds

of cups—the others are *carchesia, canthari,* and *scyphi*—whose names in some way are related to boats. *Carchesia* are named after the topmost part of the sail (5.21.4–5), and *canthari* and *scyphi* are both boatshaped (5.21.14–16). Though there is a theory that the word *cymbium* is a syncopated form of *cissybium,* the word for another kind of cup (5.21.11), Macrobius argues that it is actually "a diminutive form of *cymba,* which both for the Greeks and for us, who derived it from the Greeks, is a kind of ship" ("diminutive a cymba dicta, quod et apud Graecos et apud nos ab illis trahentes navigii genus est"). The *cantharus, carchesion, cymbion,* and *scyphus* are also discussed in Athenaeus (11.473D–474D, 474D–475C, 481D–482E, 498A–500C). Although Macrobius never names Athenaeus as his source, he is known to have derived material from him (Cameron, 28–29). See also the notes on Harpocration fragment 17. Three fragments of Didymus's lexicon to comedy show a similar interest in cups: βαλανειόμφαλοι (frag. 24 in Schmidt, 42), κιβώριον (frag. 39 in Schmidt, 75), and λαβρώνιον (frag. 41 in Schmidt, 75). Didymus's discussion has been picked up by the scholia to Demosthenes ad loc. (Dilts 471ab; also the B scholia, ed. Baiter and Sauppe).

9. According to Harpocration, in Didymus's (lost) commentary on the (lost) oration *Against Medon* (frag. 8, Baiter and Sauppe), he used a parallel from Lysias's (lost) oration *Concerning the Daughter of Phrynichus* (frag. 125, ed. Thalheim) to explain "paying a tithe" as a metaphor for "celebrating the mysteries." The word δεκατεύειν can be used in several senses: to make a person or city pay a tithe, to offer a tithe, to be a δεκατευτής (a person who collects tithes), or to decimate. Wayte, ad loc., comments that this verb is "used quite generally for any excessive taxation." It is not possible to know whether "exacting the tithe" in the two lost orations really has anything to do with "acting the shebear." Harpocration adds, not very helpfully, that ten-year-old girls (αἱ δεκετίδες) acted the she-bear, which he says could explain why Demosthenes uses δεκατεῦσαι to mean "to act the she-bear." The Lysias fragment is also found in Harpocration, s.v. ἀρκτεῦσαι, an entry that provides no information that is not well known from other earlier sources. The locus classicus of "acting the she-bear" in honor of Artemis is Aristophanes *Lysistrata* 641, where the chorus lists it among the civic duties of young girls. For further discussion of the evidence for acting the shebear in honor of Artemis, see P. Perlman, esp. 118 n. 34, and 121 n. 46.

10. This fragment is discussed along with its parallel in the notes on Berol. 5008 (text 3).

11. The main purpose of this entry is to explain the form of the word ποδοκάκκη. Harpocration suggests that the second *kappa* is superfluous, which would leave the ending κάκη, "evil." He then reports Didymus's suggestion that ποδοκάκκη is a syncopated form of ποδοκατοχή. Wayte, ad loc., thinks that Didymus is correct. But Harpocration's view is partially followed by Boisacq, 798, who places the second *kappa* in parentheses; unlike Harpocration, Boisacq links it to the word κάκαλα (as in the expression κάκαλα τείχη, "surrounding walls") and other etymologically related words signifying "restraint." This interpretation is followed by Chantraine, 481. The word ποδοκάκκη was already archaic by the time of Demosthenes, which suggests that the law mentioning the ποδοκάκκη was also of great antiquity (Harrison, 2: 177 n. 4). On the use of imprisonment as a penalty in Athens, see Harrison, 2: 166 and 177; for other uses of imprisonment—to ensure that the defendant shows up for the trial, and, after conviction, to make sure that a fine is paid—see Harrison 2: 241–44. This discussion is picked up by the B scholia to Demosthenes ad loc. (ed. Baiter and Sauppe).

12. Harpocration explains the difference between ὅσιον and ἱερόν. Both terms refer to things that are to be respected, but ὅσια belong to human beings (they are "ours," ἡμέτερα), while ἱερά belong to the gods. According to Harpocration, Didymus had asserted that the meaning of ὅσια was once equivalent to or covered by the words ἱερά and ἰδιωτικά. It would be interesting to see Didymus's evidence for this, because he appears to be wrong: Harpocration's distinction between ὅσιον and ἱερόν is standard. For a discussion of the meanings and importance of the terms ὅσια and ἱερά in classical Greece, see Connor, " 'Sacred' and 'Secular.' "

13. Didymus suggests an unusual accent for the word φαρμακός, with a circumflex on the penult (φαρμᾶκος). Photius says that this is an Ionian usage: "The Ionians, stretching it out (ἐκτείνοντες), say φαρμᾶκον" (from Schmidt, 314). Naber, 2: 256, accents the word correctly in his edition, apparently missing the point of the remark. Didymus's suggested accentuation of the word is possible only if the second *alpha* is considered long. This is the only passage in the ancient philo-

logical and historical commentaries on Demosthenes that discusses accentuation or pronunciation. Harpocration rejects this suggestion because he has not seen a parallel for it.

14. Didymus is commenting on the fact that προστασία, πρόστασις, and προστάς are etymologically related synonyms, since they all refer to something that "stands in front" (from προΐστημι). This group of words includes anything from a human supporter to an architectural element. Didymus follows the interpretation suggested by the quotation from Aeschines 2.105.

15. Didymus gives two possible interpretations for *propempta:* the one-fifth of a disputed amount that is laid down as a deposit, or a five-days advance warning for a trial. On purely etymological grounds, either interpretation is possible, προ- meaning "in advance" or "in place of," and -πεμπτα meaning "fifths." The other fragments of the Lysias speech (whose authenticity Harpocration questions) are found in Harpocration, s.vv. Μουσαῖος, διῆρξα, ἐπιθέτους ἑορτάς, Λέχαιον, προχειροτονία (list from Thalheim's edition, 354). The two mentioned here are included as fragments 91 and 12 in Thalheim's edition. The fragment of *Against Apollodorus* is the only one extant.

In general on Athenian process at law, see Harrison, 2: 69–199; on the issuing of a summons, 85–88. Adducing Aristophanes *Clouds* 1131ff., Harrison, 2: 87, demonstrates that the summons, when required, was to be made at least four days (five, counting inclusively) before the appearance before the magistrate. In the Aristophanes passage, Strepsiades is summoned four days before the last day of the month, for a court date of the last day of the month. On the παρακαταβολή, the one-tenth of a disputed sum in an inheritance case that each claimant must put down in advance, see Harrison, 2: 179–83. The word παρακαταβολή is somewhat confusing because it has a general sense and a more specific one. Generally speaking, a παρακαταβολή is *any* deposit laid down in advance by the litigants, but the more specific meaning is "a deposit related to the value of the matter at issue, which was forfeited by the litigant, either to the other litigant or to the state, if he failed to win the case, or in some instances if he failed to secure one-fifth of the votes" (Harrison, 2: 179–80). The usual amount is one-tenth of the disputed sum, but Harrison (2: 180), relying in part on the evidence of Harpocration, s.v. παρακαταβολὴ καὶ παρακαταβάλλειν, argues that "when a property confiscated by the state was put up for auction, there was a procedure by which anyone who wished to assert a claim on that property could put in an objection (ἐνεπίσκηψις)," and this person "had to deposit before the issue was tried one-fifth of the value of his claim, which became forfeit to the state if he lost." Note, however, that the term *propempta* is not used in connection with the παρακαταβολή. It seems, then, that Didymus knows about the particular kind of case for which one might lay down a deposit of one-fifth, but he is probably incorrect to associate it with the word *propempta*. Didymus's discussion of the ἐπωβελία (unknown works, frag. 8 in Schmidt, 402) reflects similar interests.

16. Responding to Dem. 46.20, Didymus and Harpocration disagree on the meaning of the expression ἐπὶ διετὲς ἡβῆσαι, "two years after *hebe*." Didymus believes that adolescence *(hebe)* extends to age fourteen; the phrase ἐπὶ διετὲς ἡβῆσαι would thus mean age sixteen. Harpocration, on the other hand, takes the phrase to mean the two years of service normally given by an Athenian ephebe. Harpocration's explanation of the troubling phrase is anachronistic, according to Pélékedis, 52–70, who has argued that there is no conclusive evidence for an organized ephebia before 335. What, then, does the phrase ἐπὶ διετὲς ἡβῆσαι mean? The quotation from Hyperides (frag. 63, ed. Jensen) shows that enrollment in the deme register took place two years after adolescence. It is well attested that enrollment took place at age eighteen, so *hebe,* by this definition, must occur at age sixteen. Pélékedis, however, argues that ἐπὶ διετὲς ἡβῆσαι recalls an ancient two-year period of adolescence whose meaning and purpose had been forgotten by the fourth century. Although the fourth-century orators use the term, argues Pélékedis, they do not really understand to what it refers. Eventually, the end of this ancient two-year period (ages sixteen to eighteen) may have corresponded to the young man's entry into the ephebia (age eighteen). If Pélékedis is correct, other ancient sources also confuse this more ancient two-year period of adolescence with the later ephebia, instituted in 335. In addition, Pélékedis suggests that Didymus may be mistakenly applying a legal definition of *hebe* from another city-state. Only one other fragment of Hyperides *Against Chares* survives, a short lexical comment in Pollux 8.142 (frag. 193, ed. Jensen). On parental authority over children and the rights of children at Athens, see Harrison, 1: 70–81; on guardianship laws, 97–121; and on the laws of succession, 122–62. Pélékedis' book remains the only complete study of the Athenian ephebeia.

17. Didymus derived the compound Λυκιουργεῖς from Λυκίου (of Lycius) and a form of ἐργ- (work). Lycius, son and student of the famous sculptor Myron, was a bronze sculptor of the second half of the fifth century. Little is known of his life and works; see Groß; Guerrini. A parallel for the Harpocration entry is found in Athenaeus *Deipnosophistae* 11.486C–D: "In explaining this word, Didymus the scholar says that they are (the cups) made by Lycius. This man was of the Boeotian race, from Eleutherae, son of Myron the sculptor, as Polemon says in book 1 of *On the Acropolis*. But the scholar does not know that one would not find such a form made from individuals' names, but rather from the names of cities or peoples" (ὅπερ ἐξηγούμενος Δίδυμος ὁ γραμματικὸς τὰς ὑπὸ Λυκίου φησὶ κατεσκευασμένας. ἦν δὲ οὗτος τὸ γένος Βοιώτιος ἐξ Ἐλευθερῶν, υἱὸς Μύρωνος τοῦ ἀνδριαντοποιοῦ, ὡς Πολέμων φησὶν ἐν ᾱ περὶ Ἀκροπόλεως. ἀγνοεῖ δ' ὁ γραμματικὸς ὅτι τὸν τοιοῦτον σχηματισμὸν ἀπὸ κυρίων ὀνομάτων οὐκ ἄν τις εὕροι γινόμενον, ἀλλ' ἀπὸ πόλεων ἢ ἐθνῶν.). Athenaeus adds information not found in Harpocration's version: Lycius is said to be a Boeotian from Eleutherae, and this biographical information is attributed to the second-century geographer Polemon; on whom see Deichgräber, esp. 1292–94. Only one other fragment of Polemon's *On the Acropolis* is extant; see Preller, 36–38. Both Harpocration and Athenaeus give examples of similar compounds and suggest that the word in Dem. 49.31 and in Herodotus *Histories* 7.76 be corrected to another form in order to indicate "things made in Lycia" (τὰ ἐν Λυκίᾳ εἰργασμένα). There is no form attested in Greek literature or inscriptions that contradicts Athenaeus's and Harpocration's view that such compound adjectives cannot be formed from personal names. Rudolph has shown that Athenaeus used alphabetized lexica as sources. As Athenaeus's floruit was around 200 C.E., he may have been able to read some of the lexica that Harpocration draws on for his lexicon. It is interesting that the same comment of Didymus, with the same objection appended to it, has been picked up by two authors with such different interests. See also notes on Harpocration fragment 8.

18. Didymus may have observed that the adjective περιστοίχων (set round in rows) grammatically modifies ἐλαῶν (olive trees) rather than φυτευτήρια (nurseries), and concluded that the adjective denoted a particular γένος (variety) of tree rather than a method of planting. According to Jacoby on *FGrH* 328 F180, Philochorus's reference to στοιχάδες "seems to be the regular manner of planting [olive trees], known already

to the laws of Solon." Pollux 5.76 (adduced by Jacoby) says that "Solon called certain olive trees στοιχάδες, contrasting them with the μορίαι, perhaps because they were planted in rows" (Σόλων δὲ καὶ στοιχάδας τινὰς ἐλάας ἐκάλεσε, ταῖς μορίαις ἀντιτιθείς, ἴσως τὰς κατὰ στοῖχον πεφυτευμένας). Pollux also apparently understands the adjective στοιχάδες as referring to a type of tree. See Aristophanes *Acharnians* 994ff. for this method of planting. Harpocration goes on to offer his own explanation: "But perhaps the orator called περίστοιχον those trees planted in a circle around the property in a row" (μήποτε δὲ περίστοιχον κέκληκεν ὁ ῥήτωρ τὰς κύκλῳ περὶ τὸ χωρίον ἐν στοίχῳ πεφυκυίας).

19. Harpocration thinks that the word ἐξένιζε refers to the subject's nationality, while Didymus thinks that it refers only to his pronunciation of Greek—that is, he did not sound like an Athenian. It is conceivable that the Atticist controversy drew Didymus's attention to this passage; on which see G. Kennedy, *Art of Persuasion*, 330–36; Wilamowitz, "Asianismus." Some support for Didymus's interpretation can be found in Diodorus 12.53, τὸ ξενίζον τῆς λέξεως, where the participle is limited or qualified by τῆς λέξεως, "of diction." Compare also Libanius's hypothesis to this speech, where it is explained that because he was a slave taken in war, "the father foreignized in language" (ὁ δὲ πατὴρ ἐξένιζε τῇ γλώττῃ, ed. Foerster). This may imply that the word had the more general meaning preferred by Harpocration, and that further qualification was needed to show that it referred specifically to a style of speaking. The question in Dem. 57 is of course whether the man is a citizen or not, but Harpocration ignores the possibility that Demosthenes could be substituting accent for nationality by metonymy. Didymus may be correct, but it is impossible to know for certain, as Demosthenes does not develop his point further. Demosthenes also uses the verb ξενίζειν in 19.235, but there it means "to entertain guests," as in Homer.

20. Harpocration cites two instances of Didymus's discussion of the "wedding feast": one in which his bibliographical reference is allegedly mistaken, and one in which he allegedly provides no supporting evidence. Relying on the evidence of Didymus and other grammarians, Harrison, 1: 7 n. 2, describes the wedding feast as "an offering accompanied by a feast to phratry members which was customary, and even in some phratries laid down by their law, on the occasion of a marriage and the giving of which was therefore often used as one means of establishing the existence of the marriage." Jacoby (on *FGrH* 325 F17) notes that

there is a great deal of confusion among ancient scholars as to what the customs of the wedding feast actually entailed.

21. Didymus correctly points out that the word "sell" in Dem. 59.67 is a reference to prostitution. Didymus gives πορνεύωσι as a synonym for πωλῶσι. This kind of short, clarifying observation often appears in the Demosthenic scholia—a word or phrase, followed by ἀντί, followed by an equivalent word or phrase. Despite Didymus's "whence" (ὅθεν), the word πορνεύειν is not etymologically related to πωλεῖν or παρέχειν. Harpocration goes on to defend the orator's choice of the word. A parallel discussion appears in Harpocration, s.v. ἀποπεφασμένον (A 198): "Instead of 'displayed' and 'made manifest.' Thus Dinarchus and Lysias and Demosthenes, *Against Neaera*: 'they openly sell' instead of 'publicly.'" Here Harpocration says only that Demosthenes uses the word ἀποπεφασμένως rather than three other words that he could have used; he also cites Dinarchus (frag. 14, Conomis) and Lysias 10.19. This entry may have been derived from fragment 21. On prostitution in classical Athens, see Keuls, chaps. 6–7, esp. pp. 156–58. On Athenian laws regarding marriage, see Harrison, 1: 1–60.

Lexicon to Dem. 23 (P.Berol.inv. 5008)

P.Berol.inv. 5008 (Pack² 317) consists of three poorly preserved fragments of a papyrus codex dating to the fourth or fifth century C.E.
that contain a total of six lexical entries: on the recto, Μιλτοκύθης
(Dem. 23.104, 115, 169, 175) and μόραν (Dem. 23.198); on the verso,
οἰνοχόημα (?) (Dem. 23.198), ὁδός (Dem. 23.53), ὁ κάτωθεν νόμος
(Dem. 23.28), and ὅτι Θεμιστοκλῆς ὠστρακίσθη (Dem. 23.205). Since
all these words, phrases, or topics occur in Dem. 23, and since they all
begin with the letters *mu* or *omicron*, Blass, "Lexikon," 149–50, identified this text as an alphabetical special lexicon for use with Dem. 23,
Against Aristocrates. Any entries that began with *nu* or *xi* were presumably lost due to the break between the recto and verso. The text of
this papyrus has been heavily restored through comparison with Harpocration, Xenophon, and Philochorus.

The length and content of the individual entries in Berol. 5008 suggest a close connection with the ancient philological and historical commentaries on Demosthenes; on this point see Naoumides, "Greek Lexicography," 195. One entry is philological (ὁδός); the rest show interest
in Greek cultural, military, and constitutional history. The historians
Philochorus (Μιλτοκύθης, ὅτι Θεμιστοκλῆς ὠστρακίσθη), Theopompus (Μιλτοκύθης, μόραν), and Anaximenes (Μιλτοκύθης) are cited,
along with Aristotle (μόραν), Xenophon (μόραν), Ephorus (οἰνοχόημα),
and Homer (ὁδός). In addition, the entries for μόραν, ὁδός, and ὁ

κάτωθεν νόμος are similar to the corresponding entries in Harpocration's lexicon to the Attic orators (second century C.E.). Blass was able to draw heavily on Harpocration in order to restore the text of this papyrus.

The date of the lexicon from which this particular copy was made is uncertain, but it has been shown that Harpocration cannot have derived his corresponding entries from it; see Gibson, "P.Berol.inv. 5008." Rather, Harpocration and the author of this lexicon seem to have drawn on a common source, which in turn drew on Didymus and perhaps one other commentator. A terminus post quem for the original lexicon is provided by the citation of Didymus, and a terminus ante quem by the palaeographical date of this particular copy.

There are no significant or interesting correspondences in the Demosthenic scholia.

Text: From D-S^2, 43–47. Originally published with commentary by Blass, "Lexikon," then reprinted with corrections in D-S^1, 78–82. The D-S^2 text conforms more closely to modern conventions of editing than does the text of Blass, "Lexikon," but D-S^2 do not read the ends of the last eight lines in the entry on ὁ κάτωθεν νόμος. In the notes to that entry the Blass text is given and discussed.

TEXT AND TRANSLATION OF P.BEROL.INV. 5008

Recto

[**ΜΙΛΤΟΚΥΘΗΣ**.] ἱστόρησεν. ὅτι δὲ ἀπέσ[τη Κότυ]ος Φιλόχορος δεδή|λωκεν ἐν τῆι ε̄ τῆς Ἀ[τθίδος. ὅτι] δὲ ὑπὸ Κερσοβλέ|πτου ἁλοὺς Μιλτοκύ[θης ἐτελεύτησ]εν, φη[σὶ καὶ] Θεόπομπος [ἐν τῆι ̈ . τῶν Φιλιππικῶν λέγων οὕτως·] | "ὁρμώμενος δ' ἐκ τῆς πό[λ]εως . . . . . .
. . . . . | ξενολογήσας διὰ τοῦ Ἡρακλείδ[ο]υ [καὶ Π]ύθ[ωνος] | τῶν Ἀρχελάου παίδων, [τὸ] μὲν πρ[ῶτον ἐ]|κράτει τῶι πολέμωι καὶ [τ]ῶν ἐπὶ [. . . . . ἔλα]|βεν καὶ τὴν χώραν ἐπέδ[ρα]μεν κακοπ[οιῶν] | [καὶ] πορθῶν ἅπασαν τ[. . .]πρ . . . εν[. . . . . Σμι]|κυθ<ί>ωνος στρατιώτας . . . . ωρ . . . . [λα]|βεῖν καὶ ω[. . . . . .]τον . . . .
. . τρω . . . . | ἀ[π]ῆχθαι πρ[ὸ]ς τὸν Κερσο[βλέπ]την | ἄνδρ[α] καὶ π – – – – – – ." | καὶ [μ]έντοι [περὶ τούτων ἄλλοι τε εἰρήκασιν] | καὶ Ἀναξιμ[ένης, ὃς ἐν τῆι ᾱ τῶν Φιλιππικῶν] | ἱστορεῖ τὴν ἀ[πό]στασιν τὴν ἀπὸ Κότυος, ἐν] | δὲ τῆι β̄ τὴν π[ροδοσίαν τὴν ὑπὸ τοῦ Σμι]|κυθίωνος κ[αὶ τὴν ἀναίρεσιν τὴν Μιλτοκύθου."]
Miltocythes (Dem. 23.104, 115, 169, 175): (– – –) narrated. Philochorus

made it clear in book 5 of the *Atthis* (*FGrH* 328 F42) that he (Miltocythes) revolted from Cotys. And Theopompus in book (number) of the
Philippica (*FGrH* 115 F307) made it clear that Miltocythes died after he
was seized by Cersobleptes, when he says as follows: "Starting out from
the city . . . , having hired mercenaries through Heraclides and Python,
the sons of Archelaus, at first he (Miltocythes) prevailed in the war, and
he took . . . , and he attacked the land, doing harm and ravaging the
whole . . . (of) Smicythion . . . soldiers (– – –) to have become hated by
Cersobleptes (– – –)." And in fact Anaximenes, in addition to others, has
spoken on these events, narrating in book 1 of the *Philippica* (*FGrH* 72
F5) the revolt from Cotys, and in book 2 (*FGrH* 72 F6) the betrayal by
Smicythion and the destruction of Miltocythes.

ΜΟΡΑΝ. "Καὶ τὴν μ[όραν κατέκοψεν Ἰφικράτης." συν]|τ[άγματά
τινα Λακωνικά, ὥς φησιν Ἀριστο]|τέλη[ς ἐ]ν [τῆι Λακεδαιμονίων πο-
λιτείαι, ὅς] | πρα[– – – – – – –] | εἰς διαίρεσι[ν – – – – –] | δ' εἰς
μόρο[υς . . . . φησὶν ὡς εἰσὶ μόραι ἑξ] | ὠνομασμέ[ναι . . . .
. . . . καὶ] | διήιρηνται ε[ἰς τὰς μόρας Λακεδαιμόνιοι
πάν]τες· τὰς δὲ τα – – – – – |μ – – – – – – – |ξας – – – – – – – |χος.
ξ – – – – – – – | λόχους. καὶ Θ[εό]π[ομπος δ' ἐν Ἑλληνικοῖς] | τὰ
παραπλ[ήσια ἱστορεῖ τούτοις· Ξενοφῶν] δὲ ἐν τῆι Λακώνω[ν πολι-
τείαι φησίν· "ἑκά]στη δὲ τῶν πολι[τικῶν μορῶν ἔχει πολέμαρχον] |
[ᾱ, λοχαγοὺς δ, πεντηκοστύας η, ἐνωμοτάρχας ῑϛ]
    Mora (Dem. 23.198): "And Iphicrates cut the *mora* to pieces" (Dem. 23.198).
These (sc. *morae*) are certain Spartan contingents, as Aristotle says in
the *Spartan Constitution,* who (sc. Aristotle) . . . into the division . . . to
their deaths. . . . He says that there are six named *morae* (– – –) and all
the Spartans are divided into *morae* (– – –*4 lines unrestored*– – –) *lochoi.*
And Theopompus in the *Hellenica* (*FGrH* 115 F308) narrates things
similar to these. And Xenophon in the *Spartan Constitution* (11.4) says:
"Each of the civil *morae* has one *polemarch,* four *lochoi*-leaders, eight
pentecostyae, and sixteen *enomotia*-commanders."

Verso

εἰς οἰνοχόημα, ὅταν ἦι Ἅλαδε μύσται, οἱ καθιστάμε|νοι μ[υστηρίων
. . . . ἐπι]μεληταί. καὶ Ἔφορος ἐν τῆι κᾱ | τῶν [ἱ]στ[οριῶν. . . . . . .
. .] δεισεστη . . . . ν . ϛ
    [Subject unknown] (Dem. 23.198?): (– – –*unknown number of lines
missing*– – –) to the wine-festival, whenever it was "Seaward, Initiates"

Day, those who were appointed overseers . . . of the mysteries. And Ephorus in book 21 of his *Histories* (*FGrH* 70 F80) (– – –).

ΟΔΟ[Σ. "'Εν ὁδῶι καθελών" . . . . ἀντὶ τοῦ] ἐν λόχωι κ[αὶ ἐ]ν̣[έ]δρα̣[ι. τοιοῦτον δὲ εἶναι] καὶ τὸ Ὁ[μηρικὸν] δο̣κε̣ῖ· | "ἢ [ὁδὸν] ἐλθέμε[ναι], ἢ ἀνδράσιν ἶφι μά[χεσθαι."]

Road (Dem. 23.53): "Seizing on the road" (Dem. 23.53), . . . instead of "in ambush" and "in a state of lying-in-wait." This also seems to be the sense in Homer: "Either ambushing or fighting violently with men" (*Iliad* 1.151).

Ο ΚΑΤΩΘΕΝ ΝΟΜΟΣ. [Δίδυ]μος ὁ γραμματικὸς διχῶς | [ἐξ-ηγ]εῖται τὸ ε̣[ἰρημ]ένον· ἢ γὰρ διὰ τὸ τὴν ἡλ̣ι̣α̣ί̣αν̣ | δ[ι]αγιγνώσκειν [περὶ] τῶν λυμαινομένων καὶ | ἄπο[ιν]α δεχομέ[νων] οὕτως φησὶν εἰ-ρηκέναι τὸν | ῥήτορα· τῶν γὰρ [δικασ]τηρίων ἔλεγον τὰ μὲν ἄ|νωι εἶναι τὰ δὲ κ̣[άτωι]· ἢ διὰ τὸ σχῆμα τῆς ἐν τοῖς | ἄξοσι γραφῆς βου-[στροφ]ηδὸν γεγραμμένης ἐκ | μεταφορᾶς τῆς ἀ[πὸ τῶν ἀ]ρ̣ο̣ύ̣[ντ]ω̣ν̣ . . . . | γὰρ ἀπὸ τῶν ἀρισ[τερῶν . . . .] | . εν ἀ[ν]αστρέφ[εσθ]α̣[ι] – – – – – |ρ – – – – – – – – – | – – – – – – – – |κα – – – – – – – – |δε – – – – – – – – |ξ – – – – – – – – |πολ – – – – – – – |τε – – – – – – – – |τη – – – – – – – –

The law (from) below (Dem. 23.28): Didymus the grammarian explains this phrase in two ways. For he says that the orator says this either be-cause the Heliaea gives judgment concerning those who inflict personal injury and those who receive recompense—for they used to speak of up-per and lower courts—or because the writing on the *axones* was bou-strophedon, a metaphor from plowing, . . . for from the lower left . . . to turn back (– – –8 *lines unrestored*).

ΟΤΙ ΘΕ[ΜΙΣΤΟΚΛΗΣ ΩΣΤΡΑΚΙΣΘΗ. "'Εκεῖνοι Θεμιστο]κλέ[α λαβόντες μεῖζον αὐτῶν ἀξιοῦντα φρο]ν̣ε̣[ῖν ἐξήλασαν ἐκ τῆς πόλεως." Ὅ]τι ἐστὶν ὀστρα||κισμός, ἄλλοι τε πολλοὶ εἰρήκα]σιν καὶ Φιλόχο[ρος ἐν τῆι γ̄ τῆς Ἀτθίδος οὕτω φη]σίν· "ὁ̣ δ' ὀστρα||κισμὸς τοιοῦτος· προεχειροτόν]ει [μὲν ὁ δῆμος] | [πρὸ τῆς η̄ πρυτανείας, εἰ δοκεῖ τὸ ὄστρακον] | [εἰσφέρειν· ὅτε δ' ἐδόκει, ἐφράσσετο σανίσιν ἡ ἀγο]||ρά, καὶ κατελείποντο εἴσοδοι ῑ, δι'] ὧν [εἰσ]ερχόμε[νοι . . . . κατὰ φυλ]ὰ[ς] ἐτίθεσαν τὰ | [ὄστρακα, στρέφοντες τ]ὴν ἐπιγρα-φήν· ἐπε[ιστάτουν δ' οἵ τε θ̄ ἄρχοντες κα]ὶ̣ ἡ βουλή· διαριθμη[θέντων δέ, ὅτωι πλεῖστα γέ]νοιτο, καὶ εἰ μὲν ἐ[λάττω ἑξακισχιλίων, τοῦτ]ον ἔδει, τὰ δίκαια δόν|[τα καὶ λαβόντα ὑπὲρ τῶν ἰδίων συναλλαγμά]|[των, ἐν ι̅ ἡμέραις μεταστῆναι τῆς πόλεως ἔτη ι̅."]

(Where it says) that Themistocles was ostracized (compare Dem. 23.205): "Taking Themistocles, who thought that he knew better than them, those men drove him from the city." As to what ostracism is, Philochorus, in addition to many others, says as follows in book 3 of the *Atthis* (*FGrH* 328 F30): "Ostracism was as follows. The people voted before the eighth prytany on whether they wanted to propose an ostracism. When they voted to do so, the Agora was fenced in with planks, and ten entrances were left open, through which those entering . . . placed their ostraca tribe by tribe, turning the inscribed side down. And the nine archons and the Council presided. When the ostraca had been counted, whoever received the most votes—and provided there were fewer (sic) than six thousand—it was required that he, paying the penalty and taking care of private commitments, leave the city within ten days for a period of ten years."

NOTES ON P.BEROL.INV. 5008

Miltocythes: The first extant entry in this special lexicon to Dem. 23 identifies Miltocythes and gives information about his revolt and death. Miltocythes is mentioned four times in *Against Aristocrates* (Dem. 23.104, 115, 169, and 175). Miltocythes is also mentioned in Dem. 50.5 and by the three historians who were consulted for this lexical entry. He is not, however, the same Miltocythes who appears in Xenophon *Anabasis* 2.2.7, a Thracian who fought at Cynaxa in 401 (Geyer, 1708). What is known about our Miltocythes can be summarized as follows: He was a Thracian commander who revolted against the Thracian king Cotys in 363 (Philochorus *FGrH* 328 F42, Anaximenes *FGrH* 72 F5, Dem. 23.115) and then offered to help Athens (Dem. 50.4–5). In response to a special command granted to the general Autocles, Miltocythes left Athens in 361, believing that the Athenians no longer liked him (Dem. 23.104). King Cotys was killed in 360 by Heraclides and Python, and Miltocythes used the mercenaries provided by Heraclides and Python to achieve military victories (Theopompus *FGrH* 115 F307). In 359 Miltocythes was betrayed by Smicythion (Theopompus *FGrH* 115 F307, Anaximenes *FGrH* 72 F6) to Charidemus. Charidemus believed that Cersobleptes (the son of Cotys) would not punish Miltocythes harshly enough, so he handed Miltocythes and his son over to the Cardians, current enemies of Athens, who executed them both at sea (Theopompus *FGrH* 115 F307, Anaximenes *FGrH* 72 F6, Dem. 23.169 and 175). How this entry opened is unknown, but the surviving portion suggests that its purpose was to provide a brief sketch of Miltocythes' life as it related to Dem. 23, and to note historical sources that discussed him in greater depth. On these events, see Parke, *Greek Mercenary Soldiers*, 131; Geyer; A. Schaefer, 1: 153, 157 n. 3; Jacoby, *FGrH* 3b suppl. vol. 1, pp. 325–26 and *FGrH* 2c, 107–8.

A text of Dem. 23.103–4 (text 7 in Schwendner) dating to the third century C.E. contains some scholia written between the columns, next to lines 14–23 of the first column. The scholia that are legible correctly explain Demosthenes' reference to τοὺς μὲν ἀσθενεῖς as τοὺς ἑτέρους βασιλ(έας) and identify the referent of τὸν δ' ἕνα ὄντα ἰσχυρόν as Cersobleptes.

Mora: The purpose of this entry is to define and discuss the place of the contingents called *morae* within the Spartan military. The lemma mentions the destruction of the Spartan *mora* by Iphicrates, which was one of Athens's most celebrated historical victories, mentioned frequently in literature both by the Athenians and about them. In *Against Demosthenes* 75, the orator Dinarchus (ed. Conomis) includes the event as part of Athens's glorious history, along with Conon's victory at Cnidus, Chabrias's victory at Naxos, and Timotheus's victory at Corcyra. In his *Life of Iphicrates* 2.3, Nepos describes the Athenian victory as "especially celebrated in all of Greece" ("quod maxime tota celebratum est Graecia"; ed. P. K. Marshall). Plutarch's *Life of Agesilaus* 22.3–6 portrays the famous event as divine punishment of the Spartan king Agesilaus for his shabby treatment of the Thebans (22.1–2); on which see Shipley, 266–70. The scholia to Aelius Aristides' *Panathenaicus* (ed. Dindorf, 273–74) even mention a commemorative place name called *Mora* near Lechaeum.

The event is narrated in Xenophon *Hellenica* 4.5.11–18 and Diodorus 14.91.2; other relevant sources are discussed in Lammert. In the summer of 390, a *mora* of hoplites stationed at Lechaeum was escorting the Amyclaeans who were serving in the Spartan army to Sicyon for a festival; a short distance from Sicyon, the hoplites turned back while the cavalry continued on with the Amyclaeans. When the Athenian Callias and his hoplites, together with the Athenian Iphicrates and his peltasts, saw the returning *mora* greatly reduced in numbers and capability, they attacked and utterly defeated the Spartan *mora*. This was a major defeat for Sparta and resulted in more widespread use of peltasts in battle;

see Parke, *Greek Mercenary Soldiers,* 53–54; Lazenby, 148–50; Cartledge, 223–25.

An entry from Harpocration's lexicon is relevant here: "A mercenary force at Corinth (Ξενικὸν ἐν Κορίνθωι, Ξ 2): Demosthenes in the *Philippics* (4.24) and Aristophanes in the *Plutus* (line 173). Conon originally gathered it, and later Iphicrates and Chabrias took it over. Using it, they cut to pieces the *mora* of the Spartans, with Iphicrates and Callias leading them, as both Androtion (*FGrH* 324 F48) and Philochorus (*FGrH* 328 F150) say" (Δημοσθένης Φιλιππικοῖς καὶ Ἀριστοφάνης Πλούτῳ. συνεστήσατο δ' αὐτὸ πρῶτον Κόνων, παρέλαβε δ' αὐτὸ Ἰφικράτης ὕστερον καὶ Χαβρίας· ᾧ χρησάμενοι τὴν Λακεδαιμονίων μόραν κατέκοψαν στρατηγοῦντος αὐτοῖς Ἰφικράτους καὶ Καλλίου, καθά φησιν Ἀνδροτίων τε καὶ Φιλόχορος.). At issue for military historians is the chronological relationship of Conon, Iphicrates, and Chabrias; the exact position of Iphicrates (was he a *strategos* or not?); and the financing of the mercenary force. Other relevant ancient evidence includes Androtion *FGrH* 324 F48, Philochorus *FGrH* 328 F150, and the scholia to Aristophanes' *Plutus.* For discussions of these and related issues, see Parke, *Greek Mercenary Soldiers,* 50–54; Pritchett, 62–72, 117–25; Harding, *Androtion,* 169–71; Jacoby, *FGrH* 3b suppl. vol. 1, pp. 156 and 521. On foreign mercenaries and mercenary generals in the fourth century, see Parke, *Greek Mercenary Soldiers,* 48–57, and Pritchett, 59–125, esp. 117–25. See also notes on fragment 1 in Harpocration.

The lexicographer is not interested in the destruction of the Spartan *mora* by Iphicrates but rather sets out to describe what a *mora* is for a reader interested in details of the Spartan military. Three pieces of evidence are adduced: a quotation from Aristotle's *Spartan Constitution* (frag. 540, ed. Rose); a corroborating footnote from Theopompus (*FGrH* 115 F308); and a brief quotation from Xenophon's *Spartan Constitution* (11.4). The Aristotle and Xenophon quotations are both concerned with the titles and interrelationships of Spartan military contingents. After a careful study of the relevant ancient evidence, Lazenby, 205, concludes that: a Spartan *mora* at full strength consisted of 1,280 men; the *polemarch* was the name given to the commander of a *mora*; the *lochos* at its best was a unit of 640; the *pentekostys* was a unit of 160; and the *enomotia* was a unit of 40 men. On the *morae*, see also Cartledge, 427–31; see Ollier, 56–57, on the passage from Xenophon. For a detailed discussion of the Spartan military in the time of Xenophon, see Lazenby, 3–40.

There is a parallel discussion in Harpocration, s.v. μόραν (M 41), which Blass, "Lexikon," used to restore the corresponding discussion in the papyrus: "Certain Spartan contingents are called by this name. Aristotle discusses them in the *Spartan Constitution*. He says that there are six named *morae*, and all the Spartans are divided into *morae*. Xenophon in the *Spartan Constitution* (11.4) says: 'Each of the civil *morae* has one *polemarch*, four *lochoi*-leaders, eight *pentecostyae*, and sixteen *enomotia*-commanders'" (συντάγματά τινα Λακωνικὰ οὕτω καλεῖται. διείλεκται δὲ περὶ τούτων Ἀριστοτέλης ἐν τῇ Λακεδαιμονίων πολιτείᾳ. φησὶ δὲ ὡς εἰσὶ μόραι ἓξ ὠνομασμέναι, καὶ διήρηνται εἰς τὰς μόρας Λακεδαιμόνιοι πάντες. Ξενοφῶν δὲ ἐν τῇ Λακώνων πολιτείᾳ φησὶν: "ἑκάστη δὲ τῶν πολιτικῶν μορῶν ἔχει πολέμαρχον ἕνα, λοχαγοὺς δ̅, πεντηκοστύας η̅, ἐνωμοτάρχας ι̅ϛ̅.") The entry in Berol. 5008 is longer than the one in Harpocration, though both entries apparently begin and end with essentially the same information. In comparison with the author of the entry in Berol. 5008, Harpocration says less about the Aristotle passage and makes no reference to Theopompus.

Subject unknown: The next entry begins on the verso, but the lemma and an unknown number of lines from the beginning of the discussion are missing; see Blass, "Lexikon," 149. As Blass, "Lexikon," 155–56, points out, the word in question should occur in Dem. 23 and should fall alphabetically between μόρα and ὁδός. He suggested οἰνοχόημα, Νάξος, and ναυμαχία as possibilities. All three words are found in Dem. 23.198, which encouraged him to connect this entry with the discussion of Chabrias in Plutarch's *Life of Phocion* 6. In his treatment of the Athenian victory at Naxos (376) and the subsequent celebration, Plutarch says that the Athenians "won during the Great Mysteries, and Chabrias provided for a wine festival (οἰνοχόημα) each year on the sixteenth of Boedromion." Blass, "Lexikon," 156, uses Plutarch to restore the sense of the fragmentary discussion as follows: "Chabrias furnished the Athenians with wine for an οἰνοχόημα, which previously the overseers of the Mysteries had furnished on this day." D-S², 45, also usefully adduce Polyaenus 3.11.2: "Fighting a naval battle at Naxos, Chabrias won on the sixteenth of Boedromion (Βοηδρομιῶνος ἕκτῃ ἐπὶ δέκα); he judged this day suitable for a naval battle, because it was one of the days of the Mysteries (μία τῶν μυστηρίων)" (ed. Krentz and Wheeler). Instead of Blass's ὅταν πάλαι δὲ μύσται, D-S² read ὅταν ἦι Ἅλαδε μύσται, "whenever it was 'Seaward, Initiates!' Day" (Parke's rendering of the name). This was a rite of purification held on the second day of the Eleusinian Mysteries, the sixteenth of Boedromion. D-S²'s reading, then, both supports and is supported by Blass's identification of the topic as Chabrias's οἰνοχόημα to the Athenians on the sixteenth of Boedromion. On this day the initiates were driven in carts either to the Piraeus or to the beach of Phaleron. Each carrying a young pig, the initiates walked into the sea and cleansed both the pigs and themselves; they later sacrificed the pigs and were sprinkled with their blood. See Parke, *Festivals*, 62–63; on the schedule of events for the Eleusinian mysteries in general, see 55–72. The four "overseers of the mysteries" (ἐπιμεληταὶ τῶν μυστηρίων), according to the *Athenian Constitution* 57, were chosen by vote of the people, two coming from the Athenians at large, one from the Eumol-pidae, and one from the Heralds. They were assisted in overseeing the Eleusinian Mysteries by the *archon basileus*. See Rhodes, *Commentary*, 636–37. Book 21 of Ephorus's *Histories* was probably adduced at the end of the entry for a discussion of the naval battle at Naxos; see Blass, "Lexikon," 156. On the fourth-century universal historian Ephorus, see Barber.

Road: Interest in Demosthenes' language, even if only on the level of a simple gloss, is common throughout the ancient philological and his-torical commentaries on Demosthenes. The phrase "seizing on the road" in Dem. 23.53 occurs within a statute listing examples of situations in which a homicide does not have to be punished with exile. After the statute is read, Demosthenes discusses every example of unintentional or otherwise excusable homicide contained within it except for this one. Perhaps he did not understand the archaic expression "seizing on the road" and was thus unable to use it in his argument. The lexicographer suggests that a line of Homer provides a parallel, but while the expres-sion that is quoted (ὁδὸν ἐλθέμεναι) might have a similar meaning, it does not provide an exact parallel to Demosthenes' ἐν ὁδῶι καθελών. It is possible that the lexicographer confused the second aorist parti-ciple ἑλών (from αἱρέω) with the second aorist participle ἐλθών (from ἔρχομαι); note Homer's ἐλθέμεναι. Whatever the reason, the Homeric phrase is better understood as meaning "going the journey" (cognate ac-cusative) or "traveling." The scholia to *Iliad* 1.151a (ed. Erbse), inci-dentally, mention this possibility but reject it: "Some say that he is talk-ing about an expedition. But I say that it is an ambush" (φασὶ μέν τινες περὶ τοῦ πλοῦ λέγειν. ἐγὼ δὲ τὸν λόχον φημί). Two entries in Harpo-cration are relevant here. The first is an entry for ἢ ἐν ὁδῶι καθελών (H 6): "Instead of grabbing him who is lying in wait, namely, seizing in a lying-in-wait" (ἀντὶ τοῦ ἐνεδρεύοντα ἑλών, τουτέστι ἔν τινι ἐνέδρᾳ καταλαβών). Harpocration seems to be trying to understand the expression in context, where it should refer to a case of unintentional or otherwise excusable homicide. So Harpocration interprets "seizing on the road" to mean "seizing in ambush," but with a very sensible twist: the excused homicide is Person A who seizes (and kills) Person B when B is lying in wait to attack A. But this interpretation is different from the one given in Berol. 5008, and it is also different from Harpocration's entry on ὁδός (O 2): "Demosthenes in *Against Aristocrates* (23.53) says 'either seizing on the road' instead of in ambush and in a state of lying-in-wait. And they say that this is also the sense in Homer: 'Either ambushing'" (Δημοσθένης ἐν τῷ Κατ᾽ Ἀριστοκράτους φησὶν "ἢ ἐν ὁδῷ καθελών" ἀντὶ τοῦ ἐν λόχῳ καὶ ἐνέδρᾳ. τοιοῦτον δὲ εἶναι καὶ τὸ Ὁμηρικόν φασιν "ἢ ὁδὸν ἐλθέμεναι").

The law (from) below: In Dem. 23.28, Demosthenes asks the clerk to read a law concerning the treatment of murderers. The expression he uses—ὁ κάτωθεν νόμος—is not used elsewhere in Demosthenes or in the Attic orators. The lack of parallels for the expression, its proximity in the text to another expression meaning the next law on a list (αὐτὸν τὸν νόμον τὸν μετὰ ταῦτα), and an overly literal interpretation of the –θεν suffix in κάτωθεν as indicating the source "from which" led some ancient commentators to believe that the easiest interpretation was not the correct one. Weil, *Plaidoyers,* ad loc. glosses ὁ κάτωθεν νόμος as "the law after these" (ὁ νόμος ὁ μετὰ ταῦτα), while C. R. Kennedy, 176, describes it as the "law written under the one last cited on the board exhibited to the jury." Three ancient explanations were generated, all taking the –θεν suffix on κάτωθεν to indicate "from below" rather than simply "below": Didymus's view that it refers to a law coming from lower courts of the Heliaea; Didymus's view that it refers to a law written on the *axones,* whose text began from the lower left; and a third view (represented by Harpocration as Didymean) that it is a law coming from down below in the Agora, with respect to the Acropolis. The first two views were loosely inspired by the surrounding text in Dem. 23.28, as the orator discusses the Heliaea's jurisdiction over cases in which murderers have been unlawfully abused (though he says nothing about upper and lower courts), and he mentions that a particular law regarding the arrest of murderers appeared on the *axones* (though he says nothing about the manner in which they were written).

On the Heliaea, see MacDowell, *Law in Classical Athens,* 29–33.

There are no parallels for upper and lower courts related to the Heliaea. Didymus's only other discussion of the Heliaea concerned its etymology, in his commentary on Aristophanes (frag. 59 in Schmidt, 259). Didymus's second interpretation may have come from his *Reply to Asclepiades Concerning the Axones of Solon* (Περὶ τῶν ἀξόνων τῶν Σόλωνος ἀντιγραφὴ πρὸς Ἀσκληπιάδην), of which only one uninformative fragment is preserved (see Schmidt, 399). The third interpretation is a misreading of Anaximenes, according to Jacoby on *FGrH* 72 F13: Ephialtes' removal of the laws from the Acropolis to the Agora is a figurative way of saying that he made the Council and the Assembly a more important part of Athenian politics. Stroud, 12–13 and 42, disagrees, preferring a literal interpretation: the *axones* and *cyrbeis* were located on the Acropolis until Ephialtes in 461 moved the *axones* to the Prytaneum and the *cyrbeis* to the Agora. On the location of laws in Athens, see also MacDowell, *Law in Classical Athens*, 45–48.

This lexical entry opens with the statement that Didymus explains the phrase "the law (from) below" in two ways. Didymus's two explanations included the one about the lower courts of the Heliaea and the one about boustrophedon writing on the *axones*. In the corresponding entry from Harpocration (text 2, frag. 10), however, the picture is somewhat different: "Didymus says: 'Either the orator means the Heliaea because the courts were called upper and lower, or because the layout of the writing on the *axones* was boustrophedon, in which a law that begins from the left Demosthenes calls "from below." For,' he says, 'Euphorion in *Apollodorus* made it clear that that the *axones* and the *cyrbeis* were written boustrophedon. Or,' he says, 'because Ephialtes moved the *axones* and the *cyrbeis* from the Acropolis down to the Bouleuterion and the Agora, as Anaximenes says in the *Philippica*" (*FGrH* 72 F13) (Δίδυμος· "ἤτοι," φησί, "τὴν ἡλιαίαν λέγει ὁ ῥήτωρ διὰ τὸ τῶν δικαστηρίων τὰ μὲν ἄνω τὰ δὲ κάτω ὀνομάζεσθαι, ἢ διὰ τὸ σχῆμα τῆς ἐν τοῖς ἄξοσι γραφῆς βουστροφηδὸν γεγραμμένης ἧι τὸν ἀπὸ τῶν εὐωνύμων ἀρχόμενον νόμον κάτωθεν ὀνομάζει ὁ Δημοσθένης· ὅτι γάρ," φησί, "βουστροφηδὸν ἦσαν οἱ ἄξονες καὶ οἱ κύρβεις γεγραμμένοι δεδήλωκεν Εὐφορίων ἐν τῷ Ἀπολλοδώρῳ. ἢ ἐπεί," φησί, "τοὺς ἄξονας καὶ τοὺς κύρβεις ἄνωθεν ἐκ τῆς ἀκροπόλεως εἰς τὸ βουλευτήριον καὶ τὴν ἀγορὰν μετέστησεν Ἐφιάλτης, ὥς φησιν Ἀναξιμένης ἐν Φιλιππικοῖς."). In Harpocration's version, Didymus is credited with three unnumbered interpretations: the one about upper and lower courts of the Heliaea, the one about boustrophedon texts on *axones*, and the one—

not found in Berol. 5008—about laws coming from below in the Agora. That Harpocration considered all three to be by Didymus is clearly indicated by the repetition of the postpositive φησί (he says), which concatenates the three different explanations given in the entry. With its "in two ways," Berol. 5008 could not have contained a third explanation by Didymus in what is lost, though there was certainly room for a third interpretation by somebody.

The relationship between these two texts is interesting. It is unlikely that Berol. 5008's entry for "the law below" was derived directly from Harpocration, since Harpocration gives three explanations by Didymus and Berol. 5008 states that only two exist. Might Harpocration's entry have been derived from the one in Berol. 5008? If so, one of two things must have happened. Harpocration independently found and appended a third explanation by Didymus, as a correction to his source that stated that only two Didymean explanations existed. Or the original lexicon behind Berol. 5008 contained a third explanation (not attributed to Didymus), which Harpocration misread as a third explanation by Didymus. Neither of these possibilities is especially persuasive. A lost source in common is possible but not necessary. This is as far as one can go using D-S²'s edition of the text, which essentially breaks off here, with only one or two letters visible at the beginning of each of the final eight lines.

In the original edition of twenty-two years before, however, Blass, "Lexikon," was able to see more: "Didymus the grammarian explains this phrase in two ways. For he says that the orator says this either because it is the Heliaea that gives judgment concerning those who inflict personal injury and those who receive recompense—for they used to speak of upper and lower courts; or because the layout of the writing on the *axones* was boustrophedon, a metaphor from plowing, for they normally started from the lower left, so that (a law) would turn back from the top from right to left (– – –). But it is also possible that 'from below' is said because Ephialtes moved the *axones* and the *cyrbeis* from the Acropolis down to the Bouleuterion and the Agora, as Anaximenes says in the (n)th book of the *Philippica* (*FGrH* 17 F13)" (Δ[ίδ]υμος ὁ γραμματικὸς διχῶς | ἐξη[γ]εῖται τὸ ε[ἰρημ]ένον· ἢ γὰρ διὰ τὸ τὴν ἡλιαίαν | δ[ι]αγιγνώσκειν [περὶ] τῶν λυμαινομένων καὶ | ἄπο[ι]να δεχομένων οὕτως φησὶν εἰρηκέναι τὸν | ῥήτορα· τῶν γὰρ [δικασ]τηρίων ἔλεγον τὰ μὲν ἄ|νωι εἶναι τὰ δὲ κ[άτωι]· ἢ διὰ τὸ σχῆμα τῆς ἐν τοῖς | ἄξοσι γραφῆς βου[στροφ]ηδὸν γεγραμμένης ἐκ | μεταφορᾶς τῆς ἀ[πὸ τῶν ἀ]ρού[ντ]ων· [ἐκ τῶν κ]άτ[ωι] | γὰρ ἀπὸ τῶν ἀρισ[τερῶν ἤρχοντο, ὥσ]τε τὸ[ν] ἑ[ξ]ῆς ἄνω][θ]εν ἀ[ν]αστρέφ[εσθ]α[ι ἀπὸ τῶν δ]εξιῶν εἰς

τὰ ἀ|ρ[ιστ]ε̣ρ[ά] . . . . . . αυ . . . . ουδε τ̣ὸ̣ν̣ νό[μο]ν̣ | [τὸν] . . . . . .
[ἀπὸ τῶν εὐωνύμω]ν̣ ἀρχό[με]νον | κά[τωθεν– – –εἶ]ναι. δύναται] | δὲ
[καὶ διὰ τοῦτο κάτωθεν λέγ]εσθαι, ὅτι τοὺς ἄ̣|ξ[ονας καὶ τοὺς κύρβεις
ἄνωθε]ν̣ ἐκ τῆς ἀκρο|πόλ[εως εἰς τὸ βουλευτήριον καὶ τ]ὴ̣ν ἀγορὰν
με|τέ[στησεν Ἐφιάλτης, ὥς φησιν Ἀνα]ξ̣ιμένης ἐν̣ | τῆ(ι) ˙ [τῶν
Φιλιππικῶν].).

As is seen in Blass's edition, there is no room to fit in the citation of
Euphorion (frag. 6, Powell) found in Harpocration's report of Didymus's second explanation. Unless Harpocration added the citation himself—which is unlikely, since he directly attributes this explanation to
Didymus—it must have come from somewhere other than Berol. 5008.
In a 1997 article that relied on Blass's edition of the text, I argued that
the discussions of "the law (from) below" in Berol. 5008 and Harpocration derive from a common source commentary or lexicon dating from
no later than the second century C.E. (the date of Harpocration's lexicon). This common source contained two explanations by Didymus and
a third, non-Didymean explanation. When they copied their discussions
from this common source, the author of the entry in Berol. 5008 correctly maintained the distinction between Didymus and the anonymous
third view, while Harpocration incorrectly attributed the third explanation to Didymus. See Gibson, "P.Berol.inv. 5008."

(Where it says) that Themistocles was ostracized: This entry discusses
the procedure for carrying out an ostracism. Most of it has been restored
by comparison with entries on ostracism in two other sources: a lexicographical work by Claudius Casilo (fourth century C.E.) and the so-called
Lexicon Rhetoricum Cantabrigiense, which is found in the margins of
some manuscripts of Harpocration and consists of excerpts from other
lexica such as that of Claudius Casilo (ed. Houtsma, 23–24); see D-S²,
46–47; Jacoby, 3b, 107–8, for collation of the texts; see also 3b suppl.
vol. 1, pp. 315–16, for other ancient parallels. Its partially restored
heading (ὅτι Θε[μιστοκλῆς ὠστρακίσθη]) does not occur in the speech,
though the subsequent lemma does if Blass's restorations, based on
Dem. 23.205, are correct. The absence of a precisely corresponding
lemma might have made it hard for someone encountering the unknown
name Themistocles to find this entry, which has been alphabetized
according to the word ὅτι, "(where it says) that" or "(the fact) that."
For the use of ὅτι with paraphrased lemmata, see the introduction to
Stras. 84. Rather than discussing the specific circumstances of Themistocles' ostracism, the lexicographer apparently quotes Philochorus on

the procedure. This passage nicely illustrates how the commentators and lexicographers to Demosthenes sometimes apparently regarded history as important for its own sake, since a detailed discussion of the procedure of ostracism does not seem particularly helpful for understanding the passage in question. After Themistocles was ostracized (sometime in the 460s), he was accused of Medism and fled to Persia. See Thucydides 1.135–38, Plutarch's *Life of Themistocles* 22–31, and the discussion in Rhodes, *Commentary,* 319–20, on the portrayal of Themistocles in *Athenian Constitution* 25.3. For the occurrence of Themistocles' name on ostraca, see Thomsen, *Origin of Ostracism,* 79–80 (with n. 170), 95. According to a much-debated passage in the *Athenian Constitution* (22), ostracism was instituted by Cleisthenes in 508/7 as a democratic measure against potential tyrants and other powerful individuals and was used for the first time in 488/7 against Hipparchus. According to Androtion (*FGrH* 324 F6), however, the institution of ostracism corresponded with its first use against Hipparchus. Scholars have tried to reconcile the apparent conflicts in the sources or have preferred one source over the other for various reasons; for surveys and detailed discussions with extensive bibliography, see Rhodes, *Commentary,* 267–71; Thomsen, *Origin of Ostracism,* 11–60 (on the apparent conflict between the two sources), 61–108 (on whether Hipparchus was the first to be ostracized), and 109–42 (on whether Cleisthenes is to be credited with the invention of ostracism).

The Athenian assembly voted in the sixth prytany whether to hold an ostracism. If they decided to hold one, then they actually held it in the Agora in the eighth prytany. They used potsherds *(ostraca)* to record their choices. If at least six thousand total votes were cast, the "winner" was exiled for ten years with no loss of property. Philochorus, however, is represented here as saying two things that contradict the picture assembled from other sources. First, that "the people voted before the eighth prytany on whether they wanted to propose an ostracism." Scholars are generally in agreement that this statement has been garbled in transmission. The Athenians voted in the sixth prytany whether to conduct an ostracism, and, if they decided to, they carried it out in the eighth prytany. For the vote in the sixth prytany, see *Athenian Constitution* 43.5; Rhodes, *Commentary,* 270; Jacoby, *FGrH* 3b suppl. vol. 1, p. 316. Second, that the man who received the most votes would be ostracized, "provided there were fewer than six thousand (votes against him)." This is in error for "provided there were *no* fewer than six thousand (votes against him)," reading μή for our lexicon's μέν (see Jacoby,

FGrH 3b suppl. vol. 1, pp. 316–17 and 3b suppl. vol. 2, pp. 227–28). For extensive bibliography on the question whether the six thousand votes mentioned here "represents a quorum of 6,000 voters present in the Ekklesia or, instead, the minimum number of votes required for banishing the top candidate in the ostrakaphoria," see Thomsen, *Origin of Ostracism,* 66 n. 23; Jacoby, *FGrH* 3b suppl. vol. 1, pp. 316–17; Rhodes, *Commentary,* 270–71. On the mistakes in the Philochorus passage that are supposedly due to the lexicographer's garbling of "Didymus," see Jacoby, *FGrH* 3b suppl. vol. 1, pp. 315, 317; Thomsen, *Origin of Ostracism,* 44, 47. Other ancient sources represented Philochorus differently, also attributing to him (correctly or incorrectly) a description of the origins of ostracism. For the text, see *FGrH* 328 F 30. For discussion, see Jacoby, *FGrH,* 3b suppl. vol. 1, pp. 315–18 and 3b suppl. vol. 2, pp. 227–28; Thomsen, *Origin of Ostracism,* 44, 47, 139.

Commentary on Dem. 5
(P.Berol.inv. 21188)

P.Berol.inv. 21188 is a papyrus from Hermoupolis dating from the second century C.E. that consists of one large fragment and ten smaller ones. The large fragment (frag. 1) preserves part of a commentary on the phrase "about the shadow of an ass" from Dem. 5.25, *On the Peace*. The reference in fragment 2 to "renting" (μεμισθωμέ[νῳ]) the ass continues the discussion of the proverb. The "shadow" is still apparently under discussion in col. 2, line 14 (σκια.[– – –]), which would suggest that this comes from a commentary rather than from a lexicon. There is a parallel treatment of the proverb in Harpocration, s.v. περὶ τῆς ἐν Δελφοῖς σκιᾶς (Π 54), which is discussed below.

There are no significant correspondences in the Demosthenic scholia.

Text: Text and commentary in Maehler. Republished with fewer restorations in Ioannidou.

TEXT AND TRANSLATION OF P.BEROL.INV. 21188

[Οὐκοῦν εὔηθ]ες πρὸς ἄπαντα[ς] πε‖[ρὶ τῆς ἐν] Δελφοῖς σκιᾶς πο-
λεμῆσαι· | [παρα]πεποιῆσθαί φησιν ὁ Δίδυ‖[μος παρὰ τὴν θρυλου]-
μένην [π]αροι‖[μίαν ὑπὸ τῶν π]ροτέρων τὴν οὕτως | [φερομέν]ην περὶ
ὄνου σκιᾶς· οὐ γὰρ | [παρέλαβε]ν ὁ Δημοσθένης ἕνεκα | [τοῦ γραφέ]ν-
τος ὑπὸ τῶν Ἀμφικτυ‖[όνων ψ]ηφίσματος, Φιλίππου | [δέ, διὰ Δελ]-
φοὺς καὶ τὰ Φωκικά· | [ἐπαινῶν τὴν π]ρὸς αὐτὸν εἰρήνην | [προύτρεψε
μεί]ζοσι κ[αὶ] χρησιμω‖[τέροις προσέχειν ἡ]συχάσα[ν]τας κατε‖[ναν-

τίον τῷ ὀνηλ]άτῃ τῇ ὄνου σκιᾷ | [κερδαίνοντι· οὖ]τος ἀπ[ο]χρήσας
πο|[τὲ] ἀπολογούμενον | [– – –]ους̣..σι | [– – –]υ̣
    "[Therefore silly] . . . to fight against everyone about the shadow at Delphi" (Dem. 5.25). Didymus says that this was adapted from a proverbial expression—the one that goes "about the shadow of an ass"—which had commonly been used by earlier authors. For Demosthenes did not use the expression because of the decree made by the Amphictyons, but because of Philip, on account of his behavior with regard to Delphi and the Phocian affairs. Praising (Athens's) peace with him (sc. Philip), he (Demosthenes) encouraged them, while at peace, to direct their minds to better and more useful things, in contrast to the ass driver who wants to make a profit with the shadow of an ass. (– – –*at least 3 lines unrestored* – – –).

NOTES ON P.BEROL.INV. 21188

The proverbial expression "about the shadow of an ass" was already current in the fifth century (see, for example, Aristophanes *Wasps* 191) and occurred frequently in Greek literature. The fifth-century poet Archippus even wrote a comedy entitled *Shadow of an Ass* (ὄνου σκιά); see fragments 35–36 in vol. 3.2 of Kassel and Austin. It is not known whether the expression "about the shadow of an ass" preceded the aetiology of the expression, or vice versa; see Maehler, 631 and 633 nn. 8–10, for the loci classici of both the expression and its aetiology. The standard aetiology of the expression is found in one of the biographies of Demosthenes: "A young man in the summer rented an ass from the city to go to Megara. At midday, when the sun became very hot, each of them (sc. the young man and the owner of the ass) wanted to get under its shadow. Each tried to keep the other away, the owner saying that he had rented him the ass, not its shadow, and the renter saying that he had control over the whole thing" (Ps.-Plutarch *Moralia* 848a–b, ed. Fowler).
    There is a parallel discussion of the phrase in Harpocration (text 2, frag. 2):

    (Π 54) Περὶ τῆς ἐν Δελφοῖς σκιᾶς· Δημοσθένης Φιλιππικοῖς. Δίδυμός φησι τὴν περὶ ὄνου σκιᾶς παροιμίαν παραπεποιῆσθαι ὑπὸ τοῦ ῥήτορος λέγοντος περὶ τῆς ἐν Δελφοῖς σκιᾶς, λέγεσθαι δ' αὐτὴν ἐπὶ τοῖς περὶ τῶν μηδενὸς ἀξίων μαχομένοις.
    "About the shadow at Delphi: Demosthenes in the *Philippics*. Didymus says that the proverbial expression 'about the shadow of an ass' was

adapted by the orator when he says 'about the shadow at Delphi,' and that the expression was directed at those who were fighting about things that were worth nothing."

Both entries mention that Demosthenes "adapted" (παραπεποιῆσθαι) the popular saying "about the shadow of an ass," and both explain that his intention was to reproach those who were wasting their time quarrelling about trivialities. Earlier scholars or popular opinion may have regarded the "shadow" as an Amphictyonic decree, referring perhaps to the ones (plural) mentioned in Dem. 5.19. This could explain why Didymus quickly dismisses that view before arguing for his own interpretation of the shadow as Philip's "behavior with regard to Delphi and the Phocian affairs." It is unclear how the version from Harpocration is related to the version in Berol. 21188. Both speak of the orator as "adapting the proverbial expression" (παροιμίαν παραπεποιῆσθαι), but there are otherwise no telling verbal similarities between them. The extract preserved in Harpocration could be an abbreviated and colorless version of the account in Berol. 21188, or both may have been derived independently from Didymus. Modern opinion on the meaning of this expression in its context seems to side with Weil, *Harangues,* ad loc., who interprets it as referring to the meaninglessness of participation in the Amphictyonic Council; similarly, Sandys, *Demosthenes,* 107–8.

Didymus is known from other sources to have been interested in proverbial expressions. For fragments of his *On Proverbs* (Περὶ Παροιμιῶν), see Schmidt, 396–98. In general on proverbs and the genre of paroemiography in antiquity, see the two articles by Rupprecht. Other fragments of Greek works on proverbs are collected and discussed in Leutsch and Schneidewin.

Commentary on Dem. 22
(P.Stras.inv. 84)

P.Stras.inv. 84 (Pack[2] 310) is a commentary on Dem. 22, *Against Androtion,* dating to the late first century C.E. The width of the papyrus varies from 8.1 to 10.0 cm; its length is 18.2 cm. The recto contains accounts from the first half of the century. The verso contains our text, a single column consisting of the ends of twenty-six lines; the restorations of the beginnings of these lines and the final entry are conjectural. Lines 3–26 are written by a second hand. The length of the undamaged lines is debated, with estimates for the portion in lacuna ranging from c. 22 to c. 32 letters; see the editions listed below. The debate over the nature of the text and the length of the original lines has led to some quite different restorations of the text. The most cautious edition and the one that has been used here is that of Wade-Gery and Meritt, though Sealey, "P.Strassburg," 442–43, questions their methodological assumption that one should try to restore the lost parts of lines with as few letters as possible (but see Wade-Gery and Meritt, 165 and n. 8).

   The surviving commentary consists of a series of discussions of eight lemmata from Dem. 22, as was first recognized by Wilcken, "Der Anonymus Argentinensis," 375–77, and as has been correctly followed by all subsequent scholars. An earlier theory proposed by the first editor, B. Keil, had incorrectly regarded the text as an epitome of a history of the Periclean age. Of the massive, now mostly irrelevant commentary produced in support of that view, Meiggs, 516, aptly says: "Few first edi-

tions have illustrated more nakedly the danger of going too far too fast."
Where they survive, the lemmata from Stras. 84 offer the unusual feature of not being direct quotations from Demosthenes, but rather paraphrases introduced by the word ὅτι. In this context, the word ὅτι seems
to mean "(where Demosthenes says) that. . . ." The words following the
word ὅτι represent the gist of Demosthenes' words but are not precise
quotations; nor do they so closely resemble his words that one might
think that the commentator had an unusual edition of Demosthenes in
front of him.

Two other explanations for the lemmata have been proposed. Laqueur thought that Stras. 84 was a "*capitulatio*" (summary or table of
contents) of one of the books of Didymus's *On Demosthenes,* adducing the column headers from Berol. 9780 in support of this view. See
Laqueur, esp. 220–21. Besides the fact that he too readily attributes the
original commentary behind Stras. 84 to the ubiquitous Didymus, Laqueur apparently does not realize that the column headers in Berol. 9780
—unlike the paraphrased lemmata in Stras. 84—indicate topics that are
discussed therein by the commentator. Several of them cannot be directly related to topics raised by Demosthenes. For example, the header
to col. 9 contains the words "That (ὅτι) there are two men named Aristomedes, one from Pherae, the other an Athenian nicknamed 'Brazen.'"
To distinguish between two fourth-century men by the name Aristomedes was Didymus's topic, not that of Demosthenes. The header to col. 10
reads: "That (ὅτι) the speech is by Anaximenes." This topic is, of course,
not raised in the (spurious?) speech. Likewise with the header to column 13: "That (ὅτι) the speech is not of one of the *Philippics,* but is otherwise by Demosthenes." Laqueur's view is incorrect. See Wade-Gery
and Meritt, 168–69; followed by Arrighetti, 66 n. 30.

Wilcken, "Der Anonymus Argentinensis," esp. 377 and 415–18, argued that the word ὅτι introduced quotations that our commentator
excerpted from a lost original commentary. The word ὅτι would then
mean "(the commentator says) that. . . ." He argued that Stras. 84 is
a series of excerpts taken from such a commentary, owing his inspiration for the theory of a lost, excerpted text to D-S[1] and their treatment
of Berol. 9780. Wade-Gery and Meritt, 166–72, have to some extent
followed Wilcken's theory of excerption, noting that this excerptor
seems to be especially interested in the constitutional history of Athens.
However, unlike Wilcken, they correctly regard the introductory clauses
as paraphrased lemmata from Demosthenes. Our commentator's use

of paraphrased lemmata may indicate greater interest in the historical topics themselves than in the passages of Demosthenes to which those comments were originally directed; this is also the view of Arrighetti, 50, 65–66.

The contents of the papyrus are as follows. The first discussion concerns the office of the *epistateis* or the *proedroi* (see Dem. 22.5–9); its lemma probably appeared in the previous column, now lost. The other seven paraphrased lemmata include [ὅτι ὠκοδόμησαν τὰ Προπύλαι]α καὶ τὸν Παρθενῶνα (compare Dem. 22.13), ὅτι τρισὶν ἡμέραις ἐβοή-θησαν | [Εὐβοεῦσιν] (compare Dem. 22.14), ὅτι | [Δεκελικὸς εἴρηται ὁ πόλεμος] (compare Dem. 22.15), ὅτι τῶι πο[λ]έμωι | [παρέστησαν] (compare Dem. 22.15), ὅτι τῶν τριηρο||[ποιῶν ἀποδρὰς ᾤχετο ὁ τα-μίας] (compare Dem. 22.17), ὅτι οἱ θεσ[μοθέτ]αι | [εἰσῆγον τὰς περὶ τῆς ἑταιρήσεως δίκας] (compare Dem. 22.21), and ὅτ[ι] δημοτι[κὸν τ]ὸ [κα]||[κῶς λέγειν τοὺς ἄρχοντας] (compare Dem. 22.32). Note that these paraphrased lemmata, as with the other commentaries surveyed in this book, are discussed in order as they appear in Demosthenes.

Since every discussion in this commentary is of a historical nature, it is easy to connect Stras. 84 with the ancient philological and historical tradition of commentaries on Demosthenes. Though no specific sources are cited within the commentary—which makes it different from most of the surviving examples of this branch of scholarship—its author apparently consulted reference materials on the Athenian constitution (lemmata 1, 6, and 7) and historical sources on fifth- and fourth-century Athens (lemmata 2, 4, 5, and perhaps 3), including a decree or decrees of Pericles (lemma 2). Lines 3–11 have been frequently discussed and are important for anyone interested in fifth-century Athenian finance, the maintenance of the navy, or the policies of Pericles.

There are no obvious or significant correspondences in the Demosthenic scholia. Wade-Gery and Meritt, 168, note that our commentator's interests are different from those of the scholiasts.

Text: From Wade-Gery and Meritt, 164. Other editions with full or partial commentary by Keil, 75–77 (not to be trusted: see above); Wilcken, "Der Anonymus Argentinensis," 414–15; de Ricci; and Sealey, "P.Strassburg," 443–44. Sealey's restorations of lines 1–8 offer an interesting alternative to those of Wade-Gery and Meritt and are given and discussed below.

TEXT AND TRANSLATION OF P.STRAS.INV. 84

[- - -ὥστε εἶναι τοῖς τε πρυτάνεσι] | [τοῖς πεντήκοντα καὶ τοῖς
προέδροις το]ῖς ἐννέα ἐπιστάτας δύο, καὶ πρόβου|[λοι καὶ συγγρα-
φεῖς ὁπότε δέοι δέκα ἦσα]ν· ἑκάστης γὰρ φυλῆς ἕνα ᾑροῦντ᾽ ἄν |
[ἑκάστοτε. **Ὅτι ᾠκοδόμησαν τὰ Προπύλαι]α καὶ τὸν Παρθενῶνα.**
μετ᾽ ἔτη τρι̣|[άκοντα μάλιστα ταῦτα ὕστερον τῶν Μηδι]κῶν ἤρξαντο
οἰκοδο[με]ῖ̣ν̣, ἐποι̣|[ήσαντο δ᾽ ἀπὸ τῶν φόρων εἰπόντος ἐπ᾽ Εὐ]θυδήμου
Περικλέους γνώμη[ν] εἰ̣ς̣ | [τὰ Παναθήναια ἀνενεγκεῖν τῆι Ἀθηνᾶι]
τὰ ἐν δημοσί<ωι> ἀποκείμενα τάλαν|[τα ἅπερ συνηγμένα παρὰ τῶν
πόλεων ἦν πε]ντακισχείλια κατὰ τὴν Ἀριστεί̣|[δου τάξιν καὶ ἄλλα
τρισχείλια ἀναφέρ]ειν εἰς τὴν πόλιν μετ᾽ ἐκεῖνο γινο̣|[μένων τῶν
ἔργων· θαλάσσης δ᾽ ὅπως ἂν κρατ]ῶσι, τὴν βουλὴν τῶν παλαιῶν
τριή|[ρων ἐπιμελεῖσθαι ὥστε ὑγιεῖς παραδι]δόναι, καινὰς δ᾽ ἐπι-
ναυπηγεῖν ἑκάσ|[του ἐνιαυτοῦ πρὸς ταῖς ὑπαρχούσαις δ]έκα. **Ὅτι
τρισὶν ἡμέραις ἐβοήθησαν | [Εὐβοεῦσιν.** τούτοις μὲν παρεγένοντο]
Ἀθηναῖοι πολεμουμένοις, Θη[β]αίων | [δ᾽ ἐκράτησαν βοήθειαν λα-
βόντες καὶ π]ρὸς τοῦ ῥήτορος τριήρει ἐπιδρ[σίμωι·] **Ὅτι | [Δεκε-
λικὸς εἴρηται ὁ πόλεμος.** τὸν Πελοπ]ονησιακὸν πόλεμον Δεκελικὸν
ἔφη | [κατὰ μέρος· οὕτω δὲ καὶ Σικελικὸς εἴρητ]α̣ι καὶ Ἀρχιδάμιος.
Ὅτι τῶι πο[λ]έμωι | [παρέστησαν. προδόντος τὰς ναῦς Ἀδειμ]άν-
του ἡττήθησαν. **Ὅτι τῶν τριηρο|[ποιῶν ἀποδρὰς ᾤχετο ὁ ταμίας.**
οὗτος ἦ]ν̣ ταμίας τ[ῶν] ὑπὸ τῆς βουλῆ[ς ἐψη]|[φισμένων τοῖς τριηρο-
ποιοῖς χρημάτ]ων ἐπὶ τὰ ἀναλώματα τὰ ἑκά[στου ἐνιαυ]|[τοῦ ὧν
πρότερον αὐτοῖς ταμίαι ἦσαν οἱ] πάλαι κωλακρέται. **Ὅ{ι}τι οἱ θεσ-
[μοθέτ]αι | [εἰσῆγον τὰς περὶ τῆς ἑταιρήσεως δίκας.**] διὰ τὸ
δίκας ἐ[πι]δεταγμένα[ς διδόνα]ι | [ἑαυτοῖς οὗτοι κύριοι ἦσαν ταύτας
εἰσάγειν αὐτο[ί]· μ[ε]τέβαινον δ[ὲ] ο[ἱ ἄρξα]ν̣|[τες τὴν ἀρχὴν τὴν
τῶν θεσμοθετῶν εἰς] Ἄρειον Πάγο[ν], τ[οῖ]ς δ᾽ ἐξ θε<σ>μ[οθέταις] |
[προσετίθεντο οἴδε τρεῖς ὅ τε ἐπώνυμος] πρὸς ὃν αἱ χρ[ο]νογραφίαι
καὶ βα[σ]ι̣|[λεὺς ὁ τὰ ἀσεβειῶν διοικῶν καὶ ὁ πολέ]μαρχος, κα̣<ὶ> νομο-
φυλάκων ἀρχα̣[ὶ δια]|[φέρουσαι ἦσαν καὶ δεσμοφυλάκων ἥτις ἀν]δρῶν
ῑᾱ. **Ὅτ[ι] δημοτι̣[κὸν τ]ὸ [κα]|[κῶς λέγειν τοὺς ἄρχοντας.** οἷαι
ἦσαν κατὰ τῶ̣ν̣ πρότερον ἀρχ[όντων παρ]ρησίαι δηλοῦσιν οἱ κωμι-
κοί - - -]

[Lemma missing (compare Dem. 22.5, 9)]: [- - -] with the result that
there were two *epistateis* for the fifty *prytaneis* and the nine *proedroi*,
and, when necessary, there were ten *probouloi* and *syngrapheis*. For they
would choose one from each tribe each time.

That they built the Propylaea and the Parthenon (compare Dem. 22.13): They began to build these things about thirty years after the Persian Wars, but they did so using the tribute payments, when Pericles in the archonship of Euthydemus (450/49) proposed to dedicate to Athena at the Panathenaea the 5,000 talents available in the public treasury, which had been collected from the cities in accordance with the tribute assessment of Aristides, and to dedicate the other 3,000 talents to the city thereafter while the buildings were under construction. And in order to assure control of the sea, he proposed that the Council take care of the old triremes so as to hand them over in good shape, and every year to build ten new ones in addition to the existing ones.

That they helped the Euboeans in three days (compare Dem. 22.14): The Athenians supported them when they were at war, but receiving aid and also the trireme lent by the orator, they defeated the Thebans.

That the war was called the Decelean (compare Dem. 22.15): He said that the Peloponnesian War was partially Decelean. The terms "Sicilian" and "Archidamian" are also used in this way.

That they were reduced to submission in the war (compare Dem. 22.15): They were defeated when Adimantus betrayed the ships.

That the treasurer of the trireme builders ran away (compare Dem. 22.17): This man was a treasurer of the money for the trireme builders that was voted on by the Council toward the yearly expenses. Before this the old *colacretae* were their treasurers.

That the *thesmothetae* introduced charges of prostitution (compare Dem. 22.21): Through handing out assigned cases, they were in charge of introducing these cases themselves. But those who had held the office of *thesmothetes* passed into the Areopagus, and these three were added to the six *thesmothetae*: the eponymous archon, after whom the annalistic writings are arranged; the *basileus,* who manages things related to impiety; and the *polemarch*. And the offices of the *nomophylakes* and the *desmophylakes,* an office of eleven men, were different.

That it was typical in democracies for people to speak badly of leaders (compare Dem. 22.32): The comic poets make evident the sort of verbal abuse that existed against former leaders (– – –*unknown number of lines lost*).

NOTES ON P.STRAS.INV. 84

Lemma missing (compare Dem. 22.5–9): In this entry the commentator
gives the names and numbers of certain Athenian officials. The surviving
portion of the commentary opens with the end of a comment on an unknown lemma, but it is not difficult to guess what it was. Since the next
lemma is taken from Dem. 22.13 and each successive lemma follows the
order of the speech, it is reasonable to assume that the missing lemma
preceded 22.13 and in some way concerned Athenian governmental officials. Dem. 22.5–9 offers two possibilities. In this section of the speech,
Demosthenes says that Androtion had failed to seek a preliminary decree before proposing a vote before the Council; he incidentally refers to
the *epistates* (22.5) and the *proedroi* (22.9). Either of these references
could have motivated the commentator's remark, which ends with a discussion of the offices of the *epistateis, prytaneis, proedroi, probouloi,*
and *syngrapheis.* The comment apparently distinguishes between the
two kinds of *epistateis,* the one who presided over the *prytaneis,* and
the one who presided over the *proedroi.* This might have been useful to
the ancient reader and student of Athenian constitutional history who
had encountered both kinds of *epistateis* in classical authors. Both kinds
of *epistateis* are discussed in the *Athenian Constitution* 44. The *epistates*
of the prytany, according to 44.1, was chosen by lot to serve one time
for a single day; he oversaw the public seal and the keys to the sanctu-
aries containing the state funds and records and remained on duty in
the Tholos with a third of the current *prytaneis.* The *epistates* of the
proedroi (44.2–3) is chosen by the *epistates* of the prytany whenever the
prytany calls a meeting of the Council or Assembly; see 43.3–4, and
Rhodes, *Commentary,* 520–26. This second *epistates* oversees the board
of nine called the *proedroi* (also chosen by the *epistates* of the prytany);
the *proedroi* were responsible for seeing that meetings of the Council and
Assembly ran smoothly and for putting questions to the vote in them.
The *epistates* of the *proedroi* is the official referred to in Dem. 22.5 and
22.9. On the two officials, see Rhodes, *Commentary,* 531–35.

The restored text goes on to mention the ten *probouloi* and *syngrapheis.* The office of the *probouloi* was created in 413, according to
Thucydides 8.1.3. Thucydides does not call them *probouloi* but says
that they were appointed to be the ones "who would *probouleuein*
about present circumstances whenever it was proper" (οἵτινες περὶ τῶν
παρόντων ὡς ἂν καιρὸς ᾖ προβουλεύσουσιν). According to the *Athenian
Constitution* 29.2, there were ten *probouloi* who held office until the

summer of 411, when twenty new ones were added to their number (Thucydides 8.67.1 refers to a total of ten; on which see Gomme et al., ad loc.). Their job was to draft legislation (συγγράψειν) to help keep the city safe; for the title ξυγγραφεῖς, see Thucydides 8.67.1. These *syngrapheis* were the men who helped to put the oligarchy of the Four Hundred into power in 411, who in turn put the Five Thousand into power; see *Athenian Constitution* 29–33; Rhodes, *Commentary*, 372–75; Gomme et al. on Thucydides 8.1.3 and 8.67.1.

Sealey, "P.Strassburg," 443–44, restores lines 1–3 differently: "with the result that there were two *epistateis* for the *prytaneis* and the nine *proedroi*. And they established ten *probouloi* after the defeat in Sicily. For they chose from each tribe one man over forty years old" ([ὥστε] | [εἶναι τοῖς τε πρυτάνεσι καὶ τοῖς προέδροις το]ῖς ἐννέα ἐπιστάτας δύο. καὶ προβού|[λους μετὰ τὴν ἐν Σικελίᾳ ἧτταν δέκα κατέστησα]ν. ἑκάστης γὰρ φυλῆς ἕνα ἡροῦντ' ἄν|[δρα ὑπὲρ μ̄ ἔτη γεγονότα.]) Sealey's restorations have certain advantages that should be considered. The *probouloi* were established after the Sicilian disaster in 413. The *Athenian Constitution* 29.2 says that the *probouloi* were to be over forty years old (compare Thucydides 8.1.3, πρεσβυτέρων ἀνδρῶν). The substitution of the word ἄν[δρα] for Wade-Gery and Meritt's conjecture of ἄν with the imperfect converts the selection of *probouloi* from a procedure that was periodically repeated (but see Wade-Gery and Meritt, 174–75) to the attested one-time event of 413.

That they built the Propylaea and the Parthenon (Dem. 22.13): In this entry the commentator discusses the financing and date of construction of the Propylaea and Parthenon. The actual lemma is οἱ τὰ προπύλαια καὶ τὸν παρθενῶν' οἰκοδομήσαντες ἐκεῖνοι ("those men having built the Propylaea and the Parthenon"), which the commentator has perhaps paraphrased as [ὅτι ᾠκοδόμησαν τὰ Προπύλαι]α καὶ τὸν Παρθενῶνα. When he refers to the historic success of the Athenian navy at Salamis during the Persian Wars, Demosthenes incorrectly attributes to that same generation the construction of the Propylaea and Parthenon. Most modern commentators have been quick to point this out. See Weil, *Plaidoyers*, ad loc.; Wayte, 19–20; Wade-Gery and Meritt, 182. As Wade-Gery and Meritt, 182, have plausibly suggested, the original commentary probably pointed out Demosthenes' error by showing that the Periclean decree of some years later provided for the construction of these buildings. The excerpting commentator of Stras. 84, on the other hand, seems more interested in the details of dates and financing than in using that information against Demosthenes. This is in keeping with the ancient philological and historical commentators' apparent lack of interest in discussing how Demosthenes sometimes reshapes historical detail to fit the rhetorical needs of the moment.

The decree of Pericles and its provisions have been exhaustively treated by scholars interested in the fifth century. Several key questions have been raised. First, do lines 3–11 represent one continuous section of commentary, as with Wade-Gery and Meritt, or are they to be divided by a new lemma somewhere in the middle? Wilcken, "Der Anonymus Argentinensis," 382–86, separated lines 3–4 from lines 5–11. Sealey divides the passage at line 8, so that whatever is being said about the navy in lines 9–11 does not have to be connected with the discussion of financing for the building program in lines 3–8. The words at the end of line 8 (μετ᾽ ἐκεῖνο γινο) are difficult no matter how the text is divided. Sealey takes them as the beginning of a new comment on a lemma about shipbuilding introduced in the first part of that line, e.g., [ὅτι ἔδει τριήρεις ποι]εῖν εἰς τὴν πόλιν, with τὴν πόλιν perhaps in error for τὸν πόλεμον; see Wilcken, "Der Anonymus Argentinensis," 393–94; Meiggs, 517. Similarly, Meiggs, 517–18, prefers to see a new lemma introduced at or near the γινο|[μένων τῶν ἔργων] of lines 8–9, because in his view there is "no logical connection between financial arrangements for the building programme and regulations for ship-building. These cannot surely have been included in the decree, but they are relevant to Demosthenes' emphasis on the fleet." But Wade-Gery, 222–24, argues that the Congress Decree (c. 450–447?) of Plutarch's *Life of Pericles* 17 is an excellent parallel to the decree in the papyrus, as it too concerns both the building program and the navy. Meiggs, 512–15, defends the Congress Decree as an essentially authentic fifth-century decree.

Whatever the correct attribution of lines here, in treating lines 3–11 as a continuous comment on a single lemma, Wade-Gery and Meritt have reconstructed a decree of Pericles with some interesting connections to epigraphical and literary evidence. According to their restoration, in 450/49 Pericles proposed a decree with the following features:

Provision 1: Athena was immediately, in the archonship of Euthydemus (450/49), to receive the 5,000 talents currently in the treasury. This sum, the result of the tribute assessment of Aristides, would allow Athens to start building the Parthenon and Propylaea.

The archonship of Euthydemus presents the main problem here. There is literary and inscriptional evidence for a Euthydemus as archon

of both 450/49 and 431/o, and a Euthydemus or Euthynus as archon
for 426/5. See Wade-Gery and Meritt, 183, and Bloedow, esp. 67, for
discussions of the evidence, with extensive bibliography (Bloedow does
not discuss this papyrus). Wade-Gery and Meritt's text rests on the assumption that the commentator's "Euthydemus" refers to the archon of
450/49 (this is followed, though cautiously, by Meiggs, 518), though
Wilcken, "Der Anonymus Argentinensis," and Sealey, "P.Strassburg,"
make him the archon of 431/o and consequently interpret the passage
differently.

The tribute assessment was made by Aristides in 478/7, according to
the *Athenian Constitution* 23.5. Meiggs, 58–60, suggests on the basis
of Plutarch's *Life of Aristides* 24.1–2 that Aristides may have taken several years to complete the assessment, and that 478/7 is only the year
in which he was appointed to carry it out. On the date and method of
collection and the amount of the assessment, see Meiggs, 58–65. On
the costs of and schedule for building the Parthenon and Propylaea, see
Gomme et al., 20–25.

Provision 2: An additional 3,000 talents were to be brought to the
Acropolis while the buildings were under construction.

This restoration is based on Wade-Gery and Meritt's argument that
payments totaling 3,000 talents were made over fifteen years, from 449
to 434. They suggest (1) that the 3,000 talents are the same as the ones
mentioned in a decree of Callias (434) as being currently available; see
D1, lines 3–4, in Meritt et al., 2: 46–47; and (2) that the payment
of 200 talents to the "other gods" (see D2, line 22, in Meritt et al., 2:
47), multiplied by fifteen years (449–434), would account for the total
of 3,000 talents. Furthermore, these 3,000 talents, when added to the
5,000 talents of the papyrus (lines 6–7), might yield the 8,000 talents of
Isocrates 8.126 (ed. Benseler), where Pericles is said to have "brought up
to the Acropolis 8,000 talents, not counting the sacred moneys" (εἰς δὲ
τὴν ἀκρόπολιν ἀνήνεγκεν ὀκτακισχίλια τάλαντα χωρὶς τῶν ἱερῶν).

This reconstruction has not met with wide approval. Gomme, 337–
38, argues that a fifteen-year financial plan yielding the supposed 3,000
talents could never have passed in the Assembly. Sealey, "P.Strassburg,"
446, doubts whether the 5,000 talents can plausibly be combined with
the (restored) 3,000 talents to yield the 8,000 talents of Isocrates. For
further discussion of the relevance of Stras. 84 to the question of the
8,000 talents of Isocrates 8.126 and Diodorus 12.38.2 and also the
10,000 talents of Isocrates 15.234 (ed. Benseler), see Meritt, esp. 216–

26; Wade-Gery and Meritt, 188–97; Sealey, "P.Strassburg," 446; Meiggs, 517–18.

Provision 3: Each year's Council would be charged with maintaining the fleet and adding ten new triremes so that Athenian naval supremacy might be maintained.

Themistocles is said to have decreed after the Persian Wars that twenty new ships be built each year (Diodorus 11.43.3). If the reading "ten" in line 11 is correct, then perhaps, as Wade-Gery and Meritt, 187, suggest, this decree of Pericles represents a peacetime reduction of that quota. Both the reading "ten" and the assumption that that number (even if it is correct) refers to a number of ships have been questioned. Eddy, 146, argues that a quota of ten new ships per year would not have been sufficient to maintain the navy in the time of Pericles, and so suggests the reading δέκα may not be correct. Rhodes, *Athenian Boule,* 115–16, suggests that even if "ten" is correct, it may refer, for example, to ten trireme builders; similarly, Jordan, 28, notes that "ten" could be part of a longer word. Rhodes also notes that the Assembly and the Council seem to have shared some of the responsibility for shipbuilding. While the Assembly chose the chief engineer and decided on the number of ships to be built, the Council (as represented by ten trireme builders) oversaw the actual construction and handled the funds; see Rhodes, *Athenian Boule,* 115–22, esp. 117. Jordan, 27, finds the restorations here implausible, because the text now "implies that it was the duty of the council to inspect and judge the condition of each ship as its trierarch brought it back from sea," although, according to Jordan, this was actually the job of the overseers of the shipyards. Though he does not suggest restorations to the Greek text, Jordan, 28, argues that the fragmentary decree may have instructed the Council to sell "obsolete or useless equipment" from Athens's triremes. On the maintenance of the Athenian navy in the time of Pericles, see Eddy. On fifth-century Athenian finance in general, see Meiggs. On this section of the papyrus, see Wade-Gery and Meritt, 181–88.

Sealey, "P.Strassburg," 443–44, offers significantly different restorations of lines 3–8: "That they built the Propylaea and the Parthenon. When the money had been transferred from Delos, they began to build the temples from the allies' contributions, but they made a decree concerning the balance. For in the archonship of Euthydemus (431/o), with Pericles making a proposal at the beginning of the war, the people voted to spend the talents lying in the treasury, whenever necessary. And more than five thousand talents were already available, having been collected in accordance with the tribute assessment of Aristides. That it was necessary to build triremes for the city" ([ὅτι ᾠκοδόμησαν τὰ Προπύλαι]α καὶ τὸν Παρθενῶνα. μετε[ν]ην̣ε̣[γ]][μένων τῶν χρημάτων ἐκ Δήλου τὰ ἱερὰ ἐκ τῶν συμμαχι]κῶν ἤρξαντο οἰκοδο[με]ῖν, ἐποί[ησαν δὲ δόγμα περὶ τῶν ὑπολοίπων. ἐπὶ γὰρ Εὐ]θυδήμου Περικλέους γνώμη[ν] εἰσ][ηγησαμένου ἐν ἀρχῇ τοῦ πολέμου ἔδοξε τῷ δήμῳ] τὰ ἐν δημο- σί<ῳ> ἀποκείμενα τάλαν[τα ἀναλίσκειν ὅτε δέοι. ὑπῆρχε δὲ πλέον ἢ πε]ντακισχείλια κατὰ τὴν Ἀριστεί[δου τάξιν συνηγμένα. ὅτι ἔδει τριήρεις ποι]εῖν εἰς τὴν πόλιν.). Sealey's reconstruction of these lines contains some significant differences from that of Wade-Gery and Meritt. The restored date of "thirty years after the Persian Wars" has disappeared, to be replaced with a reference to a transfer of funds from Delos. Pericles' decree has been moved from 450/49 to 431/0 (the archonship of another Euthydemus), and so now represents a wartime rather than a peacetime policy. The 3,000 talents have disappeared, and there is a new lemma in line 8, which introduces a separate discussion of the Council's obligations regarding the navy.

These are clearly complex and interesting textual and historical issues. Three points should be emphasized. First, the exact number of letters lost at the beginnings of these lines cannot be known, whether it is the average twenty-four of Wilcken, "Der Anonymus Argentinensis," or the thirty-three to forty-one letters of Sealey, "P.Strassburg." But within this range there is quite a bit of room for disagreement and creative speculation. Second, the question whether a new lemma is introduced in line 8 is crucial to the interpretation of this passage, but it is unfortunately also made indeterminable by the fact that our commentator does not use precise quotations for lemmata. Thus the break in thought can only be conjectural. Third, one cannot assume that whatever the commentator had to say in these lines would necessarily correspond to or be verifiable by other evidence, whether literary or epigraphical. Sealey, "P.Strassburg," 445, comes closest to agreeing with this last point (but contrast Jordan, 27).

That they helped the Euboeans in three days (Dem. 22.14): This entry provides additional historical information to supplement the target passage. The actual lemma is ὅτι πρώην Εὐβοεῦσιν ἡμερῶν τριῶν ἐβοηθήσατε ("that recently you helped the Euboeans within three days"), which the commentator has paraphrased as ὅτι τρισὶν ἡμέραις ἐβο- ήθησαν | [Εὐβοεῦσιν]. The commentator substitutes ἐν with the dative

for Demosthenes' time expression in the genitive. Dem. 22.14 mentions
Athenian aid to the Euboeans in 357 as a more recent example of an
Athenian military success that was attributable to its powerful navy. According to Aeschines 3.85, it took Athens five days to get there and an
additional thirty days to convince the Thebans to surrender: ἐν πέντε
ἡμέραις ἐβοηθήσατε αὐτοῖς καὶ ναυσὶ καὶ πεζικῇ δυνάμει, καὶ πρὶν
τριάκονθ' ἡμέρας διελθεῖν ὑποσπόνδους Θηβαίους ἀφήκατε, κύριοι
τῆς Εὐβοίας γενόμενοι. The event is mentioned in passing, without detail, in Dem. 18.99.

The phrase "and also the trireme lent by the orator" ([καὶ π]ρὸς τοῦ
ῥήτορος τριήρει ἐπιδο[σίμωι]) in line 13 does not follow the grammatical construction introduced by the proposed restoration of [βοήθειαν
λαβόντες] that immediately precedes it, but its sense is clear enough. On
this first occasion when rich citizens volunteered for the trierarchy, Demosthenes served as a volunteer trierarch. He also mentions this in orations 18.99 and 21.161. On the campaign and the volunteer trierarchy,
see MacDowell, *Meidias*, 380–81, with bibliography.

That the war was called the Decelean (Dem. 22.15): The purpose of this
entry is apparently to give some of the names of parts of the Peloponnesian War. The actual lemma is ἐπὶ τοῦ Δεκελεικοῦ πολέμου ("in the
Decelean War"), which the commentator may have paraphrased as ὅτι
| [Δεκελικὸς εἴρηται ὁ πόλεμος]. Demosthenes mentions the Decelean
War as a historic example of an Athenian military failure that was due
to a poorly maintained navy. The term "Decelean War" refers to the
period from the Spartan fortification of Decelea in 413 (see Thucydides
7.19) to the end of the war in 404. Two other names for periods within
the so-called Peloponnesian War are then given as parallels. One is the
Archidamian War (431–421), otherwise known as the Ten Years' War
(for the latter term, see Thucydides 5.25.1). Harpocration, s.v. Ἀρχι-
δάμιος πόλεμος, says this term refers to the first ten years of the war and
is named "after (the Spartan king) Archidamus's attack on Attica" (ἀπὸ
τοῦ τὸν Ἀρχίδαμον εἰς τὴν Ἀττικὴν ἐμβαλεῖν); for which see Thucydides 2.10–12. The second name for a war is in lacuna; proposals
have included "Sicilian" ([Σικελικό]ς or [Σικελικός]) (Wilcken, "Der
Anonymus Argentinensis"; Wade-Gery and Meritt) and "Mantinean"
([Μαντινικός]) (Sealey). Strauss, esp. 166–69, discusses the ancient terminology and dates for the different parts of what is today customarily
called the Peloponnesian War.

That they were reduced to submission in the war (Dem. 22.15): This entry states that the military loss was due to Adimantus's betrayal. The actual lemma is οὐ πρότερον τῷ πολέμῳ παρέστησαν πρὶν τὸ ναυτικὸν αὐτῶν ἀπώλετο ("they were not reduced to submission in the war until their fleet was destroyed"), which the commentator has paraphrased as ὅτι τῶι πο[λ]έμωι | [παρέστησαν]. This lemma comes from the same sentence as the previous one, in which Athens is described as having lost in the Decelean War because of a weak navy. The commentator simply notes here that Athens finally lost when the Athenian general Adimantus betrayed the fleet. According to Xenophon *Hellenica* 2.1.32, there were some who accused Adimantus of betraying them and thus causing Athens to lose at Aegospotami in 406; Xenophon does not comment further on the accusation and, in fact, seems to append it only as an afterthought.

That the treasurer of the trireme builders ran away (Dem. 22.17): This entry defines the duties of a certain Athenian official and identifies his fifth-century counterpart. The actual lemma is ὁ τῶν τριηροποιῶν ταμίας ἀποδρὰς ᾤχετ' ἔχων πένθ' ἡμιτάλαντα ("the treasurer of the trireme builders went fleeing with 2 1/2 talents"), which the commentator has perhaps paraphrased as ὅτι τῶν τριηρο|[ποιῶν ἀποδρὰς ᾤχετο ὁ ταμίας]. In this passage of the speech, Demosthenes anticipates that Androtion will defend his decision to propose that a crown be awarded to the outgoing Council even when they failed to maintain the navy, excusing himself and the Council on the grounds that the treasurer of the trireme builders stole the money that they were to use for that purpose. This treasurer is not discussed in the *Athenian Constitution*, but section 49.4 of that text says the Council (or, on an alternate reading, the fund for invalids) had a treasurer in the late fourth century; on which see Rhodes, *Commentary*, 570–71. There was also a treasurer for two specific ships, the *Paralus* and the ship called *Ammon's*; see *Athenian Constitution* 61.7 and Rhodes, *Commentary*, 687–88. Rhodes, *Athenian Boule*, 121–22, suggests that the Council would have appointed this official only with the approval of the Assembly. As a historical footnote, the commentator notes that the now defunct *colacretae* used to take care of the task of managing the funds for shipbuilding. In the late fifth century, the *colacretae* were in charge of disbursing funds from the state treasury. The position was abolished in 411, and their duties were taken over by the *hellenotamiae*. See Rhodes, *Commentary*, 139–

40. Jordan, 28–29, objects to Wade-Gery and Meritt's restorations in lines 17–18 on the grounds that it was the demos, and not the Council, that allocated money for the construction of ships. He proposes [οὗτος ἦ]ν ταμίας τ[ῶν] ὑπὸ τῆς βουλ[ῆς αἱρεθ]][έντων τριηροποιῶν], "This man was a treasurer of the shipbuilders (who were) chosen by the Council."

That the *thesmothetae* introduced charges of prostitution (Dem. 22.21): This entry discusses the names, duties, and induction into the Areopagus of certain Athenian officials. The actual lemma is ἔτι τοίνυν ἐπιχειρεῖ λέγειν περὶ τοῦ τῆς ἑταιρήσεως νόμου, ὡς ὑβρίζομεν ἡμεῖς καὶ βλασφημίας οὐχὶ προσηκούσας κατ' αὐτοῦ ποιούμεθα. καὶ φησὶ δεῖν ἡμᾶς, εἴπερ ἐπιστεύομεν εἶναι ταῦτ' ἀληθῆ, πρὸς τοὺς θεσμοθέτας ἀπαντᾶν ("Furthermore, he tries to say with regard to the law concerning prostitution that we are abusing him and slandering him in an unseemly fashion. And he says that if we think the charges are true, we should take him to court before the *thesmothetae*"), which the commentator has perhaps paraphrased as ὅτι οἱ θεσ[μοθέτ]αι | [εἰσῆγον τὰς περὶ τῆς ἑταιρήσεως δίκας]. Demosthenes has raised the question of his opponent's sexual immorality. He anticipates that Androtion will object to such accusations, on the grounds that Demosthenes and friends did not take him before the *thesmothetae* for his alleged offenses. On the duties of the *thesmothetae,* see the *Athenian Constitution* 59.1–3 and Rhodes, *Commentary,* 657–68; the oversight of cases involving prostitution is not discussed in the *Athenian Constitution.* The commentator's statement that ex-*thesmothetae* entered the Areopagus after their term is corroborated by the *Athenian Constitution* 3.6, which also says that they were members of the Areopagus for life. The eponymous archon, the archon *basileus,* and the polemarch existed in the earliest Athenian constitution, according to the *Athenian Constitution* 3, but their duties had changed significantly by the end of the fourth century, according to *Athenian Constitution* 55–59; see Rhodes, *Commentary,* 612–68. Lines 24–25 have been restored to say that "the offices of the *nomophylakes* and the *desmophylakes,* an office of eleven men, were different." The editors' inspiration here comes from Harpocration, s.v. νομοφύλακες (N 19), who says that the office of *nomophylakes* "is different from that of the *thesmothetae*" (ἀρχή τις . . . διαφέρουσα τῶν θεσμοθετῶν). For the question whether the office of *nomophylakes* was a fourth-century revival of an office originally established in 462/1, see Jacoby, *FGrH* 3b suppl. vol. 1, pp. 337–39; Rhodes, *Commentary,* 315.

The eleven *desmophylakes,* more often simply called the Eleven, played
a key role in the oligarchic revolutions at the end of the fifth century. See
Athenian Constitution 29.4, 35.1, 39.6; on their duties, see *Athenian
Constitution* 52; Rhodes, *Commentary,* 579–88.

**That it was typical in democracies for people to speak badly of lead-
ers** (Dem. 22.32): This lemma is only partially preserved, and the comments following it almost completely lost. The actual lemma is ἐν γὰρ
ταῖς ὀλιγαρχίαις . . . οὐκ ἔστι λέγειν κακῶς τοὺς ἄρχοντας ("for
in oligarchies, . . . it is not permitted to speak badly of the leaders"),
which the commentator has perhaps paraphrased as ὅτ[ι] δημοτι[κὸν
τ]ὸ [κα][κῶς λέγειν τοὺς ἄρχοντας]. But he is more specifically following up on 22.31, where Demosthenes characterizes the Solonian de-
mocracy as a system whereby the wicked were excluded from the possibility of misleading the rest of the city, since Athenian freedom of speech
could target such men and make their crimes known to everyone. Under
an oligarchy, Demosthenes continues, this is not allowed. More specific
to the case against Androtion, Dem. 22.30 says that the Solonian constitution forbade those guilty of prostitution to participate in leadership
roles in the government. Of this almost entirely lost section of the discussion, Wade-Gery and Meritt, 181, suggest that the commentator may
have "noted the parrhesia of Old Comedy, and perhaps subsequent re-
straints." It is important to note, however, that all that survives of the
commentator's remarks are (perhaps) the words "of former leaders," so
that anything beyond this is entirely speculative.

TEXT 6

Lexicon to Dem. 21
(P.Rain.inv. 7)

P.Rain.inv. 7 (Pack² 308) is a sheet of a papyrus codex dating to the fourth or fifth century C.E. that contains part of a special lexicon to Dem. 21, *Against Meidias*. The sheet is torn on all four sides. The recto preserves part of a single entry for the word διαιτητής (Dem. 21.83). The verso contains brief entries for six other lemmata: ἕτεροι δεύτεροι μετὰ ταῦτ[α] (Dem. 21.161), ἐγὼ νομίζω πάντας ἀνθρ[ώπους ἐράνους φέρειν οὐχὶ μόνον ὧν πληρ]ωταὶ γίγνονται (184–85), ἡγεμὼν συ[μμορίας] (157), θέ[μ]ενος τὰ ὅπλ[α] (145), [εἰσι]τήρια (114), [σ]εμναῖς θε[α]ῖς ἱεροποιὸν αἱρηθ[– – –] (115). The organization is roughly alphabetical, beginning on the recto with the letter *delta,* continuing on the verso with *epsilon, eta,* and *theta,* and apparently ending with *iota.* The first, third, fourth, and fifth entries on the verso are ordered by initial letter. The second entry (ἐγώ) should properly precede the first (ἕτεροι), but as other ancient lexica show, absolute alphabetization was more often the exception than the rule. Similarity in sound between the presumed ει of [εἰσι]τήρια and the letter *iota* accounts for this entry's placement after θέ[μ]ενος τὰ ὅπλα; see Naoumides, "Greek Lexicography," 183, 188–89. Unless this special lexicon contained no words from *kappa* to *rho* (which does not seem likely), the sixth and final entry on the verso was ordered by the third word of the lemma (ἱεροποιόν).

This text can be connected with the ancient philological and historical scholarship on Demosthenes in several ways. As with Berol. 5008,

several of the entries in this lexicon bear a close resemblance to entries
in Harpocration; this has been recognized by both Wessely in his edition
and Naoumides, "Literary Papyri," 243. Wessely in *Archiv* attributed
authorship to Didymus, but this is not necessary. The entry on the recto
(διαιτητής) consists of a lengthy quotation from the Aristotelian *Athenian Constitution* (53), but according to Naoumides, "Literary Papyri"
241, the author must have been either quoting it from memory or using
a text representing a very different branch of the ancient manuscript
tradition. Constitutional histories are used alongside quotations from
fourth- and third-century historians throughout the ancient philological
and historical commentaries on Demosthenes. The first entry on the
verso (ἕτεροι δεύτεροι μετὰ ταῦτ[α]) dates Athenian aid to Olynthus
to 349/8. Dionysius of Halicarnassus *First Letter to Ammaeus* 9 shows
that the Atthidographer Philochorus discussed this event under the year
349/8 (*FGrH* 328 F49). The length of the lemmata and the nature of the
comments on them suggest that these entries are abbreviated discussions
excerpted from commentaries; see Naoumides, "Greek Lexicography"
187, 195. The entries for ἡγεμὼν συ[μμορίας] and [εἰσι]τήρια focus on
aspects of classical Athenian culture that might not have been familiar
to readers in the fourth or fifth century C.E. The entry for ἐγὼ νομίζω
πάντας ἀνθρ[ώπους ἐράνους φέρειν οὐχὶ μόνον ὧν πληρ]ωταὶ γίγνονται brings out an important facet of ancient social and economic life,
while primarily emphasizing the etymology of the word πληρωτής. The
entry for θέ[μ]ενος τὰ ὅπλ[α] focuses entirely on word choice.

    There are no significant or interesting correspondences in the Demos-
thenic scholia.

Text: From Wessely's edition, with corrections by Naoumides, "Literary
Papyri." Brief commentary in Wessely's articles and Naoumides, "Literary Papyri."

TEXT AND TRANSLATION OF P.RAIN.INV. 7

Recto

[. . . . καὶ τὰ μὲν μέχρι δέκα δραχμῶν αὐτοτελεῖς εἰσι δικ]άζειν
τὰ | [δ' ὑπὲρ τοῦτο τὸ τίμημα τοῖς διαιτηταῖς παραδιδόασιν. οἱ] δὲ
λαβόντε[ς] | [ἐὰν μὴ δύνωνται διαλῦσαι γιγνώσκουσι κἂ]ν μὲν ἀμφο-
τέροις ἀρ[έσ]][κῃ τὰ γνωσθέντα καὶ ἐμμένωσιν τέλος ἔχ]ει ἡ δίκη. ἐὰν

δὲ ὁ ἕτερ[ος] | [ἐφῇ τῶν ἀντιδίκων εἰς τὸ δικαστήριο]ν̣ ἐμβαλ[ό]ντες
τὰς μαρτυρία[ς] | [καὶ τὰς προκλήσεις καὶ τοὺς νόμους] εἰς τοὺς
ἐχ[ί]νους χωρὶς μὲν | [τὰς τοῦ διώκοντος χωρὶς δὲ τὰς τ]οῦ φεύ-
γοντος καὶ τούτους κατ[α][σημηνάμενοι καὶ τὴν γνῶσιν τὴν τ]οῦ
διαιτητοῦ γεγραμμένην | [ἐν γραμματείῳ παραδιδόασι προσ]αρτή-
σαντες τηρεῖν τέταρσι | [τοῖς τὴν φυλὴν τοῦ φεύγοντο]ς δικάζουσιν.
οἱ δὲ παραλαβόν[τες εἰσάγουσιν εἰς τὸ δικαστ]ήριον. οὐκ ἔξεστι δὲ
γὰρ οὐδὲ νόμοις | [οὔτε προκλήσεσι οὔτε μαρ]τυρίαις ἄλλαις χρήσα-
σθαι ἢ ταῖς παρὰ | [τοῦ διαιτητοῦ ταῖς εἰς τοὺς ἐχίνους] προβεβλη-
μέναις. διαιτηταὶ δέ εἰσιν | [οἷς ἂν ἑξηκοστὸν ἔτος ᾖ. καὶ με]τ᾽ ὀλίγα·
ὁ γὰρ νόμος· ἐάν τις μὴ [γένηται τῆς ἡλικίας αὐτῷ καθη]κ̣ο̣ύσης
διαιτητὴς τῆς αὐτῷ | [καθηκούσης ἄτιμον εἶναι κε]λεύει πλὴν ἐὰν
τύχῃ ἀρχὴν | [ἄρχων τινὰ ἐν ἐκείνῳ τῷ ἐνι]αυτῷ ἀποδημῶν οὐκ
ἀτελεῖς. | [ἔστι δὲ καὶ εἰσαγγέλλειν] εἰς τοὺς διαιτη[τ]άς, ἄν τις
ἀδι[κηθῇ ὑπὸ τοῦ διαιτητοῦ. καὶ ἀτί]μους εἶναι κελεύουσιν οἱ νόμοι |
[ἄν τινων ἀδικίαν καταγνῶσιν]. ἔφεσις δέ ἐστι [κ]αὶ [το]ύτοις.

Arbitrators (Dem. 21.83): "(– – –) and they (the Forty) have absolute
power to judge cases involving up to 10 drachmas, but ones above this
amount they hand over to the arbitrators. And the arbitrators, taking
over the cases—if they are not able to settle them—give a decision on
them, and if the decision is agreeable to both parties and they abide by it,
the case is ended. But if one of the two parties appeals to the jury court,
they put the depositions and the challenges and the laws into jars—those
of the prosecutor and those of the defendant separately—seal them up,
affix to them the decision of the arbitrator written on a tablet, and hand
them over to watch over for safekeeping to the four men who judge the
defendant's tribe. And receiving these things, they introduce them to the
jury court. And it is not permitted to use laws or challenges or depositions other than those from the arbitrator that have already been put
into the jars. Arbitrators are those who are in their sixtieth year." And
after a few words: "If anyone, when he is of the proper age, does not become an arbitrator, {when he is of the proper age}, the law prescribes
that he is to be deprived of his rights as a citizen, unless he happens to be
holding some office in that year or to be abroad, in which case he is {not}
immune. It is also permitted to bring impeachment charges to the arbitrators (as a group), if someone is wronged by an (individual) arbitrator.
And the laws prescribe that (such arbitrators) be deprived of their rights
as citizens, if they find them guilty of wrongdoing. And there is also an
appeals process for these cases" (*Athenian Constitution*, 53.2–6).

Verso

1 [– – –]ọ[.]ισθαι [– – –]

2 [– – –]τανοντες κα[– – –]

3 [– – –]ματικῶς εἰσαγομ[ε].[– – –]

4 [– – –ὁ] ῥήτωρ ἐπέδειξεν τὸ μη[– – –]

5 [– – –].αμενος τὰ μετ[. .].υνεισ.[– – –]

6 [– – –ἁ]γματα κατὰ πηλι[κό]τητα πρọ[– – –]

7 [– – –]μη· ἕτεροι δεύτεροι μετὰ ταῦτ[α – – –]

8 [– – –]ạ ἐπὶ Καλλιμάχου ἔπραξαν Ἀθην[αῖοι – – –]

9 [– – –]· ἐγὼ νομίζω πάντας ἀνθρ[ώπους ἐράνους φέρειν
   οὐχὶ μόνον ὧν]

10 [πληρ]ωταὶ γίγνονται. πληρωτὰς ἔλεγο[ν τοὺς ἀποδιδόντας
   τοῖς ἤ-]

11 [τοι ἐ]πιλαχοῦσιν ἢ ἐωνημένοις τὸν ἔ[ρανον – – –]

12 [– – –]ιον πλήρωμα ἐκπιμπλάντας φαρ[– – –]

13 [– – –πλήρω]μα εἰς τὸν ἔρανον· ἡγεμὼν συ[μμορίας
   ἐκαλεῖτο ὁ μείζω τῶν]

14 [ἄλλω]ν ἔχων περιουσίαν κα[ὶ] διὰ τοῦτ[ο τῶν ἄλλων ἡγεμονεύειν ἐπ-]

15 [ειλη]μμένος· θέ[μ]ενος τὰ ὅπλ[α] ἀντὶ [τοῦ περιθέμενος,
   ὁπλισάμενος]

16 [– – –εἰσι]τήρια οἱ λαχόντες βουλεύειν τοι[– – –]

17 [– – –]αι πάντες καὶ αὐτὴ ἡ θυσία οὕτω [ἐκαλεῖτο – – –]

18 [– – –σ]εμναῖς θε[α]ῖς ἱεροποιὸν αἱρηθ[– – –]

1–3 (– – –)

4 . . . the orator showed . . .

5 (– – –)

6 . . . according to the importance . . .

7 . . . A second call for donations after this (Dem. 21.161) . . .

8 . . . in the archonship of Callimachus (349/8), the Athenians
   made . . .

9 . . . I think that all men support the *eranoi*, not only those of
   which

10   they are "completers" (Dem. 21.184–85). They used to call
      "completers" those who paid the ones who

11   either attained by lot or purchased an *eranos* . . .

12   . . . fulfilling their "completing" . . .

13   . . . the "completing" for the *eranos*. Leader of the symmory
      (Dem. 21.157). This was the name for the one who had

14   more wealth than the others and because of this was ap-
      pointed to lead

15   the others. Placing arms (Dem. 21.145) instead of putting
      them on, arming . . .

16   . . . Inaugural rites (Dem. 21.114). Those who were allotted
      to be on the Council . . .

17   . . . all of them, and the sacrifice itself was thus named . . .

18   . . . elected as *hieropoios* for the hallowed goddesses
      (Dem. 21.115) . . .

NOTES ON P.RAIN.INV. 7

Arbitrator (διαιτητής): The first extant entry of the lexicon draws on
the Aristotelian *Athenian Constitution* 53.2–6 to identify the constitutional position of the "arbitrator" mentioned in Dem. 21.83. The passage describes the appointment of arbitrators, their duties, the procedure for arbitration and appeals, and the checks that were in place to
regulate their behavior. Appointed for the next Athenian year after they
reached the age of fifty-nine, public arbitrators were not technically government officials, but the Athenian government did regulate the process
of arbitration and seek to discourage the arbitrators from wrongdoing.
The system of public arbitration at Athens, according to MacDowell,
Meidias, 303, was "evidently intended to save the time and expense of a
trial by jury in cases in which a settlement could be reached without it."
See Harrell, esp. 10–20 and 21–35; Harrison, 2: 64–68; Rhodes, *Commentary*, 588–96. The passage from the *Athenian Constitution*, here re-
worked as a lexical entry, could serve as useful background for an ancient reader's understanding of Dem. 21.83–101, where Demosthenes
describes in detail Meidias's mistreatment of the arbitrator Strato of
Phaleron. On this section of the speech see MacDowell, *Meidias*, 302–
25; Harrell, 16–18. The divergences between the *Athenian Constitution*

(collated from the edition of Chambers) and Rain. 7 are as follows, ignoring passages that are entirely in lacunae:

Athenian Constitution	Rain. 7
(53.2) δὲ παραλαβόντες	δὲ λαβόντε[ς]
ἔχει τέλος	[τέλος ἔχ]ει
δίκη ἂν δ'	δίκη ἐὰν δὲ
εἰς ἐχίνους	εἰς τοὺς ἐχ[ί]νους
προσαρτήσαντες παραδιδόασι	[παραδιδόασι προσ]αρτήσαντες
το[ῖ]ς δ̄	τηρεῖν τέταρσι
(53.3) τὰ μὲν ἐντὸς . . . τετρακοσίους	*om.*
ἔξεστι δ' οὔτε	ἔξεστι δὲ γὰρ οὐδὲ
ἀλλ' ἢ ταῖς παρὰ τοῦ διαιτητοῦ χρῆσθαι	ἄλλαις χρήσασθαι ἢ ταῖς παρὰ [τοῦ διαιτητοῦ]
(53.3–4) ἐμβεβλημέναις διαιτηταὶ δ'	προβεβλημέναις διαιτηταὶ δέ
(53.4–5) τοῦτο δὲ δῆλον λάχῃ διαίτας ἐκδιαιτᾶν	*om.*
(53.5) νόμος ἂν	νόμος ἐὰν
γένηται διαιτητὴς	[γένηται τῆς ἡλικίας αὐτῷ καθη]κούσης διαιτητὴς
ἐνιαυτῷ ἢ ἀποδημῶν οὗτοι δ'	[ἐνι]αυτῷ ἀποδημῶν οὐκ
(53.6) διαιτητὰς ἐάν	διαιτη[τ]ὰς ἄν
ἀτιμοῦσθαι κελεύουσιν	[ἀτί]μους εἶναι κελεύουσιν
ἔφεσις δ'	ἔφεσις δέ

Collation of the two texts reveals that Rain. 7 routinely reverses the order of individual words and phrases, routinely substitutes ἐάν for ἂν and δέ for δ', omits without acknowledgement sixteen words from 53.3, substitutes a simple verb form (λαβόντες) for a compound one (παραλαβόντες) in 53.2, and substitutes one prefix (προ-) for a different one (ἐμ-) in 53.3.

Verso

Lines 1–6: The contents of these lines are unknown. They should contain an entry or entries beginning with the letters *delta* or *epsilon*.

Lines 7–8: This entry concerns a lemma from Dem. 21.161: ἕτεροι δεύτεροι μετὰ ταῦτ[α], "a second call for donations after this." All that is intelligibly preserved of the lexicographer's comment is a reference to a date (349/8) and the fact that the Athenians did something at that time. It is likely that the lexicographer correctly identified ἕτεροι δεύτεροι μετὰ ταῦτ[α] as a reference to Athenian aid sent to Olynthus in 349/8. A brief identification of an event and its date is certainly in keeping with the agenda of the philological and historical commentators. This date for Athenian aid is confirmed by Philochorus (*FGrH* 328 F49), as preserved in Dionysius of Halicarnassus *First Letter to Ammaeus* 9; on whose dates see Sealey, "Dionysius of Halicarnassus." Demosthenes delivered the *Olynthiacs* (orations 1–3) to encourage the Athenians to help the Olynthians when they were under attack by Philip. See MacDowell, *Meidias*, 380–82, with bibliography.

Lines 9–13: This entry identifies the "completers" of the *eranoi* and justifies their name with an etymology. Its target is an adapted lemma from Dem. 21.184–85: ἐγὼ νομίζω πάντας ἀνθρ[ώπους ἐράνους φέρειν οὐχὶ μόνον ὧν πληρ]ωταὶ γίγνονται, "I think that all men support the *eranoi*, not only those of which they are 'completers.'" If this restoration is correct, the adapted lemma omits the words παρὰ πάντα τὸν βίον αὐτοῖς (after the word φέρειν) and omits the words τούσδε μόνους οὓς συλλέγουσί τινες καὶ (after the word οὐχί). Naoumides, "Literary Papyri," restored the rest of the lacunae with reference to Harpocration's entry on πληρωτής (Π 71): Δημοσθένης Κατ' Ἀριστογείτονος. πληρωτὰς ἐκάλουν τοὺς ἀποδιδόντας τὸν ἔρανον τοῖς ἤτοι λαχοῦσιν ἢ ἐωνημένοις . . . , "Demosthenes in *Against Aristogeiton* (25.21): They used to call 'completers' those who paid the ones who either attained by lot or purchased an *eranos*. . . . " The lexical entry in Rain. 7 focuses on the meaning and etymology of the word πληρωταί (completers). It first identifies them as "those who paid the ones who either attained by lot or purchased an *eranos*," and then apparently gives an etymological explanation for their name: the "completers" (πληρωταί) are those who bring the *eranos* to "completion" (πλήρωμα). The word "completion" appears in lines 12 and 13, in line 13 as a cognate accusative with the participle ἐκπιμπλάντας.

The word *eranos* originally referred to a club dinner that club members took turns providing or whose cost was offset for the provider by contributions of gifts from the other members. This seems to be the sense implied by Harpocration and by the author of Rain. 7. But by the time of Demosthenes, the term more frequently referred to a friendly interest-free loan whose attested uses include providing start-up funds for a new business, ransoming someone from foreign slavery, and buying back lost citizenship rights (see MacDowell, *Meidias*, 322–24). The *plerotes* collected the money for the loan, gave the loan to the borrower, and ensured that the terms of the loan were carried out. For an overview of the *eranos* arrangement, with attention to the relevant ancient literary sources, see Millett, 153–59. On *eranoi* in the *horos* inscriptions, see Finley, 100–106; Harris, "Women and Lending." Demosthenes compares life to one of these friendly interest-free loans in 21.101 and 184–185, with the message being (in MacDowell's paraphrase) "Whatever you lend to other people, they should make a similar loan to you on another occasion."

Lines 13–15: This entry defines the term "leader of the symmory" mentioned in Dem. 21.157. Naoumides, "Literary Papyri," has restored the lacunae in the lexicon with reference to Harpocration's entry for ἡγεμὼν συμμορίας (H 2): Δημοσθένης ἐν τῷ ὑπὲρ Κτησιφῶντος. ἡγεμὼν ἐκαλεῖτο συμμορίας ὁ προέχων τῷ πλούτῳ καὶ διὰ τοῦτο τῶν ἄλλων ἡγεμονεύειν ἐπειλημμένος. . . , "Demosthenes in *For Ctesiphon* (18.103, 212). 'Leader of the symmory' was the name of the man who was wealthiest and because of this was appointed to lead the others. . . . " Perhaps first introduced in 378/7, the symmories were groups of people who paid the *eisphora*, a levy made on the rich when the Assembly thought it necessary to raise emergency money. The so-called "leader of the symmory" was the wealthiest member of the group. Demosthenes was leader of his symmory for *eisphora* for many years (Dem. 21.157, 27.7–9, 28.4) and paid one-fifth its burden (Dem. 27.7–9). See MacDowell, *Meidias*, 368–69, 375–76. The historical development of the symmories and the *eisphora* is the subject of a number of scholarly treatments. On the collection of the *eisphora*, see the three articles by Ruschenbusch; Rhodes, "Athenian Eisphora"; MacDowell, "Law of Periandros." On its importance and historical development, see also Thomsen,

Eisphora. The purpose of this entry, however, is simply to identify what is meant by the term "leader of the symmory."

Lines 15–16: This entry explains the expression "placing arms" by glossing the word "placing." Its target is a lemma from Dem. 21.145: θέ[μ]ενος τὰ ὅπλα. Naoumides, "Literary Papyri," has restored this entry with reference to the corresponding entry in Harpocration (Θ 2): ἀντὶ τοῦ περιθέμενος καὶ ὁπλισάμενος . . . , "instead of putting them on and arming." Harpocration's entry goes on to cite parallel usages of unaffixed forms of the verb τίθημι from Homer *Iliad* 3.336 and Aeschines 1.29. The scholia to Aeschines 1.29 (ed. Baiter and Sauppe), commenting on Aeschines' use of the phrase τὰ ὅπλα μὴ τίθεσθαι, says that "he says 'to put' on occasions of taking weapons off and putting them on and clothing oneself with them" (τὸ τίθεσθαι λέγεται καὶ ἐπὶ τοῦ ἀποτίθεσθαι τὰ ὅπλα καὶ ἐπὶ τοῦ περιτίθεσθαι καὶ ἐνδύεσθαι). They also cite Thucydides 2.2.4 as a parallel for τίθεσθαι meaning περιτίθεσθαι; the scholia to Thucydides (ed. Hude) agree with this. Gomme et al., ad loc., gloss the phrase in Thucydides (τίθεσθαι παρ' αὐτοὺς τὰ ὅπλα) as "to take his place with them" or "take sides with them." MacDowell, *Meidias,* 360, translates the Demosthenic phrase as "bearing arms."

Lines 16–17: This entry concerns the word [εἰσι]τήρια (inaugural rites) in Dem. 21.114. The manuscripts give εἰσιτήρια in Dem. 21.114 and 19.190, but in contemporary Athenian inscriptions the form is εἰσιτητήρια; see MacDowell, *Meidias,* 338; Rhodes, *Athenian Boule,* 12–13. According to MacDowell, these particular inaugural rites were carried out at the beginning of the calendar year 347 when Demosthenes was elected to the Council (compare Dem. 21.111). The lexical entry mentions "those who were allotted to be on the Council," perhaps indicating that the original entry described who carried out these rites and when (compare line 17).

Line 18: Unless there were no entries for the letters *kappa* through *rho,* this entry is apparently ordered by the word ἱεροποιόν, the third word in a lemma from Dem. 21.115: [σ]εμναῖς θε[α]ῖς ἱεροποιὸν αἱρη-θ[– – –], "elected as *hieropoios* for the Hallowed Goddesses." Demosthenes was elected to this position for the year 347/6; the lost comment may have discussed this or may simply have defined the term *hieropoios*.

Hieropoioi were not priests per se, but officials (sometimes from the Council) who managed religious festivals or parts of religious festivals not managed by the priests; see MacDowell, *Meidias,* 338–39. On the religious duties of the Council, see Rhodes, *Athenian Boule,* 127–31. The "Hallowed Goddesses" were the Eumenides, whose conversion from the unpleasant Erinyes (Furies) is celebrated in Aeschylus's *Eumenides.*

Rhetorical Prologue and Commentary on Dem. 21 (*P.Lond.Lit.* 179)

P.Lond.Lit. 179 (more properly *P.Lond.* I 131) (Pack[2] 307) is a rhetorical prologue and commentary on Demosthenes *Against Meidias* 1–11, which dates to the late first or early second century C.E.[1] Three different texts were written on this papyrus. First, some accounts dated to 78–79 C.E. were written on the recto. Then another scribe turned the roll over and transcribed the commentary on Demosthenes on the verso, starting at the beginning of the roll. This hand has been dated on palaeographical grounds to the end of the first or beginning of the second century C.E. Finally, a third hand shortly thereafter turned the papyrus upside down and, still on the verso, began transcribing the pseudo-Aristotelian *Athenian Constitution* at the opposite end of the roll. When he reached the commentary on Demosthenes (now located in the lower half of the *Athenian Constitution*'s col. 10 and all of the unnumbered column following), he crossed it out, wrote around it, and attached another piece of papyrus in order to complete col. 11, the last column of the roll.

The text, translation, and notes on the earliest-known rhetorical commentary on Demosthenes has been included as an appendix in order to illustrate the differences between the rhetorical tradition and the philological and historical traditions of scholarship on Demosthenes. The author of this commentary treats select words, phrases, and topics in Dem. 21.1–11, with predominantly rhetorical interests. Sources include the first-century rhetorician Caecilius of Calacte, the first-century philological and historical commentator Didymus, and Aeschines' speech *Against Timarchus* (*Oration* 1). The commentator is also familiar with

---

1. Lossau, 112–13 and 119–22, argues that *P. Lond. Lit.* 179 is a copy made in approximately 40–50 C.E. of an original dating to the mid-first century B.C.

the *stasis* theory of the second-century rhetorician Hermagoras (Lossau, 111–18), though no specific passages are cited and Hermagoras is not cited by name. *P.Lond.Lit.* 179 discusses seven passages also discussed by the Byzantine scholiasts, but with no significant verbal similarities that indicate borrowing: compare lines 22–28 with the scholia to 21.1 (Dilts 2b); lines 29–32 with the scholia to Dem. 21.1 (Dilts 5); lines 35–36 with the scholia to Dem. 21.3 (Dilts 19ab); lines 43–48 with the scholia to Dem. 21.5 (Dilts 25d); lines 50–61 with the scholia to Dem. 21.9 (Dilts 38a); line 62 with the scholia to Dem. 21.9 (Dilts 39abcd); and lines 63–66 with the scholia to Dem. 21.11 (Dilts 47).

Text: Text from Kenyon, 215–19. Printed with discussion in Blass, "Demosthenica," 29–33; MacDowell, *Meidias,* 425–26, 430. Description in Milne. Plates in ΑΘΗΝΑΙΟΝ ΠΟΛΙΤΕΙΑ. Lines 1–21 printed as Caecilius fragment 163 (ed. Ofenloch). Detailed discussion in Lossau, 111–23.

TEXT AND TRANSLATION OF *P.LOND.LIT.* 179

Lines 1–21: Μειδίας εἰς τὰ μάλιστα ἐχθρὸς ἦν τῷ Δημοσθένει, καὶ διὰ πολλῶν μὲν καὶ ἄλλων ἐνεδείξατο εἰς αὐτὸν τὴν ἔχθραν, καί ποτε χορηγὸν ὄντα αὐτὸν τῆς Πανδιονίδος φυλῆς ἐν μέσῃ τῇ ὀρχήστρᾳ κονδύλοις ἔλαβεν. ὁ δὲ ἐγράψατο αὐτὸν δημοσίων ἀδικημάτων, συμπεριλαβὼν τοῖς δημοσίοις ἀδικήμασι τὴν ἑαυτοῦ ὕβριν· ἐπεὶ ἐξῆν ἐκείνῳ λέγειν ὅτι "ὑβριστής² · λαβὲ τῆς ὕβρεως τὸ πρόστιμον." ἔχει δ' ἡ ὑπόθεσις κατὰ μὲν Καικίλιον δύο κεφάλαια, εἰ δημόσιόν ἐστιν ἀδίκημα, καὶ εἰ μεγάλα τὰ πεπραγμένα ἐστίν. προσθετέον δὲ κἀκεῖνο, εἰ ὕβρις ἐστὶν ἡ γενομένη· ὅπερ ἀθετεῖ Καικίλιος, κακῶς· ἔσται γὰρ ἐναντίως αὐτῷ γεγραμμένον τὸ προοίμιον καὶ ἡ τοῦ χρυσοχόου μαρτυρία. ὅτι δὲ δῆλός ἐστι συμπεριλαβὼν τοῖς δημοσίοις ἀδικήμασι τὴν ἑαυτοῦ ὕβριν ἐξ ἐκείνου φανερόν, ὅταν λέγῃ, "ἐπειδὰν ἐπιδείξω Μειδίαν τοῦτον μὴ μόνον εἰς ἐμὲ ἀλλὰ καὶ εἰς ὑμᾶς καὶ εἰς τοὺς ἄλλους ἅπαντας ὑβρικότα," καὶ τὰ ἑξῆς. αἱ δ' ὑποθέσεις ὅταν μὴ ἔχωσιν ζητήματα μηδ' ἀμφισβητήσεις λελυμέναι εἰσί, καὶ τόπον τῷ ῥήτορι οὐ καταλείπουσι· οἷον περὶ φόνου τις ἐγκαλεῖται καὶ λέγει "ἀπέκτεινα μὲν τὸν δεῖνα, δικαίως δέ," τότε ὁμολογήσαντος αὐτοῦ τὸν φόνον ζητεῖται πότερα δικαίως ἢ ἀδίκως ἀπέκτεινε· ὅταν δὲ λέγῃ ὁ ἐγκαλούμενος ὅτι ἀπέκτεινε καὶ ἀδίκως ἀπέκτεινε, τότε λέλυται ἡ ὑπόθεσις. οὕτως καὶ περὶ ταύτης τῆς ὕβρεως ῥηθήσεται.

Meidias was a great enemy to Demosthenes, and he demonstrated his hatred toward him in many different ways; at one point he even struck him with his fists in the middle of the orchestra when he (Demosthenes) was chorus leader of the tribe Pandionis. But Demosthenes indicted him for public offenses, including under the rubric of public offenses the assault committed against him, since it was possible for him to say: "You are guilty of assault. Pay the penalty for assault." According to Caecilius the *hypothesis* has two main points: whether the offense

2. Correcting ὑβρίσθης.

is a public one, and whether the things done were important. But to these must also be added the question whether what occurred was assault. This point Caecilius rejects, wrongly, for the written introduction and the deposition of the goldsmith are against him. It is evident that he is clearly including under the rubric of public offenses the assault committed against him, when he says: "since I shall show that this Meidias has committed assault not only against me but also against you and against all the others" (Dem. 21.7), et cetera. And *hypotheses* fall apart when they have neither questions nor disputes and they do not leave the orator an occasion. For example, someone is accused of murder and says: "I killed so-and-so, but I did it justly"; then, since he agrees that it was murder, it is inquired whether he killed him justly or unjustly. But when the accused says that he killed somebody and did it unjustly, then the *hypothesis* falls apart. The same will be said of this case of assault.

Lines 22–28: τὴν μὲν ἀσέλγειαν ᾧ, καὶ τὰ ἑξῆς· Σελγοὶ ἔθνος ἐστὶν ἐπὶ τῆς Ἰταλίας, δίκαιον καὶ ὅσιον· οἱ οὖν παραβαίνοντες τὸ δίκαιον εἰκότως ἂν κληθεῖεν ἀσελγεῖς. ταῦτα μὲν Δίδυμος λέγει· τινὲς δὲ λέγουσιν ὅτι, "πῶς περὶ δημοσίων ἀδικημάτων ὄντος τοῦ ἀγῶνος λέγει καὶ τὴν ὕβριν;" ἐπιλύεται οὖν αὐτὸς ἐπιφέρων ὅτι, ἢ πρὸς ἅπαντας ἀεὶ χρῆται Μειδίας, ὡς καθολικῶς ὑβριστοῦ πρὸς πάντας ὄντος.

The bullying, O, et cetera (Dem. 21.1): The Selgoi are a people in Italy, just and reverent. So those who overstep justice would naturally be called *aselgeis* (un-Selgoi-like). That is what Didymus says. But some say: "How can he also speak of assault when this is a trial about public offenses?" He himself (sc. Demosthenes) solves this problem in this way, adding the phrase "which Meidias always employs toward everyone" (Dem. 21.1), since in general a hubristic person behaves that way toward everyone.

Lines 29–32: καὶ προὐβαλόμην ἀδικεῖν τουτονί· προὐβαλόμην· εἰς δίκην κατέστησα. ἀδικεῖν· περὶ τὴν ἑορτήν. προβολὴ γὰρ κυρίως ἡ μετὰ Διονύσια δίκη ἡ γινομένη περὶ τῶν ἡμαρτημένων ἐν τοῖς Διονυσίοις, μεταφορικῶς δ' ἐπὶ πάσης δίκης.

And I instituted a *probole* against him for committing an offense (Dem. 21.1): "I instituted a *probole*" (means) "I have brought him to court." "Of committing an offense," (understand) "concerning the festival." For a *probole* is properly a trial that arises concerning offenses committed at the Dionysia, but it is by extension applied to any trial.

Lines 33–34: εἰς τὰς οὐσίας τὰς τούτων οὐδ' εἰς τὰς ὑποσχέσεις· ὡς δωροδοκούντων.

To the wealth or the promises of these men (Dem. 21.2): As with those who take bribes.

Lines 35–36: ἐπειδή τις εἰσάγει· δηλονότι ὁ ὑπηρέτης· οὐ γὰρ χωρὶς τούτου ἐξῆν τοῖς λέγουσιν εἰσελθεῖν.

Since someone is leading in (Dem. 21.3): Evidently the aide. For it was impossible for speakers to come in without him.

Lines 37–39: πολλὰ μὲν χρήματ' ἐξόν μοι λαβεῖν, καὶ τὰ ἑξῆς· τοῦτο ὡς δικαίως ἀγωνιζόμενος καὶ μὴ ἀργύριον εἰληφώς· ὅμως δὲ χιλίας λαβὼν καθυφείκατο τὴν δίκην, ὡς ἐν τῇ ἱστορίᾳ φέρεται.

Although it was possible for me to get a lot of money, et cetera (Dem. 21.3): (He says this) on the pretense that he is contending in a just manner and has not taken any money. But nevertheless, having taken a thousand (drachmas), he withdrew the charge, as is transmitted in history.

Lines 40–42: πολλὰς δὲ δεήσεις καὶ χάριτας καὶ νὴ Δία ἀπειλὰς ὑπομείνας· εἰκότως, ἃ συμβαίνει τοῖς παρακαλοῦσι καὶ ἐν ὀργῇ πᾶσι γινομένοις.

Having held out against many requests and favors and, by Zeus, even threats (Dem. 21.3): Naturally. These things happen to those who give summons and make everybody angry.

Lines 43–48: εἰ μὲν οὖν παρανόμων ἢ παραπρεσβείας ἤ τινος ἄλλης τοιαύτης ἔμελλον αὐτοῦ, καὶ τὰ ἑξῆς· εἰκότως· οἱ γὰρ περὶ ἰδίων πραγμάτων ἀγωνιζόμενοι ὀφείλουσιν οἰκτίζεσθαι εἰς τὸ ἐλέου τινὸς τυχεῖν, οἱ δὲ περὶ δημοσίων αὐτὸ μόνον λέγειν καὶ ἐνδεικνύναι, ὡς τοῦ δήμου ἀκούοντος καὶ ὑπὲρ ἑαυτοῦ ἀγωνιουμένου.

So if I intended (to prosecute) him for illegal motions or misconducting an embassy or some other such charge, et cetera (Dem. 21.5): Naturally. For those who are contending about private matters have to lament in order to receive a measure of pity, but those who are contending about public matters only have to state (their case) and to demonstrate (the wrongdoing), since their audience is the people and they will be contending on their own behalf.

Line 49: προπηλακισμός· πληγή.

An occasion of disrespectful treatment (Dem. 21.7): A blow.

Lines 50–61: ὁ μὲν νόμος οὗτός ἐστιν ᾧ, καὶ τὰ ἑξῆς· τὸ εἶδος τοῦτο πρόθεσις λέγεται, ὅταν ὁ ῥήτωρ τὸ πρᾶγμα περὶ οὗ λέγει ἐκ τῶν ἐναντίων αὐξάνῃ· ὥσπερ καὶ Αἰσχίνης ἐν τῷ κατὰ Τιμάρχου, περὶ ἑταιρήσεως οὔσης τῆς δίκης, ἀντιπαρατέθεικε τοὺς τῆς εὐκοσμίας νόμους. ὅμοιον κἂν εἴ τις περὶ ἱεροσύλου λέγων αὐξάνῃ τὸ ἁμάρτημα ἐγκωμιάσας τὸ θεῖον, οὕτω καὶ ὁ Δημοσθένης πρῶτον τὸν περὶ αὐτῶν τῶν Διονυσίων νόμον ἀνέγνω, δεύτερον δὲ τὸν περὶ τῆς ὕβρεως, ἐπιδεικνὺς ὅτι καὶ τοὺς ἐκ καταδίκης εἰσπραττομένους καὶ ὀφείλοντας ἀνυβρίστους ἀνίησιν ταύτας τὰς ἡμέρας τῶν Διονυσίων. ὅπου δὲ τιμωρίας ἄξιοί εἰσιν οἱ ὑβρίσαντες τοὺς κατακρίτους, πόσῳ οἱ μὴ τοὺς κατακρίτους ἀλλ' ἐλευθέρους ὑβρίσαντες;

This is the law, O, et cetera (Dem. 21.9): This figure is called *prothesis*, when the orator amplifies the thing that he is discussing by bringing up its opposite. For instance, Aeschines in *Against Timarchus*, a case about prostitution, contrasts the laws and customs of decent behavior. Just as if someone in speaking about a temple robber were to amplify the crime by delivering an encomium to the divinity, in this same way also Demosthenes first read the law about the Dionysia itself, and then the law about assault, demonstrating that for these days of the Dionysia they leave unharassed (ἀνυβρίστους) even debtors and those who have to pay a fine as a result of a judgment against them. But in a situation where those who harass condemned criminals are deemed worthy of punishment, how much more worthy of punishment are those who have assaulted not condemned criminals but free men?

Line 62: Πάνδια· ἑορτή
Pandia (Dem. 21.9): A festival.

Lines 63–66: ἀλλὰ καὶ τὰ δίκῃ καὶ ψήφῳ τῶν ἑλόντων γινόμενα τῶν ἑαλωκότων· ὃ λέγει τοιοῦτόν ἐστιν· ἃ καὶ τῶν νικησάντων δίκῃ γινόμενα τῶν νικηθέντων δεδώκατε ταύτην τὴν ἑορτήν.

But (you have) also (granted that) the things that by trial and vote belong to the successful prosecutors should remain with the unsuccessful defendants (Dem. 21.11): What he means is this—You have also granted that the things that belong to the winners as the result of a trial should remain with the losers for the duration of the festival.

NOTES ON *P.LOND.LIT.* 179

Lines 1–4: The commentary opens with a rhetorical analysis of the speech, for which one might compare the other surviving hypotheses to the speech printed and discussed in MacDowell, *Meidias,* 424–30. The bad blood between Meidias and Demosthenes was long-standing; see MacDowell, *Meidias,* 1–13. The commentator quickly passes over this history to arrive at the final straw, when Meidias punched Demosthenes in the theatre at the City Dionysia of 348. Although this event is the ostensible occasion for the speech *Against Meidias,* it receives surprisingly little specific attention in the speech. Perhaps Demosthenes decided that it was ill advised to cover the event again, since everybody saw it happen or at least heard about it (as is suggested in Dem. 21.74). The contemporary orator Aeschines mentions it as a familiar event (3.52). It appears in Plutarch's biography of *Demosthenes* (12.1–3) as well as in the biography of him in the *Moralia* (844d).

Lines 4–7: The commentator points out that Demosthenes has managed to make an essentially private matter a public one. The orator bridges the gap between private and public in the introduction (21.1–8) and emphasizes it repeatedly throughout the speech (see esp. 21.29–35, 123–27). He fully expects Meidias to argue for a distinction between personal and public affairs (21.29–35), but he answers this hypothetical objection by saying that the nature and seriousness of the act makes Meidias's behavior a matter of public concern (21.42–76). The rhetorician Hermogenes (second century C.E.), in *On Staseis* 63 (ed. Rabe; trans. Heath), discusses Demosthenes' strategy here under the heading of "inclusion" (σύλληψις; note also line 5, συμπεριλαβών), which Heath, 255, defines as a "species of definition in which the opponent's description of the act is accepted, and another description added to it"—"When Meidias maintains that there was an assault and a private wrong rather than a crime against the public interest respecting the festival, Demosthenes draws the two together (the assault and the crime with respect to the festival), to avoid undermining the crime with respect to the festival by dismissing the assault; for unless the assault is established in advance, the crime with respect to the festival does not stand up either." For further discussion of the term συμπεριλαβών and its significance for *stasis* theory, see Lossau, 113–19. On Hermogenes' attitude toward Demosthenes, see Wooten, 21–45.

Lines 7–10: Caecilius wrote histories and rhetorical works in the Augustan period. His most important treatise (now lost) was *On the Style of the Ten Orators* (περὶ τοῦ χαρακτῆρος τῶν δέκα ῥητόρων; *Suda,* s.v. Καικίλιος). On Caecilius, see G. Kennedy, *Art of Rhetoric,* 364–69. He is sometimes incorrectly credited with the creation of the canon of the ten Attic orators; on which see Smith; Douglas, "Canon of Ten Attic Orators." Caecilius was cited by contemporary and later literary critics, at times unfavorably; see Dionysius of Halicarnassus *Letter to Gnaeus Pompeius* 3; Longinus *On Sublimity* 1–2 (ed. Russell); Plutarch *Life of Demosthenes* 3. The commentator rejects Caecilius's two-part classification of the *hypothesis* and adds a third question: whether Meidias's actions in fact constituted assault. The slippery term ὕβρις (assault) does occur throughout the speech. However, in categorizing different sorts of disreputable acts under the rubric of assault, Demosthenes seems more concerned with generally condemning Meidias's entire modus vivendi than with arguing that his behavior actually constituted assault in any sort of legal sense. See MacDowell, *Meidias,* 18–23, 425–26.

Lines 10–11: The commentator adduces the "written proem" (21.1–8) and "the deposition of the goldsmith" (referred to in 21.16, actually given in 21.22) as evidence for the argument against Caecilius. The proem (introduction) of Demosthenes' speech does refer to assault but not to the specific question whether Meidias's actions legally constituted assault. According to the deposition of the goldsmith (Dem. 21.22), Demosthenes ordered a gold crown and a gold-inlaid cloak for use in the festival, and Meidias later broke into the shop and tried to destroy them.

Lines 11–15: The commentator quotes from Dem. 21.7 to show how Demosthenes turns a personal offense into a public one. According to the commentator's reading of Demosthenes, Meidias has behaved hubristically toward Demosthenes, the jury, and the Athenians in general (compare Dem. 21.1). He is a public nuisance.

Lines 15–21: *Hypothesis* is used here in the rhetorical sense of a specific rhetorical theme (e.g., "Is a specific act just?") as opposed to a *thesis,* which typically deals with general principles (e.g., "What is justice?"). See Heath, 47 n. 17, with further bibliography. The term is used in rhetoric to determine the exact nature of an "issue" *(stasis).* As our commentator observes, when a rhetorical *hypothesis* has no particular points of contention ("neither questions nor disputes"), it falls apart. The term "falls apart" (λελυμέναι) comes from the verb λύειν, which is equivalent in meaning to the more commonly used ἀναιρεῖν (Meijering, 118).

When a *hypothesis* "falls apart," one side has a case, and the other does not. The commentator may be drawing on the *stasis* theory of the second-century rhetorician Hermagoras (Lossau, 111–18), whose works are all lost but whose influence was widespread; see G. Kennedy, *Greek Rhetoric* 52–132. The rhetorician Hermogenes (*On Staseis* 32–34) discusses situations in which a *stasis* cannot be located. In our commentary, the commentator adduces an example in which someone kills someone else (this act is not in doubt) and admits that he did it unjustly (so the justice of the act is not in doubt); there is therefore no specific point of contention. The commentator then says, without further elaboration or explanation, that "the same will be said of this case of assault." This seems to imply that the situation described in Dem. 21 has no *stasis,* which is not actually the case. There are two other possibilities: the commentator may be alluding to a topic to be discussed farther along in the commentary, or referring to the unjustifiable objections that Demosthenes expects Meidias to make (see Dem. 21.25–41).

Lines 22–28: The commentator cites Didymus on the etymology of *aselgeia* as *a-* (*alpha* privative, meaning "not") plus *selgeia,* the kind of behavior exhibited by the Selgoi. This could have come from Didymus's commentary on Dem. 21, but not necessarily so, as Didymus's discussion (as reported here) is not keyed explicitly to this particular occurrence of the word. It could have come from a lexicon or even a commentary on another author. Selgoi in Italy are unknown; the closest parallel is the Selgeis of Selge in Pisidia (Strabo 12.570). The rest of the comment again discusses how Demosthenes extends his private concern to the public realm. A hypothetical question is posed of the text—"How can (Demosthenes) also speak of assault when this is a trial about public offenses?"—and Demosthenes himself is adduced to "solve" (ἐπιλύεται, line 26) it. As a rhetorical term, λύσις can refer to an orator's "response to an argument attributed to the opposing side" (Heath, 259). But λύσεις also appeared in ancient scholarly literature as solutions to scholarly questions, problems, or difficulties; see Gudeman, "Λύσεις"; also G. Kennedy, *Greek Rhetoric,* 87–88. The verb ἐπιλύεται here may reflect either or both of these concerns.

Lines 29–32: Of these three glosses, the second explains the particular "offense" as one "concerning the festival." This seems unnecessary, since these words appear together (separated only by τοῦτον) in Dem. 21.1. The words could have been missing from the commentator's text of Demosthenes, but not necessarily so: the commentator could just as easily be noting that the subsequent words "concerning the festival" explain and/or limit the "offense" described by ἀδικεῖν. The first and third glosses extrapolate an apparently unjustified general sense from the specific sense of *probole.* In the first one, "I instituted a *probole* against him" is equated in general with taking someone to court. In the third, *probole* is first defined (correctly) as a trial conducted after the Dionysia for offenses committed at the festival, but the commentator adds (incorrectly) that the term is used by extension to refer to any sort of trial. However, one should remember that the commentator's purpose is not to explain the nitty-gritty details of classical Athenian legal procedure (as a philological and historical commentator might try to do), but rather to help the contemporary student of rhetoric understand the verb προὐβαλόμην by giving equivalent expressions that are more likely to be seen or used in practice. Demosthenes quotes the laws concerning the *probole* in 21.8–12. See MacDowell, *Meidias,* 13–16, on the procedure, for which Dem. 21 is our main evidence.

Lines 33–34: The commentator is referring to the story of how Demosthenes is said to have taken a bribe to drop his case against Meidias. See below on lines 37–39.

Lines 35–36: The "someone" here in Demosthenes refers to the *thesmothetes* who presided over the earlier *probole*. See MacDowell, *Meidias,* 222–23. C. R. Kennedy, ad loc., sees this section of Dem. 21 as "a slight reflexion upon the tardiness of the magistrate in bringing the cause to trial"; similarly, Weil, *Plaidoyers,* ad loc. The commentator has had some difficulty with the vagueness of the orator's phrasing. The commentator takes the "someone" to refer to a lower-level official whose job it was to "lead in" (εἰσάγειν) the speakers. It is unclear whether this is understood as a physical or a verbal "leading in." Demosthenes uses the term ὑπηρέτης in the general sense of an aide and also in reference to various governmental officials (19.70, 21.179, 47.35, 50.46, 50.51). In Dem. 25.23 there is a ὑπηρέτης who prevents regular citizens from entering the Council or the Areopagus, but he is not mentioned as being responsible for introducing speakers. Aeschines 2.37 mentions ὑπηρέται at the court of Philip who summon the Athenian ambassadors to hear Philip. None of these is satisfactory. The commentator is most likely guessing from the context.

Lines 37–39: Demosthenes says in 21.3 that he could have taken a bribe but chose not to. The commentator replies to this statement by saying that Demosthenes took a bribe of 1,000 drachmas and dropped the charge against Meidias. This popular anecdote has been used to support the view that *Against Meidias* was never delivered. See MacDowell, *Meidias,* 23–25, with further bibliography. The anecdote may ultimately stem from Aeschines 3.52, where Aeschines says that Demosthenes accepted an out-of-court settlement (ἀπέδοτο) from Meidias, but the amount given there is the more usual 30 *minae* (3,000 drachmas). In his biography of Demosthenes (12.1–3), Plutarch says that Demosthenes accepted an out-of-court settlement of 3,000 drachmas from Meidias because he thought that he could not actually win the case against him. The "1,000" of the papyrus could be the result of an error in copying, an alternate tradition, a lapse in memory on the part of the commentator, or from confusion with the 1,000 drachmas assessed as an earlier fine against Meidias (on which see Dem. 21.88). The final words of this comment (ὡς ἐν τῇ ἱστορίᾳ φέρεται) seem to be a vague reference to a fact from "history" that all readers would presumably know, as in the colloquial English expressions "history states" and "we know from history." I have translated "as is transmitted in history." The word "history" seems to be used in this general sense in the *Suda*'s list of the writings of Caecilius, among which is "Concerning things said in the orators that are in accordance with history or contrary to history" (Περὶ τῶν κατὰ ἱστορίαν ἢ παρὰ ἱστορίαν εἰρημένων τοῖς ῥήτορσι). Expressions identical or nearly identical to the one here are also found in late-ancient Christian authors (e.g., Eusebius, Gregory of Nyssa, and Origen), who also seem to be recalling facts from "history." In Greek scholia to the poets, according to Meijering, 77, ἱστορίαι referred to "those matters that the author and his public are accustomed to consider as historical, . . . as far as common sense does not contradict their historical nature." Sometimes this amounted to "legendary matter" rather than "true facts of history" (Meijering, 78). See also the discussion of *historia* and related terms in Potter, 9–19.

Lines 40–42: The word "naturally" (εἰκότως) can be used as a literary critical term. Blass, "Demosthenica," 33, suggests that the commentator has not used it correctly. The term occurs in lines 22–28 (within a sentence) and in lines 43–48. It does not occur in the scholia to Demosthenes.

Lines 43–48: On the term "naturally," see above on lines 40–42. The rest of this comment draws a general moral for the aspiring speaker, giving instructions for the ideal rhetorical strategy in private court cases as opposed to public ones. These instructions are based heavily on Dem. 21.5–6.

Line 49: This provides a simple gloss on an unusual word.

Lines 50–61: The commentator's definition of the term *prothesis* is not standard. Blass, "Demosthenica," 33, suggests that the commentator should have used the word ἀντιπαράθεσις, adducing the use of the verb ἀντιπαρατέθεικε in line 53 (as also Lossau, 120 n. 159). Aeschines' speech *Against Timarchus* discusses Timarchus's unchaste behavior in an attempt to discredit him before the Assembly; see esp. 1.19–21 and 160. The subsequent anecdote about the temple robber sounds as though it might have been taken from a rhetorical handbook. The commentator's "law about the Dionysia" is found in Dem. 21.8. The subsequent law in Dem. 21.10 is not a "law about assault," contrary to the commentator's characterization of it. However, in the subsequent explication of the law (Dem. 21.11), the orator does represent it as prohibiting assault at the festival. In the closing sentence of this section, the commentator paraphrases Dem. 21.11 so as to draw a more general lesson from the passage, as previously in lines 43–48.

Line 62: The commentator identifies the Pandia only as "a festival." This festival of Zeus occurred at Athens in the month of Elaphebolion, almost immediately after the City Dionysia; see Parke, *Festivals,* 135–36; MacDowell, *Meidias,* 227–28.

Lines 63–66: The commentator paraphrases this rather difficult passage of Dem. 21.11 by substituting active and passive forms of νικάω for the technical terms αἱρέω (to prosecute successfully) and ἁλίσκομαι (to defend unsuccessfully). See MacDowell, *Meidias,* 236, on the vocabulary.

Bibliography

FREQUENTLY CITED ANCIENT AUTHORS AND WORKS

Aeschines	M. R. Dilts, ed. *Aeschinis Orationes*. Stuttgart, 1997.
[Aristotle] *Ath. Pol.*	M. Chambers, ed. Aristoteles ΑΘΗΝΑΙΩΝ ΠΟΛΙΤΕΙΑ. Leipzig, 1986.
Athenaeus	G. Kaibel, ed. *Athenaei Naucratitae Dipnosophistarum Libri XV*. 3 vols. Leipzig, 1887–90.
Demosthenes	S. H. Butcher and W. Rennie, eds. *Demosthenis Orationes*. 3 vols. Oxford, 1903–31.
Diodorus Siculus	F. Vogel and C. Fischer, eds. *Diodori Bibliotheca Historica*. 6 vols. Leipzig, 1888–1906.
Dionysius of Halicarnassus	H. Usener and L. Radermacher, eds. *Dionysii Halicarnasei Opuscula*. 2 vols. Leipzig, 1899–1929.
Harpocration	J. J. Keaney, ed. *Harpocration: Lexeis of the Ten Orators*. Amsterdam, 1991.
Plutarch, *Lives*	C. Lindskog and K. Ziegler, eds. *Plutarchi Vitae Parallelae*. 4 vols. Leipzig, 1914–39.
Pollux	E. Bethe, ed. *Pollucis Onomasticon*. Lexicographi Graeci, vol. 9, pts. 1–3. Leipzig, 1900–1937.
Quintilian	M. Winterbottom, ed. *M. Fabii Quintiliani Institutionis Oratoriae Libri Duodecim*. 2 vols. Oxford, 1970.
Seneca the Younger	L. D. Reynolds, ed. *L. Annaei Senecae ad Lucilium Epistulae Morales*. 2 vols. Oxford, 1965.

Suda   A. Adler, ed. *Suidae Lexicon.* 4 vols. Leipzig,
                         1928–35.
Thucydides   C. Hude, ed. *Thucydidis Historiae.* 2 vols. Leip-
                         zig, 1913–25.
Xenophon   E. C. Marchant, ed. *Xenophontis Opera Omnia.*
                         5 vols. Oxford, 1900–1920.

MODERN WORKS

Adams, C. D. *Demosthenes and His Influence.* New York, 1927.
Adler, A. "Suidas (1)." *RE* 4A.1 (1931) 675–717.
Anderson, W. "Juvenal and Quintilian." *Yale Classical Studies* 17 (1961) 3–93.
Arrighetti, G. "*Hypomnemata* e *scholia:* Alcuni problemi." In *Museum Philologum Londiniense,* vol. 2, edited by G. Giangrande, 49–67. Uithoorn, 1977.
ΑΘΗΝΑΙΩΝ ΠΟΛΙΤΕΙΑ, *Aristotle on the Constitution of Athens.* Facsimile of Papyrus CXXXI in the British Museum. Oxford, 1891.
Austin, C., ed. *Comicorum Graecorum Fragmenta in Papyris Reperta.* Berlin, 1973.
Badian, E. "Harpalus." *Journal of Hellenic Studies* 81 (1961) 16–43.
———. "The King's Peace." In *Georgica: Greek Studies in Honour of George Cawkwell,* BICS 58, edited by M. Flower and M. Toher, 25–48. London, 1991.
Baiter, J. G., and H. Sauppe, eds. *Oratores Attici.* Hildesheim, 1850.
Balsdon, J. P. V. D. *Romans and Aliens.* Chapel Hill, 1979.
Barber, G. L. *The Historian Ephorus.* Cambridge, 1935.
Bekker, I., ed. *Harpocration et Moeris.* Berlin, 1833.
Benseler, G. E., ed. *Isocratis Orationes.* 2 vols. Leipzig, 1889–1902.
Blass, F. "Demosthenica aus neuen Papyrus." *Jahrbücher für classische Philologie* 38 (1892) 29–33.
———. "Lexikon zu Demosthenes' *Aristokratea.*" In "Neue Papyrusfragmente im Ägyptischen Museum zu Berlin," *Hermes* 17 (1882) 148–63.
———. "Literarische Texte mit Ausschluss der christlichen." *Archiv für Papyrusforschung und verwandte Gebiete* 3 (1906) 284–92.
Bliquez, L. J. "Anthemocritus and the ὀργάς Disputes." *Greek, Roman and Byzantine Studies* 10 (1969) 157–61.
———. "A Note on the Didymus Papyrus XII.35." *Classical Journal* 67 (1972) 356–57.
Bloedow, E. F. "Hipponicus and Euthydemus (Euthynus)." *Chiron* 11 (1981) 65–72.
Bloomer, W. M. *Valerius Maximus and the Rhetoric of the New Nobility.* Chapel Hill, 1992.
Boisacq, É. *Dictionnaire étymologique de langue grècque.* 3d ed. Heidelberg, 1938.
Bömer, F. "Der Commentarius." *Hermes* 81 (1953) 210–50.
Bonner, S. F. *The Literary Treatises of Dionysius of Halicarnassus: A Study in the Development of Critical Method.* Cambridge, 1939.

Bruce, I. A. F. "Athenian Embassies in the Early Fourth Century B.C." *Historia* 15 (1966) 272–81.

Brunt, P. A. "Euboea in the Time of Philip II." *Classical Quarterly* 19 (1969) 245–65.

———. "On Historical Fragments and Epitomes." *Classical Quarterly* 30 (1980) 477–94.

Buchanan, J. J. *Theorika: A Study of Monetary Distributions to the Athenian Citizenry during the Fifth and Fourth Centuries B.C.* Locust Valley, 1962.

Bühler, W. "Die Philologie der Griechen und ihre Methoden." In *Jahrbuch der Akademie der Wissenschaften in Göttingen für das Jahr 1977, 44–62.* Göttingen, 1978.

Bury, J. B., S. A. Cook, and F. E. Adcock, eds. *The Cambridge Ancient History.* Vol. 5, *Athens: 478–401 B.C.* 2d ed. Cambridge, 1964.

———, eds. *The Cambridge Ancient History.* Vol. 6, *Macedon: 401–301 B.C.* 2d ed. Cambridge, 1964.

Cameron, A. "The Date and Identity of Macrobius." *Journal of Roman Studies* 56 (1966) 25–38.

Cartledge, P. *Agesilaos and the Crisis of Sparta.* Baltimore, 1987.

Cawkwell, G. L. "Anthemocritus and the Megarians and the Decree of Charinus." *Revue des Études Grecques* 82 (1969) 327–35.

———. "Demosthenes' Policy after the Peace of Philocrates." *Classical Quarterly* 13 (1963) 120–38, 200–213.

———. "Euboea in the Late 340s." *Phoenix* 32 (1978) 42–67.

———. "Eubulus." *Journal of Hellenic Studies* (1963) 47–67.

Chantraine, P. *Dictionnaire étymologique de la langue grecque: Histoire des mots.* 4 vols. Paris, 1968–80.

Clarysse, W. *The Leuven Database of Ancient Books.* CD-ROM. Leuven, 1998.

Clausen, W. V., ed. *A. Persi Flacci et D. Iuni Iuvenalis Saturae.* Oxford, 1992.

Clinton, K. *The Sacred Officials of the Eleusinian Mysteries.* Transactions of the American Philosophical Society, n.s., 64:3. Philadelphia, 1974.

Cohn, L. "Didymos (8)." *RE* 5.1 (1903) 445–72.

Connor, W. R. "Charinus' Megarian Decree." *American Journal of Philology* 83 (1962) 225–46.

———. "Charinus' Megarian Decree Again." *Revue des Études Grecques* 83 (1970) 305–8.

———. " 'Sacred' and 'Secular': Ἱερὰ καὶ ὅσια and the Classical Athenian Concept of the State." *Ancient Society* 19 (1988) 161–88.

Conomis, N. C., ed. *Dinarchus: Orationes cum Fragmentis.* Leipzig, 1975.

Constantinides, E. "Timocles' *Ikarioi Satyroi*: A Reconsideration." *Transactions of the American Philological Association* 100 (1969) 49–61.

Courtney, E. *A Commentary on the Satires of Juvenal.* London, 1980.

Cunningham, I. C. "Harpocration and the Συναγωγή." *Greek, Roman and Byzantine Studies* 27 (1986) 205–21.

Daintree, D. "The Virgil Commentary of Aelius Donatus: Black Hole or '*Éminence Grise*'?" *Greece and Rome* 37.1 (1990) 65–79.

Daly, L. W. *Contributions to a History of Alphabetization in Antiquity and the Middle Ages.* Brussels, 1967.

Davies, J. K. *Athenian Propertied Families (600–300 B.C.).* Oxford, 1971.

Deichgräber, K. "Polemon (9)." *RE* 21.2 (1952) 1288–1320.

De Ricci, S. "L'Anonymus Argentinensis." *Revue des Études Anciennes* 11 (1909) 30–32.

Devoto, J. G. "Agesilaus, Antalcidas, and the Failed Peace of 392/91 B.C." *Classical Philology* (1986) 191–202.

Diels, H., and W. Schubart, eds. *Didymos Kommentar zu Demosthenes.* Berliner Klassikertexte 1. Berlin, 1904.

———, eds. *Volumina Aegyptiaca Ordinis IV, Grammaticorum Pars I, Didymi de Demosthene Commenta cum Anonymi in Aristocratem Lexico.* Leipzig, 1904.

Dilts, M. R., ed. *Scholia Demosthenica.* 2 vols. Leipzig, 1983–86.

Dilts, M., and G. A. Kennedy. *Two Greek Rhetorical Treatises from the Roman Empire: Introduction, Text, and Translation of the Arts of Rhetoric Attributed to Anonymous Seguerianus and to Apsines of Gadara.* Mnemosyne Suppl. 168. Leiden, 1997.

Dindorf, G., ed. *Aristides.* Vol. 3. Leipzig, 1829.

Dittenberger, W., et al., eds. *Sylloge Inscriptionum Graecarum.* 3d ed. 4 vols. Leipzig, 1915.

Douglas, A. E. "Cicero, Quintilian, and the Canon of Ten Attic Orators." *Mnemosyne* 9 (1956) 30–40.

———. Review of *Untersuchungen zur antiken Demosthenesexegese* by M. Lossau. *Journal of Hellenic Studies* 86 (1966) 190–91.

Dover, K. J., ed. *Aristophanes: Clouds.* Oxford, 1968.

Drerup, E. "Antike Demosthenesausgaben." *Philologus Suppl.* 7 (1899) 531–88.

Düring, I. *Aristotle in the Ancient Biographical Tradition.* Göteborg, 1957.

Eddy, S. K. "Athens' Peacetime Navy in the Age of Pericles." *Greek, Roman and Byzantine Studies* 8 (1968) 141–56.

Edmonds, J. M., ed. *The Fragments of Attic Comedy.* 3 vols. Leiden, 1957–61.

Edson, C. "Notes on the Thracian *Phoros*." *Classical Philology* 42 (1947) 88–105.

Erbse, H., ed. "Pausaniae Atticistae Fragmenta." *Abhandlungen der deutschen Akademie der Wissenschaften zu Berlin, Philosophisch-historische Klasse* (1950) 152–221.

———, ed. *Scholia Graeca in Homeri Iliadem (scholia vetera).* 7 vols. Berlin, 1969–86.

Finley, M. I. *Studies in Land and Credit in Ancient Athens, 500–200 BC: The Horos-Inscriptions.* New Brunswick, N.J., 1952.

Florian, W. *Studia Didymea Historica ad Saeculum Quartum Pertinentia.* Leipzig, 1908.

Flower, M. A. *Theopompus of Chios: History and Rhetoric in the Fourth Century B.C.* Oxford, 1994.

Foerster, R., ed. *Libanii Opera.* 12 vols. Leipzig, 1903–27.

Foucart, M. P. "Étude sur Didymos d'apres un papyrus de Berlin." *Mémoires de L'Institut National de France, l'Académie des Inscriptions et Belles Lettres* 38 (1909) 27–218.

Fowler, H. N., ed. and trans. *Plutarch's "Moralia."* Vol. 10. Cambridge, Mass., 1936.

Fraser, P. M. *Ptolemaic Alexandria.* 3 vols. Oxford, 1972.

Frazer, J. G., ed. and trans. *Apollodorus: The Library.* 2 vols. Cambridge, Mass., 1921.

Gercke, A. "Die Überlieferung des Diogenes Laertios." *Hermes* 37 (1902) 424–25.

Geyer, F. "Miltokythes (2)." *RE* 15.2 (1932) 1708.

Gibson, C. A. "The Agenda of Libanius' Hypotheses to Demosthenes." *Greek, Roman, and Byzantine Studies* 40 (1999) 171–202.

———. "The Critical Note Above Col. 12 of the Didymus Papyrus (P.Berol.Inv. 9780)." *Zeitschrift für Papyrologie und Epigraphik* 132 (2000) 148.

———. "P.Berol.inv. 5008, Didymus, and Harpocration Reconsidered." *Classical Philology* 92 (1997) 375–81.

Gignac, F. T. *A Grammar of the Greek Papyri of the Roman and Byzantine Periods.* 2 vols. Milan, 1976–81.

Gilliam, J. F. "A Citation of Didymus." *Zeitschrift für Papyrologie und Epigraphik* 35 (1979) 41–42.

Gisinger, F. "Timosthenes (3)." *RE* 6a.2 (1937) 1310–22.

Goldstein, J. A. *The Letters of Demosthenes.* New York, 1968.

Gomme, A. W. "Thucydides ii 13.3: An Answer to Professor Meritt." *Historia* 3 (1954–55) 333–38.

Gomme, A., A. Andrewes, and K. J. Dover. *A Historical Commentary on Thucydides.* 5 vols. Oxford, 1945–70.

Groß, W. H. "Lykios (3)." *Kleine Pauly* 3 (1969) 811.

Gudeman, A. "Λύσεις." *RE* 13.2 (1927) 2511–29.

———. "Scholien (Demosthenes)." *RE* 2a.1 (1921) 697–703.

Guerrini, L. "Lykios (1)." *Enciclopedia dell'Arte Antica, Classica e Orientale,* vol. 4, 746–47. Rome, 1961.

Hager, H. "Theophrastus Περὶ Νόμων." *Journal of Philology* 6 (1876) 1–27.

Haigh, A. E. *The Attic Theatre.* 2d ed. Oxford, 1898.

Hammond, N. G. L., and G. T. Griffith. *A History of Macedonia.* Vol. 2, *550–336 B.C.* Oxford, 1979.

Harding, P. *Androtion and the Atthis.* Oxford, 1994.

———. "Androtion's Political Career." *Historia* 25 (1976) 186–200.

———. *From the End of the Peloponnesian War to the Battle of Ipsus.* Cambridge, 1985.

Harrell, H. C. "Public Arbitration in Athenian Law." *University of Missouri Studies* 11.1 (1936) 1–42.

Harris, E. M. "More Chalcenteric Negligence." *Classical Philology* 84 (1989) 36–44.

———. "Women and Lending in Athenian Society: A *horos* Re-examined." *Phoenix* 46 (1992) 309–21.

Harrison, A. R. W. *The Law of Athens.* 2 vols. Oxford, 1968–71.

Heath, M., trans. *Hermogenes, On Issues: Strategies of Argument in Later Greek Rhetoric.* Oxford, 1995.

Heckel, W. "Marsyas of Pella, Historian of Macedon." *Hermes* 108 (1980) 444–62.

Helmbold, W. C., and E. N. O'Neil. "The Form and Purpose of Juvenal's Seventh *Satire.*" *Classical Philology* 54 (1959) 100–108.

Hemmerdinger, B. "Les papyrus et la datation d'Harpocration." In "Deux notes papyrologiques." *Revue des Études Grecques* 72 (1959) 106–9.

Henry, R., ed. *Photius: Bibliothèque.* 8 vols. Paris, 1959–77.

Hercher, R. *Claudii Aeliani De Natura Animalium Libri XVII.* Leipzig, 1864.

Herington, C. J., ed. *The Older Scholia on the "Prometheus Bound."* Leiden, 1972.

Higbie, C. "Craterus and the Use of Inscriptions in Ancient Scholarship." *Transactions of the American Philological Association* 129 (1999) 43–83.

Houtsma, E. O., ed. *Lexicon Rhetoricum Cantabrigiense.* Leiden, 1870.

Hubbell, H. M. "A Papyrus Commentary on Demosthenes." *Yale Classical Studies* 15 (1957) 181–93.

Hubert, C., M. Pohlenz, and H. Drexler, eds. *Plutarchi Moralia.* Vol. 5.1. Leipzig, 1960.

Hude, C., ed. *Scholia in Thucydidem ad Optimos Codices Collata.* Leipzig, 1927.

Ioannidou, G., ed. *Catalogue of Greek and Latin Papyri in Berlin (BKT 9).* Mainz am Rhein, 1996.

Jacoby, F. *Die Fragmente der griechischen Historiker.* Berlin, 1923–58.

Jaeger, W. *Aristotle: Fundamentals of the History of His Development.* Translated by Richard Robinson. 2d ed. Oxford, 1948.

Jensen, C., ed. *Hyperidis Orationes VI cum Ceterarum Fragmentis.* Leipzig, 1917.

Jordan, B. *The Athenian Navy in the Classical Period: A Study of Athenian Naval Administration and Military Organization in the Fifth and Fourth Centuries B.C.* Berkeley, 1975.

Kassel, R., and C. Austin, eds. *Poetae Comici Graeci.* Berlin, 1983–.

Kaster, R. A. *Guardians of Language: The Grammarian and Society in Late Antiquity.* Berkeley, 1988.

Keaney, J. J. "Alphabetization in Harpocration's *Lexicon.*" *Greek, Roman, and Byzantine Studies* 14 (1973) 415–23.

———, ed. *Harpocration: Lexeis of the Ten Orators.* Amsterdam, 1991.

Kebric, R. B. *In the Shadow of Macedon: Duris of Samos.* Historia Einzelschriften 29. Wiesbaden, 1977.

Keen, A. G. "A 'Confused' Passage of Philochorus (F149A) and the Peace of 392/1 B.C." *Historia* 44 (1995) 1–10.

Keil, B., ed. *Anonymus Argentinensis: Fragmente zur Geschichte des perikleischen Athen aus einem Strassburger Papyrus.* Strassburg, 1902.

Kennedy, C. R., trans. *The Orations of Demosthenes: Against Leptines, Midias, Androtion, and Aristocrates.* London, 1856.

Kennedy, G. *The Art of Persuasion in Greece.* Princeton, 1963.

———. *The Art of Rhetoric in the Roman World.* Princeton, 1972.

———. *Greek Rhetoric under Christian Emperors.* Princeton, 1983.

———. *Quintilian.* New York, 1969.

Kenyon, F. G., ed. *Aristotle: On the Constitution of Athens.* 3d ed. Oxford, 1892.

Keuls, E. C. *The Reign of the Phallus: Sexual Politics in Ancient Athens.* New York, 1985.

Kirchner, J. "Chairestratos (1,2,3)." *RE* 3.2 (1899) 2029.

———. "Dokimos (2)." *RE* 5.1 (1903) 1274.

Kohl, R. *De Scholasticarum Declamationum Argumentis ex Historia Petitis.* Rhetorische Studien 4. Paderborn, 1915.

Körte, A. "Zu Didymos Demosthenes-Commentar." *Rheinisches Museum* 60 (1905) 388–416.

Krentz, P., and E. L. Wheeler, eds. and trans. *Polyaenus: Stratagems of War.* 2 vols. Chicago, 1994.

Lammert, F. "Μόρα (1)." *RE* 16.1 (1933) 251–52.

Laqueur, R. "Die litterarische Stellung des Anonymus Argentinensis" *Hermes* 43 (1908) 220–28.

Latte, K., ed. *Hesychii Alexandrini Lexicon.* 2 vols. Copenhagen, 1953.

Lazenby, J. F. *The Spartan Army.* Warminster, 1985.

Lehmann-Haupt, C. F. "Didymos zum Jahre 344/3." *Klio* 10 (1910) 391–93.

Leo, F. "Didymos περὶ Δημοσθένους." *Nachrichten von der Königlichen Gesellschaft der Wissenschaften philologisch-historische Klasse* (1904) 254–61.

———. *Die griechische-römische Biographie nach ihrer litterarischen Form.* Leipzig, 1901.

Leutsch, E. L., and F. G. Schneidewin, eds. *Paroemiographi Graeci.* 2 vols. Göttingen, 1839–51.

Link, H. F., and J. G. Schneider, eds. ΘΕΟΦΡΑΣΤΟΥ ΕΡΕΣΙΟΥ ΤΑ ΣΩΖΟΜΕΝΑ *Theophrasti Eresii Quae Supersunt Opera et Excerpta Librorum Quatuor [sic] Tomis Comprehensa.* 5 vols. Leipzig, 1818–21.

Lloyd-Jones, H., and P. Parsons, eds. *Supplementum Hellenisticum.* Berlin, 1982.

Long, H. S., ed. *Diogenis Laertii Vitae Philosophorum.* 2 vols. Oxford, 1964.

Lossau, M. J. *Untersuchungen zur antiken Demosthenesexegese.* Palingenesia 2. Bad Homburg, 1964.

MacDowell, D. M. *Demosthenes: Against Meidias.* Oxford, 1990.

———. *The Law in Classical Athens.* Ithaca, N.Y., 1978.

———. "The Law of Periandros about Symmories." *Classical Quarterly* 36 (1986) 438–49.

MacLeod, M. D., ed. *Luciani Opera.* 4 vols. Oxford, 1972–87.

Maehler, H. "Der Streit um den Schatten des Esels." In *Proceedings of the XIXth International Congress of Papyrology,* vol. 1, edited by A. H. S. El-Mosalamy, 625–33. Cairo, 1992.

Marrou, H. I. *A History of Education in Antiquity.* Translated by G. Lamb. New York, 1956.

Marshall, B. A. *A Historical Commentary on Asconius.* Columbia, Mo., 1985.

Marshall, P. K. *Cornelii Nepotis Vitae cum Fragmentis.* Leipzig, 1985.

Mayser, E. *Grammatik der griechischen Papyri aus der Ptolemaerzeit.* 2 vols. Berlin, 1926–70.

McComb, R. A. "The Tradition of 'The Lives of the Ten Orators' in Plutarch and Photius." Ph.D. diss., University of North Carolina, Chapel Hill, 1991.

McNamee, K. *Sigla and Select Marginalia in Greek Literary Papyri.* Papyrologica Bruxellensia 26. Brussels, 1992.

Meiggs, R. *The Athenian Empire.* Oxford, 1973.

Meijering, R. *Literary and Rhetorical Theories in Greek Scholia.* Groningen, 1987.

Meineke, A., ed. *Stephan von Byzanz "Ethnika."* Berlin, 1849.

Mejer, J. *Diogenes Laertius and His Hellenistic Background.* Hermes Einzelschriften 40. Wiesbaden, 1978.

Meritt, B. D. "Indirect Tradition in Thucydides." *Hesperia* 23 (1954) 185–231.

Meritt, B. D., H. T. Wade-Gery, and M. F. McGregor. *The Athenian Tribute Lists.* 4 vols. Cambridge and Princeton, 1939–53.

Mette, H. I., ed. *Die Fragmente der Tragödien des Aischylos.* Berlin, 1959.

Millett, P. *Lending and Borrowing in Ancient Athens.* Cambridge, 1991.

Milne, H. J. M. *Catalogue of the Literary Papyri in the British Museum.* London, 1927.

Milns, R. D. "Didymea." In *Ventures into Greek History,* edited by I. Worthington, 70–88. Oxford, 1994.

Momigliano, A. "Ancient History and the Antiquarian." In *Studies in Historiography,* 1–39. London, 1966.

———. *The Development of Greek Biography.* Expanded ed. Cambridge, Mass., 1993.

Montanari, F. "The Fragments of Hellenistic Scholarship." Translated by R. Barritt and G. W. Most. In *Collecting Fragments: Fragmente Sammeln,* edited by G. W. Most, 273–88. Göttingen, 1997.

Morgan, T. *Literate Education in the Hellenistic and Roman Worlds.* Cambridge, 1998.

Naber, S. A., ed. *Photii Patriarchae Lexicon.* 2 vols. Leiden, 1864–65.

Naoumides, M. "The Fragments of Greek Lexicography in the Papyri." In *Classical Studies Presented to Ben Edwin Perry by His Students and Colleagues at the University of Illinois, 1924–60,* 181–202. Urbana, 1969.

———. "Notes on Literary Papyri." *Transactions of the American Philological Association* 93 (1962) 240–43.

Nickau, K., ed. *Ammonii Qui Dicitur De Adfinium Vocabulorum Differentia.* Leipzig, 1966.

Nouhaud, M. *L'utilisation de l'histoire par les orateurs attiques.* Paris, 1982.

Ober, J. *Mass and Elite in Democratic Athens: Rhetoric, Ideology, and the Power of the People.* Princeton, 1989.

Ofenloch, E., ed. *Caecilii Calactini Fragmenta.* Leipzig, 1907.

O'Hara, J. J. *True Names: Vergil and the Alexandrian Tradition of Etymological Wordplay.* Ann Arbor, 1996.

Ollier, F. *Xénophon: La République des Lacédémoniens.* New York, 1979.

Osborne, K. T. "The 'Peri Demosthenous' of Didymos Grammatikos." Ph.D. diss., University of Washington, 1990.

Pack, R. A. *The Greek and Latin Literary Texts from Greco-Roman Egypt.* 2d ed. Ann Arbor, 1965.

Page, D. L., ed. *Epigrammata Graeca.* Oxford, 1975.

————, ed. *Poetae Melici Graeci.* Oxford, 1962.

————, ed. and trans. *Select Papyri.* Vol. 3. London, 1941.

Parke, H. W. *Festivals of the Athenians.* Ithaca, N.Y., 1977.

————. *Greek Mercenary Soldiers: From the Earliest Times to the Battle of Ip-sus.* Chicago, 1933.

Paton, W. R., M. Pohlenz, W. Sieveking, eds. *Plutarchi Moralia.* Vol. 3. Leipzig, 1929.

Pearson, L. "Historical Allusions in the Attic Orators." *Classical Philology* 36 (1941) 209–29.

————. *The Lost Histories of Alexander the Great.* Philological Monographs 20. New York, 1960.

Pearson, L., and S. Stephens, eds. *Didymi in Demosthenem Commenta.* Stuttgart, 1983.

Pélékedis, C. *Histoire de l'éphébie attique: Des origines à 31 avant Jésus-Christ.* Paris, 1962.

Perlman, P. "Acting the She-Bear for Artemis." *Arethusa* 22 (1984) 111–33.

Perlman, S. "The Historical Example, Its Use and Importance as Political Propaganda in the Attic Orators." *Scripta Hierosolymitana* 7 (1961) 150–66.

————. "Quotations from Poetry in the Attic Orators of the Fourth Century B.C." *American Journal of Philology* 85 (1964) 155–72.

Petrochilos, N. *Roman Attitudes to the Greeks.* Athens, 1974.

Pfeiffer, R., ed. *Callimachus.* Vol. 1, *Fragmenta.* Oxford, 1949.

————. *History of Classical Scholarship from the Beginnings to the End of the Hellenistic Age.* Oxford, 1968.

Platnauer, M. "Comedy: Old, Middle, New, Graeco-Egyptian." In *New Chapters in the History of Greek Literature,* 3d series, edited by J. U. Powell, 156–79. Oxford, 1933.

Pohlenz, M. "Philipps Schreiben an Athen." *Hermes* 64 (1929) 41–62.

Pöhlmann, E. *Einführung in die Überlieferungsgeschichte und in die Textkritik der antiken Literatur.* Vol. 1. Darmstadt, 1994.

Potter, D. S. *Literary Texts and the Roman Historian.* London, 1999.

Powell, J. U., ed. *Collectanea Alexandrina.* Oxford, 1925.

Preller, L., ed. *Polemonis Periegetae Fragmenta.* Leipzig, 1838.

Pritchett, W. K. *The Greek State at War.* Vol. 2. Berkeley, 1974.

Rabe, H., ed. *Hermogenis Opera.* Rhetores Graeci, vol. 6. Leipzig, 1913.

————. *Scholia in Lucianum.* Leipzig, 1906.

Radt, S. L., ed. *Tragicorum Graecorum Fragmenta.* Vol. 4, *Sophoclis Fragmenta.* Göttingen, 1977.

Rawson, E. *Intellectual Life in the Later Roman Republic.* Baltimore, 1985.

————. "The Romans." In *Perceptions of the Ancient Greeks,* edited by K. J. Dover, 1–28. Oxford, 1992.

Renehan, R. "Aristotle as Lyric Poet: The Hermias Poem." *Greek, Roman and Byzantine Studies* 23 (1982) 251–74.

Reynolds, L. D., and N. Wilson. *Scribes and Scholars: A Guide to the Transmission of Greek and Latin Literature.* 2d ed. Oxford, 1974.

Rhodes, P. J. *The Athenian Boule.* Oxford, 1972.

———. *A Commentary on the Aristotelian "Athenaion Politeia."* Oxford, 1993.
———. "Problems in Athenian Eisphora and Liturgies." *American Journal of Ancient History* 7 (1982) 1–19.
Riginos, A. S. "The Wounding of Philip II of Macedon: Fact and Fabrication." *Journal of Hellenic Studies* 114 (1994) 103–19.
Rigsby, K. J. "Geographical Readings." *Epigraphica Anatolica* 30 (1998) 137–38.
Robertson, N. "False Documents at Athens: Fifth-Century History and Fourth-Century Publicists." *Historical Reflections* 3 (1976) 3–25.
Roos, A. G., ed. *Flavii Arriani Quae Exstant Omnia*. Leipzig, 1907.
Rose, V. ed. *Aristotelis qui Ferebantur Librorum Fragmenta*. Leipzig, 1886.
Rudolph, F. "Die Quellen und die Schriftstellerei des Athenaios." *Philologus Suppl.* 6 (1891) 109–62.
Runia, D. T. "Theocritus of Chios' Epigram against Aristotle." *Classical Quarterly* 36 (1986) 531–34.
Rupprecht, K. "Παροιμία." *RE* 18.4 (1949) 1707–35.
———. "Paroimiographoi." *RE* 18.4 (1949) 1735–78.
Ruschenbusch, E. "Die athenischen Symmorien des 4. Jh. v. Chr." *Zeitschrift für Papyrologie und Epigraphik* 31 (1978) 275–84.
———. "Ein Beitrag zur Leiturgie und zur Eisphora." *Zeitschrift für Papyrologie und Epigraphik* 59 (1985) 237–40.
———. "Symmorienprobleme." *Zeitschrift für Papyrologie und Epigraphik* 69 (1987) 75–81.
Russell, D. A. *Criticism in Antiquity*. Berkeley, 1981.
———. *Greek Declamation*. Cambridge, 1983.
———, ed. *'Longinus' "On the Sublime."* Oxford, 1964.
Rusten, J. Review of *Didymi in Demosthenem Commenta*, by L. Pearson and S. Stephens. *Classical Philology* 82 (1987) 265–69.
Sacks, K. S. *Diodorus Siculus and the First Century*. Princeton, 1990.
Sandys, J. E. *Demosthenes: On the Peace, Second Philippic, On the Chersonesus, and Third Philippic*. London, 1900.
———. *A History of Classical Scholarship*. 3d ed. Vol.1. Cambridge, 1921.
Schaefer, A. *Demosthenes und seine Zeit*. 3 vols. Leipzig, 1885–87.
Schaefer, H. "Polytropos." *RE* 21.2 (1952) 1839.
Schmidt, M., ed. *Didymi Chalcenteri Grammatici Alexandrini Fragmenta*. Leipzig, 1854.
Schultz, H. "Hesychios (9)." *RE* 8.2 (1913) 1317–22.
Schwendner, G. W. "Literary and Non-literary Papyri from the University of Michigan Collection." Ph.D. diss., University of Michigan, 1988.
Sealey, R. *Demosthenes and His Time: A Study in Defeat*. New York, 1993.
———. "Dionysius of Halicarnassus and Some Demosthenic Dates." *Revue des Études Grecques* 68 (1955) 77–120.
———. "P.Strassburg 84 verso." *Hermes* 86 (1958) 440–46.
Seel, O., ed. *M. Iuniani Iustini Epitoma Historiarum Philippicarum Pompeii Trogi*. Leipzig, 1935.
Shipley, D. R. *A Commentary on Plutarch's "Life of Agesilaos": Response to Sources in the Presentation of Character*. Oxford, 1997.

Skutsch, O. "Euphorion (4)." *RE* 6.1 (1907) 1174–90.

Skydsgaard, J. E. *Varro the Scholar: Studies in the First Book of Varro's "De Re Rustica."* Hafniae, 1968.

Slater, W. J. "Grammarians and Handwashing." *Phoenix* 43 (1989) 100–111.

———. "Problems in Interpreting Scholia on Greek Texts." In *Editing Greek and Latin Texts: Papers Given at the Twenty-Third Annual Conference on Editorial Problems, University of Toronto, 6–7 November 1987,* edited by J. N. Grant, 37–61. New York, 1987.

Smith, R. M. "A New Look at the Canon of the Ten Attic Orators." *Mnemosyne* 48 (1995) 66–79.

Smyth, H. W. *Greek Grammar.* 2d ed. Cambridge, Mass., 1956.

Squires, S., ed. and trans. *Asconius: Commentaries on Five Speeches of Cicero.* Bristol, 1990.

Staab, K., ed. "Fragmente in Epistulam I ad Corinthios." In *Pauluskommentar aus der griechischen Kirche aus Katanenhandschriften gesammelt,* 544–83. Münster, 1933.

Stählin, F. "Die griechischen Historikerfragmente bei Didymos." *Klio* 5 (1905) 55–71, 141–54.

Stangl, T., ed. *Ciceronis Orationum Scholiastae.* Vol. 2. Leipzig, 1912.

Stephens, S., ed. *Yale Papyri in the Beinecke Rare Book and Manuscript Library* II. Chico, 1985.

Strauss, B. S. "The Problem of Periodization: The Case of the Peloponnesian War." In *Inventing Ancient Culture: Historicism, Periodization, and the Ancient World,* edited by M. Golden and P. Toohey, 165–75. London, 1997.

Stroud, R. G. *The Axones and Kyrbeis of Drakon and Solon.* University of California Publications, Classical Studies, vol. 19. Berkeley, 1979.

Szegedy-Maszak, A. *The Nomoi of Theophrastus.* New York, 1981.

Thalheim, T., ed. *Isaei Orationes cum Deperditarum Fragmentis.* Leipzig, 1903.

———, ed. *Lysiae Orationes.* Ed. maior. Leipzig, 1913.

Thompson, D. W. *A Glossary of Greek Birds.* Oxford, 1895.

Thomsen, R. *Eisphora: A Study of Direct Taxation in Ancient Athens.* Copenhagen, 1964.

———. *The Origin of Ostracism: A Synthesis.* Copenhagen, 1972.

Todd, S. "The Use and Abuse of the Attic Orators." *Greece and Rome* 37 (1990) 159–78.

Treadgold, W. T. *The Nature of the "Bibliotheca" of Photius.* Washington, D.C., 1980.

Trevett, J. "Demosthenes' Speech *On Organization* (Dem. 13)." *Greek, Roman and Byzantine Studies* 35 (1994) 179–93.

Turner, E. G. *Greek Papyri: An Introduction.* Oxford, 1968.

———. "Roman Oxyrhynchus." *Journal of Egyptian Archaeology* 38 (1952) 78–93.

Uhlig, G., ed. *Dionysii Thracis Ars Grammatica.* Leipzig, 1883.

Van der Valk, M., ed. *Eustathii Archiepiscopi Thessalonicensis Commentarii ad Homeri Iliadem Pertinentes.* 4 vols. Leiden, 1971–87.

Veyne, P. *Did the Greeks Believe in Their Myths? An Essay on the Constitutive Imagination.* Translated by P. Wissing. Chicago, 1988.

Von Arnim, J., ed. *Dionis Prusaensis Quem Vocant Chrysostomum Quae Exstant Omnia.* 2 vols. Berlin, 1893–96.
Wade-Gery, H. T. "The Question of Tribute in 449/8 B.C." *Hesperia* 14 (1945) 212–29.
Wade-Gery, H. T., and B. D. Meritt. "Athenian Resources in 449 and 431 B.C." *Hesperia* 26 (1957) 163–97.
Wagner, E. *Die Erdbeschreibung des Timosthenes von Rhodus.* Leipzig, 1888.
Walz, C., ed. *Rhetores Graeci.* 9 vols. Stuttgart, 1832–36.
Wankel, H. Review of *Didymi in Demosthenem Commenta,* by L. Pearson and S. Stephens. *Gnomon* 59 (1987) 213–23.
Wardman, A. *Rome's Debt to Greece.* New York, 1976.
Wayte, W., ed. *Demosthenes: Against Androtion and Against Timocrates.* 2d ed. Cambridge, 1893.
Weil, H., ed. *Les harangues de Démosthène.* Paris, 1912.
———, ed. *Les plaidoyers politiques de Démosthène.* 2d ed. 2 vols. Paris, 1883.
Wendel, C., ed. *Scholia in Apollonium Rhodium Vetera.* Berlin, 1935.
Wessely, C. "Fragmente eines alphabetischen Lexikons zu Demosthenes Midiana." *Studien zur Palaeographie und Papyruskunde* 4 (1905) 111–13.
———. On P.Rain.inv. 7, in *Archiv* 3 (1906) 493–94.
West, M. L. *Textual Criticism and Editorial Technique Applicable to Greek and Latin Texts.* Stuttgart, 1973.
West, S. "Chalcenteric Negligence." *Classical Quarterly* 20 (1970) 288–96.
Whitehead, D. "Competitive Outlay and Community Profit: Φιλοτιμία in Democratic Athens." *Classica et Mediaevalia* 34 (1983) 55–74.
———. *The Demes of Attica, 508/7–ca. 250 B.C.: A Political and Social Study.* Princeton, 1986.
Whittaker, J. "The Value of Indirect Tradition in the Establishment of Greek Philosophical Texts or the Art of Misquotation." In *Editing Greek and Latin Texts: Papers Given at the Twenty-Third Annual Conference on Editorial Problems, University of Toronto, 6–7 November 1987,* edited by J. N. Grant, 63–95. New York, 1987.
Wilamowitz-Möllendorff, U. von. "Asianismus und Atticismus." *Hermes* 35 (1900) 1–52.
———. *Einleitung in die griechische Tragödie.* Berlin, 1910.
———. "Lesefrüchte." *Hermes* 61 (1926) 289–91.
Wilcken, U. "Der Anonymus Argentinensis." *Hermes* 42 (1907) 374–418.
———. "Die Subskription des Didymus-Papyrus." *Hermes* 55 (1920) 324–25.
———. On P.Rain. 1.25, in *Archiv* 11 (1935) 270.
Willis, J., ed. *Ambrosii Theodosii Macrobii Saturnalia.* Leipzig, 1970.
Wilson, N. G. "A Chapter in the History of Scholia." *Classical Quarterly* 17 (1967) 244–56.
———. *Scholars of Byzantium.* Rev. ed. Baltimore, 1996.
Wimmer, F., ed. ΘΕΟΦΡΑΣΤΟΥ *Theophrasti Eresii Opera, Quae Supersunt, Omnia.* Paris, 1866.
Wooten, C. W., trans. *Hermogenes' "On Types of Style."* Chapel Hill, 1987.
Wormell, D. E. W. "The Literary Tradition Concerning Hermias of Atarneus." *Yale Classical Studies* 5 (1935) 57–92.

Worthington, I. *A Historical Commentary on Dinarchus: Rhetoric and Conspiracy in Later Fourth-Century Athens.* Ann Arbor, 1992.

Yunis, H. "What Kind of Commentary Is the περὶ Δημοσθένους of Didymus?" In *Akten des 21. Internationalen Papyrologenkongresses,* Band 2, ed. B. Kramer et al., 1049–55. Stuttgart, 1997.

Zetzel, J. E. G. *Latin Textual Criticism in Antiquity.* Salem, 1984.

———. "On the History of Latin Scholia." *Harvard Studies in Classical Philology* 79 (1975) 335–54.

Zuntz, G. *Die Aristophanes-Scholien der Papyri.* Berlin, 1975.

Concordance to the Translations

This concordance contains proper names, transliterated Greek words, and other significant words used in the translations in Part Two, including those translations that are based on alternate restorations of the Greek texts.

Academy, 87
accursed, 100
Acharnae, 89
Achilles, 87
Acropolis, 142, 143, 168
Acte, 99, 99n32
Adimantus, 179
Aegialus, 99
Aegospotami, 91
Aenianes, 95
Aeolian(s), 87, 96
Aeolis, 96
Aeschines, 140, 143, 204
Aeschylus, 99
Aetolians, 95
Agora, 142, 146, 161, 168
Ajax, 87
Alexander, 92, 97
Altar of Peace, 89
ambush, 160
Amphictyonic Council, 95
Amphictyons, 84, 173
Amphipolis, 91
Amyntas, 97
Anaphlystus, 88
Anaximenes, 87, 90n16, 90n19, 92, 94, 94n25, 142, 159, 168
Andocides, 88

Androtion, 90, 90n19, 100, 141
Antalcidas, 88, 89
Antigenides, 97
Apollodorus, 98, 142, 144
arbitrators, 192
Archelaus, 159
Archidamian (War), 179
archon, 179
archonship, 83, 84, 90, 94, 98, 179, 193
Areopagus, 179
arete, 86, 87
Arethusius, 145
Aristides, 179, 185
Aristocrates, 142
Aristogeiton, 143
Aristomedes, 92, 93
Aristophanes, 95, 96, 140
Aristophon, 91
Aristotle, 85, 86, 86n14, 87, 159
aselgeis, 203
Asia, 88
ass, shadow of, 139, 173
assault, 202, 203, 204
Assians, 86
Assos, 85, 86, 86n14
Aster, 97
Atarneus, 85, 87, 90
Athena, 179

General Index

This index excludes occurrences of proper names and other significant words in the translations of Part Two (for which see the Concordance to the Translations), as well as their mention in the corresponding notes.

Index Locorum

Abbreviations come primarily from the *Oxford Classical Dictionary* (3d edition). Asterisks (*) denote passages cited or discussed by our commentators.

Index Verborum

Compositor:	G & S Typesetters, Inc.
Text:	General: 10/13 Sabon; Greek: 10/13 GraecaII
Display:	Sabon
Printer and binder:	Maple-Vail